Psychotherapy and the Widowed Patient

E. Mark Stern, Editor
Iona College, New Rochelle, New York

The Psychotherapy Patient Series
E. Mark Stern, Editor

Routledge
Taylor & Francis Group

NEW YORK AND LONDON

First published 1990 by The Haworth Press, Inc.

Published 2009 by Routledge
711 Third Avenue, New York, NY 10017
2 Park Square, Milton Park, Abingdon, Oxfordshire OX14 4RN

First issued in paperback 2016

Routledge is an imprint of the Taylor and Francis Group, an informa business

Psychotherapy and the Widowed Patient has also been published as *The Psychotherapy Patient*, Volume 6, Numbers 3/4 1990.

Library of Congress Cataloging-in-Publication Data

Psychotherapy and the widowed patient / E. Mark Stern, editor.
    p. cm.
    "Has also been published as The Psychotherapy Patient, volume 6, numbers 3/4 1990 – T.P. verso.
    Includes bibliographical references.
    ISBN 1-56024-016-4
    1. Widows – Mental health. 2. Bereavement – Psychological aspects. 3. Psychotherapy. 4. Widowers – Mental health. I. Stern, E. Mark, 1929- .
    [DNLM: 1. Bereavement. 2. Family Therapy. 3. Psychotherapy. 4. Single Person – psychology. W1 PS87 v.6 no. 3/4 / WM 430.5.F2 P9738]
RC451.4.W53P78   1990
616.89'14'08654--dc20
DNLM/DLC
for Library of Congress   90-4502
                                                                                              CIP

ISBN 13: 978-1-138-98420-2 (pbk)
ISBN 13: 978-1-56024-016-7 (hbk)

Psychotherapy and the Widowed Patient

CONTENTS

ABOUT THE EDITOR

E. Mark Stern, EdD, ABPP, is Professor of Psychology in the Graduate Division of Pastoral and Family Counseling, Iona College, New Rochelle, New York. A Diplomate in Clinical Psychology of the American Board of Professional Psychology and a Fellow of the American Psychological Association, Dr. Stern is President of the Division of Humanistic Psychology, APA. He is in private practice of psychotherapy with offices in New York City and Dutchess County, New York. Dr. Stern completed his clinical studies at Columbia University (1955) and at the National Psychological Association for Psychoanalysis.

Psychotherapy and the
Widowed Patient

The Widowed and the Widowed Patient:
A Preface

In preparing for this monograph, I conducted an informal survey of approximately 200 practicing psychotherapists. A very few reported having had any patients who came to see them because of the loss of a spouse. The several I phoned in followup, mostly colleagues I had known over the years, could not think of why this should be. One, a pastoral counselor and recent widower, was pleased for the question. It had not dawned on him to seek psychotherapeutic help. "When Tess died," he said, "the kids began to take a greater interest in me. I didn't want to see my predicament as anything more extraordinary than essential."

Those therapists I spoke with, some whose essays appear in these pages, were quick to note that the untoward effects of the loss of a spouse did not necessarily disappear with time. Most agreed that dependency issues played a major role in how well their widowed patients developed emotionally.

In its ideal state, widowhood does little to damage a person's self-regard. The widowed, like other bereaved, move from the sadness of their loss to a gradual mixture of incorporation and detachment from the deceased spouse. Widowhood is riveted to the marriage bond. "Till death do us part" sustains the marital vows. Yet for some, the pain of loss seems to be never fully concluded. Ambivalence, guilt, and helplessness characterize a good number of those who seek psychotherapeutic help. They have often found themselves beyond the usual consolations. And where the loss is an almost "happy" occasion, questions of emotional survival can create their own impact, triggering anxiety and fear. For others, the terror is rooted in being set adrift in a world which for them is often in want of meaning.

The Widowed Patient is being issued at a time of renewed interest in the developmental challenges of the life cycle. Diversity of the

xi

many essays in this monograph points less to controversies of therapeutic approaches than to the wide scope and creative imagination
of the contributors. It is my hope that the appeal of this collection
has a direct relationship to the practitioner's need for enrichment in
working with widowed patients.

E. Mark Stern
Editor

The Widow as Survivor and "Killer"

E. Mark Stern

SUMMARY. A clinical narrative of a twice-widowed woman. Her concerns regarding guilt, anger, and anguish about her most immediate late husband. Issues which dealt with her struggles for emotional survival, and with her attitudes toward her past mode of being. How her elderly mother, with whom she continued to live, her stepson and husband's former wife, and her own childlessness contributed to her need to clarify her own position.

It was the final day of a long weekend. I checked in with my answering service from the airport of a distant city. Faye, the managing operator, who had an uncanny ear for crisis, put me on hold. I heard some serious shuffling of papers. Then: "Please attend to this as soon as you can. Mrs. Lamb has been calling since early this morning." There was an almost imperceptible hesitation just before she gave me the worst of the news. "Her husband died last night." There were a few other messages. I thought to myself, "Thank God for Faye." She was an effective link to my practice long before the days of recorded messages and answering machines.

"Alice? I'm about 25 minutes from boarding time. I know about Kurt. Tell me what happened."

"I'll make it quick. Kurt surprised us all," she spoke as if it was a by-now-many-times-repeated script. "The doctor seemed so posi-

E. Mark Stern, EdD, completed his clinical studies at Columbia University (1955) and at the Institute of the National Psychological Association for Psychoanalysis. Besides his private practice in psychotherapy and psychoanalysis, Dr. Stern is Professor in the Graduate Division of Pastoral Counseling, Iona College, New Rochelle, NY. Dr. Stern is a Diplomate in Clinical Psychology of the American Board of Professional Psychology and Fellow of the American Psychological Association. Address correspondence to the author at 215 East 11 St., New York, NY 10003.

1

tive." Her tempo changed, "Mark, could you possibly see me to-morrow? There won't be a funeral. What I need most is to talk to you." We agreed on 2 o'clock the following day.

Alice had concluded her therapy several months before. I remember well. It was on her 58th birthday. She was now a widow for the second time. Kurt, her just-now-deceased husband, had been a prosperous enough investment broker. What she claimed he lacked in sensitivity to her feelings, he made up in his desire to safeguard her. They had met 7 years earlier through a mutual friend. Kurt was just about to be divorced. Even as he was ready to move ahead, he remained quite troubled by a breakdown in his relationship with his then teenage son. Kurt obviously needed a woman to be there for him, to sympathize with his crises, to redeem him from harrowing bouts of loneliness. Yet their early courtship was not one born of desperation. Alice seemed prepared to lend just the right amount of emotional support to Kurt's changing emotional needs.

Alice felt an enthusiastic desire to make her own transition. She had held several jobs in public relations. She had a natural bent for coining slogans, planning elite promotional parties, and designing fund raisers. Alice had worked on several political campaigns as a front-line part-timer. Lately she had dropped her "company work," having found a more lucrative market in a national newspaper syndicate. This allowed her to do more work at home and to become attentive to more personal concerns.

*   *   *

Her first husband had died following a year-long battle with leukemia. There were no children. Three miscarriages occurred early in the marriage. More about the marriage later.

There had been a 10-year hiatus between George and Kurt. Though this might suggest total absence of relationship, Alice actually maintained a close relationship with her mother. Alice described her mother as "my lively sister widow." They continued to share the large apartment that she and George had shared with her. His death brought the two women closer than ever. They were feted by many friends as the "even couple." At one point they contemplated co-authoring a book on multi-generational cohabitation. Though it may be apocryphal, I believe that somewhere Freud was reported to have said that we have little idea of how many adult daughters are actually married to their mothers.

Alice arrived half an hour early. I greeted her at the door as she waved me on, mumbling something about needing the waiting room's away-from-home atmosphere. There were notes that she had wanted to get "in some order" before our meeting. Coincidentally, she was acquainted with the patient whose appointment preceded hers. The ensuing interval between sessions brought the two together for a brief updating. "My Lord, seeing Sue was like meeting up with a world I'd lost almost complete touch with." Sharing the details of Kurt's death with an unexpected friend was, for all its newness, part of the necessary healing routine. I'd left my door ajar. When she finally came in, and even before she had taken her seat: "So, you must have overheard the official story."

We stared for a time—some at each other, some into space. Finally, "I'd like to hear more, Alice."

"Funny," she began, "it was only last year that we signed up with a nonprofit memorial society. We decided between ourselves that we would respect the other's request for immediate cremation. As I mentioned to you on the phone, there will not be a funeral. This meeting will have to be my way of having a memorial service. You've known more about what goes on inside me than anyone else in my life. I need you to help me better understand the sense of where I am now." Her expression made it clear that she was still possessed more by fear than by any sort of stylized grief. Her mother, now in her 80s, was little available to her this time around. "Mother seems more stricken by Kurt's death than I am. If you can believe it, Kurt was more like Dad than Dad himself."

"And you?" I asked.

She appeared to wander off. She asked for some tissue as she began to shuffle the notes she had gathered on her lap. It was her way of getting composed. "I wanted to be sure that I'd say it all just right. It's so important for me to know that you're hearing me out. I don't care about your trying to make me feel better." She rearranged her notes. "*This* is going to be about Kurt."

I had known Kurt, but only through a variation of group therapy. Alice had been the primary member in one of my therapy groups. At one point I began experimenting with a format that allowed members to send "envoys" to substitute for them for an agreed fixed number of sessions. These envoys were usually spouses or spouse equivalents, though sometimes, parents, close friends, or even business associates. Kurt had agreed to attend group in Alice's absence for three or four sessions.

He struck some of the group members as a dapper gentleman. He was always dressed as if for a business meeting. Though self-possessed, he was hardly as intimidating as his success in a highly competitive business might have suggested. He viewed himself as an "overgrown kid from the streets of Jersey City."

Kurt let it be known that he had a limited appetite for introspection. He created much laughter during his few sessions even as he was obviously doing all he could to preserve his dignity and keep control. He did share with the group his concerns about his son's increasing distance. "Too close to his mother." Asked about what part he might be playing in creating this situation, he put up his hand, claiming it inappropriate to open up issues about his first wife during a session in which he was "supposed" to talk about his second. About Alice: "She's introduced me to values, aesthetics, and the worth of knowing how to contain my sweet tooth."

* * *

"I have to get this part off my chest." There was a sad pause. Then a gesture toward her notes. "I had, as you so well know, been concerned about Kurt's grueling work habits . . . about his constant travel. Our doctor had advised him to ease up for his health's sake. But you know me, I just couldn't let go." With some shame in her voice she continued, "I called him on his insane hours. But despite his promises, Kurt was not about to yield to anyone else's recipe for his business life.

"Just a week ago he visited a union pension-plan headquarters in New Jersey. I pleaded with him to make it a short day. Mark, I almost bribed him. In the end I guess I must have sounded like an impatient shrew. All I wanted was a comfortable evening away from Kurt's business woes. This is the hard part. On his way home — oh, I should mention that Kurt left the union office later than he said he would — he experienced severe chest pains. He had had a mild heart attack several years before I met him. He knew the signs and the dangers, but despite the pain, drove to a gas station. An attendant phoned for an ambulance which brought him to a local hospital. How much damage to his heart had occurred was uncertain. I was called, and immediately hired a cab to drive me across the river. Kurt was heavily sedated though I was able to visit with him briefly.

"The doctor gave him favorable odds. 'But we'll have to wait.' He offered to have me put up in a nearby motel for the night. But I wanted to be in my own surroundings. Besides, it was getting late and I was concerned for my mother who sounded shaky and upset on the phone. I picked up the car at the service station and returned to the hospital early the next day, this time with my mother. But that night! It was the most horrible time I'd ever spent in my life. I was afraid of falling asleep, fearing those nightmares which resound for days. Earlier I called our personal doctor, who definitely advised against having Kurt moved to his hospital in the city. He promised to be in touch with the New Jersey cardiologist. Hopeful as it all sounded, including the ECGs, I sensed I was part of a passion play which could end with Kurt's death.

"On the fourth day we had our longest visit. From all appearances I thought Kurt was well out of danger. 'I'm so sorry,' he said for the first time ever, 'I was trying my best to get home on time.'

"I knew he was trying to please me, but had obviously become tense with the traffic working against him."

She stopped short of crying. "I felt accused and frightened for both of us. I held his hand, but we spoke no more about it. I did say that I was grateful that he was getting better so fast. We even joked about how he would use this opportunity to let the stubble of his beard grow. He wanted his dignity so much.

"On Saturday I decided to drive out myself. Mother was overtired by now, and frankly she was a bit of a burden. I was comfortable reading and had even started to knit a sweater. Kurt had just about finished his dinner, and I was thinking about the best time to avoid the tunnel traffic on my return. It was then that it happened.

"The nurses station was next to Kurt's room. In a flash, he was surrounded by a team of doctors and nurses. They cut into his chest and massaged his heart. It was hopeless. How I maintained calm standing in the corner of the room remains a mystery. Then it was over. I was asked, but decided against having an autopsy and then made immediate arrangements for the memorial society's designated mortician to pick up the body for immediate cremation. It was Saturday evening. It's hard to get the clock to move ahead.''

"It's reasonable", I said, "that you'd like to go back to it all, if not just to be able to know what feelings you had.''

"Talking to mother had put me in touch with my grief. Kurt was 'alive' as I was driving back to the city. I allowed him to be dead the minute I told her. We cried and cried. Somehow, between the tears, I phoned Lois and Tony. They'd been good friends of mine before and during our marriage. They seemed to be there almost immediately, and stayed until long after midnight. Then Lois was back with me the whole of yesterday. News travels fast. Others trickled in — a combination of neighbors, friends, distant cousins. Lois took it on herself to call Kurt's son. I spoke with him, and once again surprised myself as to how unnerved I was by his cool anger. No different from what you and I have talked about for so many hours.

"What I need to tell you is that I feel horribly guilty. Have you any sense of what I mean?''

Knowing what she meant was the easy part. Helping her understand its significance would be something else again.

"Mark, please try to understand this. I feel I killed Kurt.''

We were looking straight at each other. She continued, "If only I hadn't put pressure on him . . . not only about his getting home early, but about so many day-to-day requirements of life. Let's face it, Kurt was always trying to accommodate my moods even if he ignored my requests.''

"And you?'' I hesitated. "Alice, what was happening to you during those hours of waiting for him before you were called to the hospital?''

There could be no immediate response. The answer needed to be paced accordingly. Alice reviewed her notations. She looked. This time she averted her eyes. "Of course it was horrible. I can be an impatient demanding woman . . . Yes, I'd become overwrought. There was plenty of anguish. Kurt's heart attack was a scenario I played out in my mind many times. I tried to make it not happen. I wanted him to ease up. I can anticipate your saying, what had to be, had to be."

"Perhaps," I responded, "it's always more ruthless than that. Kurt's behavior was, by any definition, like Russian roulette. And as the onlooker, while he played with the trigger, you were caused no small amount of anguish."

She nodded in assent, "Call it a continuing heartache." Yet I know she was looking for more than consolation. The wide range of meaning had first priority. However black Alice's grief, she wanted to know that her experience really mattered — what the Germans call *schlechtin unvergleichlich,* (the totally incomparable.)

"If you're willing to accept your guilt — your responsibility — you have to allow Kurt his share in the conspiracy. You implied it. At least as I heard it. Kurt had been as much a murderer as you were." I chose not to pause. "You indeed did kill one another . . . But it was not a series of isolated acts. Finely tuned relationships bless both partners with life. At the same time, the productive marriage is a killing field even as it extends the possibilities of life. Even as life is given, it is freely taken away. Look at it carefully. Kurt had a penchant for rousing your anxiety. And you in turn, you could drive him near 'crazy' by your concerns for his 'doing what was right.' Obviously the score's never even-steven. More than likely it comes to two people generating and regenerating excitement — if not challenge. The challenge was taken and successfully created the power to give each other life. But this same challenge demanded mutual sacrifices. You might have been the first to die. Kurt happened to die before you. But his work habits eroded your sense of well-being and reminded you of your own mortality."

Alice *had* heard me. She had been leading me to what I was saying to her. My sensibilities told me that she had received what she came for. We might have stopped there, but agreed that it would be helpful for her to continue our meetings for a few months.

*   *   *

Widowhood is etched into marriage. When it occurred for the second time in Alice's life, widowhood had become her opportunity for new odysseys even as it was filled with terror for her future. Opportunity is often the ripening of a burden. The burden involved the final "kill"; the marshalling of Alice's forces so that she could move beyond the last evidences of Kurt.

Widowhood is essential deconstruction. It acknowledges the temptation to immortalize the departed spouse. Though wanting to enshrine the haunting presence, the task of widowhood is to not make idols of ghosts. Alice was willing to engage in deconstruction. Kurt was no longer. Facing his death allowed the consolation that productive grieving could exist in proportion to the meaning found. To do less is to identify with the burly laborer described by C. S. Lewis (1976), who was shouting back to his friends as he made his way through the gates of a churchyard cemetery: "See you later, I'm just going to visit Mum" (p. 23). "Mum" as described had come to be a six by three foot flower-bed.

For C. S. Lewis, who was a recent widower when he described his encounter with the burly laborer, wrote on the importance of his shedding the temptation to keep alive the intense icons of his marriage. "A really good photograph," he wrote, "might become in the end a shrine, a horror, and an obstacle" (p. 76). Lewis's challenge was to let his grief introduce an enlargement of his experience.

Like C. S. Lewis and all who are widowed, Alice needed to struggle with the challenge of going it alone. Learning to discover her own text for widowhood carved out its temporality with all its tenaciousness. The death of her marriage was to allow Alice to peer into the greater terror of being a survivor. She suddenly found herself distressed at the lack of a positive relationship with her stepson. The was somehow where Kurt left off. But for Alice, the break with Kurt's son bred an even more intense dread of her own temporality. She despaired that, while still a daughter herself, no child—biological or otherwise—would ever follow her.

There was more to Ted's being a "stranger" to her. He, the child of Kurt's first marriage, began to threaten her sense of spousal and then widowed legitimacy. Stepmothers are often portrayed as prototypic intruders into intact arrangements. Ted remained forbidding, a memento that Kurt's first marriage still had a location. Alice experienced shame every time his name was mentioned. It was as if he was living evidence that Kurt's first marriage had the capacity to withstand death whereas her own did not.

She felt like "used goods" and none the better by Kurt's selection of an insensitive attorney as executor of his estate. There were times when she longed to talk to Kurt, if for no other reason than to blame him for the complications he had left her with. Dialogue with Kurt was one way of letting go of him.

She dreamed of climbing up a cliff. Kurt was by her side, then somehow paused. He was now below her somewhere in the midst of other climbers. Suddenly someone — as she recalled — it could have been Kurt, tried to grab onto her foot. Fearful that she'd lose hold, she kicked her legs to "the other side." Suddenly all of those below her fell to the ground. She felt she now had space and could reach for a rope. She knew she could now go to the top of the hill.

Another dream: She was in a small bookstore in what appeared to be a resort town. A volume grabbed her attention. The salesman said, "Oh, this is the book that lets you in on the whole of everything: creation and evolution, all of Europe and Africa, the great territories. But it is much more personal than an encyclopedia." She then moved aside and browsed through the gold-edged pages. Suddenly she began to notice that she was surrounded by three men. They seemed to be talking about closing the store for the night. Alice felt rushed, but believed that they were less concerned about closing the shop than about making sure that she buy the book.

The scene shifted. Alice was with friends in a restaurant. Kurt appeared to be resting in a corner booth. He was preparing to die. As desserts were being served, her friends suggested that she bury Kurt before the end of the meal. It was decided that he be placed under a chest which would then double as seating for a restaurant booth. She felt anxious about what was required of her.

Forceful letting go was the topic of the first dream. Alice wasn't at first sure of her own sex in the dream. "If not you, then who?"

"Maybe Ted," she replied. "No, no, it's me needing to have the strength of a man."

"And you're sure he fell behind?"

"He was just there, with the folks on the bottom of the climb."

"How about the grab for your foot?"

"That was frightening. I just needed to shift."

"To 'the other side'?"

"Yes, yes. The other side was associated to the title of a book by the widow of the late Dr. James Pike, a former Episcopal Bishop of

Northern California. Dr. Pike had disappeared on an expedition and the book was about their spirit communication.

"Did you want to communicate with Kurt?"

"Perhaps not as much as I thought . . . The rope was hope. And while we're on it, going to the top of the hill made me think I want to kill."

"Letting him go. Killing the last traces of him."

"It shocks me, but what else am I to do?"

I asked her for a heading. "Forced to Decision," she replied. The three men in the bookstore were unprincipled and high powered . . . who used every trick in the book to get me to buy."

"And the book?"

"It was a sacred epic and the gold-edged pages needed to be separated tenderly. I was afraid they'd adhere."

"And you were tending to your own business?"

"Now that I reflect on it, it could have been Kurt's will."

"And about Kurt?"

"Maybe I'm beginning to get the idea that something was a bit unscrupulous about Kurt. I have that same feeling about his lawyer and Ted."

"You'd better be gentle with the gold if you're feeling bilked. But you've got your last resort?"

The word restaurant had, for Alice, a ring similar to the sound of resort. This was a gathering place of friends who were there to urge her to bury her Caesar. The last course, like the last resort, brought her back to recalling that she had recently made a decision to take a course on the management of personal finances.

The final course — the dessert? ". . . and what about feeling deserted?"

"And the chest," she volunteered — "Ah, chest and chest pains! . . . When can I finally bury him," she volunteered. "Or are we still in a contest about who kills whom?"

"Only you can decide that in your own time."

"I was uncomfortable with the pressures of the salesmen and the others at the table."

"Without pressure you might not feel anything . . . If you can claim your right as a killer you have a legitimacy, a power base. What about the pressure you feel here, from me?"

* * *

Hannah, who had been an able-bodied companion through her daughter's first widowhood, was destined to be more helpless at the advent of the second. Kurt's death had become the widowhood of Hannah's old age. Hannah, the youngest of three girls, was raised in a cultured German-Jewish household. She, like her sisters, was graduated from a prestigious women's college. The family was disappointed when she married Anton, a handsome, though less than promising, man who had then recently emigrated from Hungary. He entered her father's business and (in contrast to his successful brothers-in-law) only marginally succeeded. He was not offered a partnership.

Alice, their only child, survived an influenza epidemic. As a result of her daughter's recovery, Hannah, undaunted by her family's tribulations, was drawn to New Thought, a religious movement in the genre of Christian Science. Hannah devoted her energies to this new-found faith. Anton resigned from the family's company and bought a dry-cleaning store in partnership with his brother. The business survived the precarious years of the great Depression. He finally sold his share of the business to his nephews the year before his death at 62.

Not long before her father's death, Alice married a distant cousin. He was 15 years her senior, and according to Alice, "an experienced lover." Frank, who, like her father, had a "weak constitution," was as "irresponsible as an investor as he was great as a lover." This, as much as the housing shortage of World War II years, forced the couple to move in with her newly widowed mother. Alice suffered two miscarriages early in the marriage. Frank died of Leukemia several months after their sixth anniversary.

Mother and daughter continued living together after Frank's death. Alice, though devoted to her mother, did what she could to claim her independence. Her inventiveness was fundamental to her drive to differentiate their distinct realms of interest and activity.

The years of her widowhood before Kurt were a revisitation of adolescence. She was then in her mid-30s, her mother almost 60. Kurt, 8 years her senior, met her shortly after her 43rd birthday. He was in the final stages of working out a separation agreement from his then wife. Soon there would be a quick Mexican divorce. Kurt moved into the apartment Alice had been sharing with her mother.

Alice had felt like a "real adult" even as she experienced a growing sense of constriction. A month after her marriage to Kurt she developed a debilitating persistent and "constricting" bronchitis. "Taking to bed" seemed to have become her way of fleeing "the new circumstance." Something in their lovemaking was unsatisfactory. Soon there was physical discomfort. Could it have paralleled the choking sensation of the bronchitis? Not long after, Alice underwent a hysterectomy for what were diagnosed as fibroid tumors. Her recovery was slow, underlining the end of all hope for a child of her late reproductive years.

Alice knew from the beginning that Kurt was a "rough-hewn gentleman." His apparent lack of aesthetic sensitivity succeeded in putting her off. He "spoke too loudly and slurped his soup." She felt all the more petty because of her intolerance. Despite these forebodings, she still wanted the marriage to work. It was because of this desire that she decided to go into psychotherapy.

* * *

We met twice a week for several months, and then replaced one of these sessions with group therapy. Kurt, who felt no need for any therapy himself, appeared to be unaware of Alice's uneasiness about him. Rather than "dig up her hidden rage," Alice shifted her focus from complaining about Kurt to her fears that he would someday abandon her. Her fear, not only of losing Kurt, but of not being tolerant of any man, translated into the terrors of loss. She feared doing anything rash, of not controlling her temper, of desiring to hurt herself. She wondered aloud how accessible Kurt could ever be. There's always been the suspicion that, since he'd left his first wife, might he not also be capable of leaving her. She feared "making any false move." Kurt had felt like a stranger. It was not her lot to feel safe with any man.

Kurt rarely paused to reflect on his effect on Alice. He did not see himself as brash and had trouble understanding Alice's distance. In her turn, Alice resented Kurt's "density." It was at this point that Kurt consented to attend the series of group sessions as Alice's surrogate. Though he was exasperating to the group, it was no surprise that he endeared himself to the majority of its members. He had a saleman's casualness. Some complained of his "irritating the serious business at hand." As a result of those few sessions, several group members were able to help Alice see that others could react to Kurt much as she had. She was encouraged by being seen as the sort of person who could have a positive impact on Kurt. People recognized his support of her. Something in his experience was seen as adding to her perspective. When Alice terminated both individual and group therapy, it was with enormous gratitude for what she had learned about Kurt.

* * *

Kurt's death came soon after she began gathering her memoirs into novel form. Kurt had declared that he would "soon" take steps toward retirement though he was reluctant to establish definitive time-tables. This created a tone of uneasiness between the two. They could well afford Kurt's cutting back. Alice felt that it was time for their marriage to be at the top of their agendas. Through it all, Alice had an ominous sense that the marriage was simply fighting for time. Death had become a central focus for her. This, despite the fact that Kurt appeared to feel immortal. His capacity for work "would have put any 35-year-old vice-president to shame." Alice needed perspective. She attended her mother's Church, hoping that it would provide a perspective. It was then that she registered Kurt and herself in the church-sponsored memorial society. It appeared prophetic. Kurt died 6 months later.

* * *

The early months of her second widowhood highlighted what was most compelling in the present moment. Kurt was no more. Master 5-and 10-year plans were laid to rest.

Hannah, now in her late 80s, was to continue living with her daughter. Hannah mourned Kurt's death. Alice tended to see her mother's grief as stemming from her sorrow that there would probably be no more "protecting male presence in the household." Alice confirmed that Hannah was feeling a certain shame at having survived her husband and her two sons-in-law.

Alice wanted to move beyond centering herself on her mother. This would be still another "failure." She wondered if she hadn't married Kurt to please her mother. Being "the child" *and* childless was experienced as her insufficiency. "Why," she asked, had she developed the fibroid tumors and faced the consequences of having her uterus removed. What way, she wondered, could the condition have had to do with resentments long stored away. She bristled over feelings of abandonment. She knew she could not trust men. And there was much indignation at her mother for having survived her uterus and her two marriages. Alice wanted something more than consolation. Yet therapy was to be a "necessary" consolation. It enabled her to hold to her course.

*   *   *

Though many hours were spent in tears and anguish over the abandonment, Alice wanted to be able to permit Kurt a right to die his own death — to complete, as it were, his own autobiography. Coming to terms with being alone at this point in her life was contingent on her acceptance of the appropriateness of Kurt's death. It was to become her task to cherish being a free and separate person without losing what she had gained from having been married.

Alice's grief would eventually move beyond sadness and guilt. Guilt and sadness are only a small part of grief. Other aspects of grieving were to include the possibility of new loyalties and encouraging the development of new engagements. More central was her obligation *to be* without Kurt. Equal in importance was the task of pursuing a relationship with the world even if this quest ultimately excluded a single other. It was a time for reformulation of what would constitute experience. Fear and expectation could have made for an uneasy frenzy.

Widowhood had now become Alice's survivorship. Were it otherwise, she might have counted herself among the emotionally and spiritually dead. Fortunately, living in or for the past was not her mode of emotional support. There were many distractions that might have diverted her: her stepson's derogation of her. And through him, the sense that Kurt's first wife had in some way triumphed. Even Hannah, with all of her professed love for her daughter, regarded her insistence on the immediate cremation as insensitive. Had she indeed robbed them all of Kurt? Ted finally retrieved his father's ashes and had them buried in the family's plot. It was a chapter that needed to be completed. There were few comforts.

The inevitable demands Kurt and Alice made on each other were necessary killers. Though exercises of mortality, they were also life signs — "un-understood experience(s) towards which they yearn(ed)" (Hillman, 1973, p. 65). What remained was Alice's even more private concern. The relationship had taken its toll on her life.

Couples destroy each other even as they demonstrate concern. Accepting this mutually wrought destruction helped Alice to give perspective and meaning to her wounds. To be aware of this cost of life can never be separated from a fully examined existence.

"Ted cut ties with me . . . It was inevitable."

"And you with him. It's been both freeing and injurious to you. It's through the project of these wounds that you continue. Even so, you've had to bear being seen as "the culprit.""

"Takes more of my strength than I'd like to think."

"It was your relationship, and you have to continue what remains of it for you even if you're counted out by the others."

"This widow's fate," she mused.

* * *

From the beginnings of their relationship, Alice was aware that she would more than likely survive Kurt. She had become his inspiration and it was her desire to transform him. Although they may not have seemed to have much in common, they had agreed that this marriage would exist, in large part, to transform Kurt from a somewhat crass character to a man with greater cosmopolitan sensibilities. He had become her "project" and was "the only woman in my life who showed she cared for me." Sensing the briefness of the marriage probably provided it with a unique worth. There is a native American myth that speaks to this worth. The Sun fell in love with the tribal princess. He descended to earth in the form of a poor and infirm youth. The Chief decided on tests that needed to be passed for his daughter's hand. Despite his background and repulsiveness, the young man passed over the others. The princess, out of loyalty to her father, took the stranger as her husband. Then they were both transformed into a greater magnificence.

Despite the marriage's toll on her, Alice's widowhood had finally become her victory. Transformation was the theme of this relationship. A deeper aesthetic was formed in each of their consciousnesses because of the other.

* * *

Widowhood ultimately involves a reevaluation of time. "Perhaps you might ask," I suggested, "what you think you'll need along the way?" Survivor time is sensitive to the fleetingness of existence. She became aware that facing each day required a consciousness of the tasks that surviving the marriage required of her. "Some people think it might help for me to break down, at least in tears. And I'm scared that it could happen."

"Would that be some sort of defeat?"

"I like the question. It makes me wonder if I'm not always having to show them all just how strong I am."

Alice's survivorship continued to take on a newer essence. Her bouts of anxiety were finally seen by her as the visible and necessary signposts of standing alone. New organizing principles came into play. Alice mobilized her resources, even as more friends faded away. Alice commented: "I've become an all-at-once odd place card at the dinner table." Given her "exclusiveness," she was not all that interested in reinvolving herself in the "marriage network." She said, smiling, that she preferred a productive exile.

* * *

There is no finalizing a case narrative. It is not necessary to know where the patient has gone since. As necessary as my presence was at that time in her life, Alice eventually passed me by. Our contacts ended within the year of Kurt's death. I trust that her resources provided amply enough to continue whatever her search was all about and what it would be.

REFERENCES

Hillman, J. (1973). *Suicide and the soul*. New York: Harper.
Lewis, C.S. (1976). *A grief observed*. New York: Bantam Books.

On Inspiration

Sharon Hymer

SUMMARY. Inspiration occurs when an individual establishes an intense object relationship which evokes creative products or ideas which would not otherwise materialize. Inspirational objects can be subdivided into "divine"; inanimate (e.g., nature, music); secular (e.g., teachers, mentors, and therapists); and the self-as-object. Inspiration in widowhood is explored in terms of the widow's transformational relationship with the self and the deceased object. In therapy, inspiration involves both access to the unconscious, and the harnessing of cognitive ego functions to carry through the inspiration to completion. Inspiration requires the coexistence of discipline and spontaneity, mindlessness and mindfulness, receptive waiting and active searching. The empathic analytic couple welcoming of paradox and novelty are most likely to experience inspiration as a catalyst in the therapeutic process.

> One hears—one does not seek; one takes—one does not ask who gives; like lightning, a thought flashes up, with necessity, without hesitation regarding its form—I never had any choice.
>
> —Nietzsche

So Nietzsche (1908/1968) in *Ecce Homo* described the inspiration he experienced while writing *Thus Spake Zarathustra* in a frenzy of energy and speed. The notion of the inspired individual as the instrument of another has found popular currency in religious, anthropological and romantic/poetic accounts of inspiration.

In Genesis, breath (inspiration etymologically equated with

Sharon Hymer, PhD, a psychologist in private practice in New York City, is Adjunct Associate Professor at New York University. She is the author of *Confessions in Psychotherapy* (New York: Gardner Press, 1988). Address correspondence to the author at 144 West 86th Street, New York, NY 10024.

17

breathing into) is a life-giving agent. "And the Lord God formed man of the dust of the ground, and breathed into his nostrils the breath of life; and man became a living soul" (Gen 11, 7). Jones (1923/1964) pointed out that in legends of the Catholic Church God's breath into the Virgin's ear became the fertilizing material for Christ's conception. Examples abound of poets who wrote their best work or could only write when inspired. Many of Blake's songs were written in visionary exaltation; Pushkin wrote poetry only when he was "possessed"; and *Kubla Khan* came to Coleridge in a trance (Bowra, 1955).

Analytic writers, with the notable exceptions of Kris and Klein, have been conspicuously silent regarding the nature of inspiration. This paper explores the reasons for this analytic lacuna and offers a theoretical framework, along with clinical examples, to illustrate how inspiration operates within therapy as well as extra-therapeutically. Further, how inspiration can generate hope and strengthen old and new self and object relations in widowhood is touched upon.

The death of a spouse has been deemed the most stressful life event (Bowling, 1987; Holmes & Rahe, 1967; Windholz, Marmar, & Horowitz 1985). Higher frequencies of illnesses and deaths along with depression, loneliness, and a sense of hopelessness are especially prevalent among widows[1] who have no or few social objects to support them through this trying period (Windholz, Marmar, & Horowitz, 1985).

Yet such dire consequences are not inevitably the lot of the widowed. Inspiration — often narrowly associated with genius and creativity — can galvanize all of us at critical junctures in our lives. Although mourning has sometimes been characterized as a time of diminished capacity and self-esteem (Abraham, 1924; Freud, 1917/1957), others view widowhood as a time of self-renewal and growth (Arens, 1982; Ferraro, 1985-1986; Lopata, 1981, 1986).

During marriage many spouses were unable to strike a balance between the self as a separate entity and the self in relation to the selfobject/spouse. The death of the selfobject can result in a resur-

---

1. I use the term widow to include both widows and widowers in order to avoid the linguistically ungainly widow/widower pairing.

gence of the self that went into hiding or never fully developed if sacrificed at the altar of the relationship. Others whose selves evolved during marriage may derive inspiration both from the deceased selfobject who may be selectively identified with (Jacobson, 1964; Klass, 1987), as well as from a multitude of objects, including the self-as-object (Bollas, 1982). Strong self and object ties thereby can become sources of inspiration rather than expiration (Bowling, 1987; Stroebe, Stroebe, Gergen & Gergen, 1982; Windholz, Marmar, & Horowitz, 1985).

Freud (1917/1957) saw the purpose of mourning as freeing the ego from the attachment to the deceased. "When the work of mourning is completed the ego becomes free and uninhibited again" (p. 245). Inspiration, *per contra*, allows the widow to transform rather than to abandon her attachment to the lost object.

Volkan (1981) described the paradoxical process of mourning: [The work of mourning comes to a practical end when the mourner no longer has a compulsive need to cling to the representation of the dead person. Meanwhile, however, paradoxically the mourner identifies with certain aspects of the dead and comes to resemble him in these particulars (p. 67)]. The inspired widow may thus selectively choose aspects of the object to boost the self. Just as the dead Osiris is regenerated in his son Horus, the widow who "breathes in" aspects of the deceased can add continuity to, rather than deplete the self.

Marris (1975) incorporated Freud's ideas regarding identification with the Gestalt concept of changing meaning structures. He noted that grief is "mastered, not by ceasing to care for the dead, but by abstracting what is fundamentally important in the relationship and rehabilitating it" (p. 38). Being inspired by the deceased can thereby result in creative self-transformation.

Inspiration during widowhood involves neither a blanket separation from the lost object (Freud, 1917/1957), nor a static incorporation of lost objects (Abraham, 1924; Klein, 1975). Rather than being regressively held onto in its archaic form, the object can be drawn upon to fit the current situation. In Marris' schema, the object is thus not regenerated as a static gestalt, but rather selectively identified with to fit in with the changed meaning of the widow's life. For example, Lopata's (1981) concept of husband sanctification in which the widow idealizes her late husband transforms the internal representation of the husband so that the widow can fashion a more satisfying self-construct.

Bowlby (1961, 1982) advocated the formation of new relationships as a means of avoiding any continued relationship with the deceased. Lindemann (1944), in his seminal study, likewise viewed "grief work" culminating in the emancipation from the deceased and the formation of new relationships. These approaches eschew the benefits that the widowed can derive from continuing to be inspired by the deceased. The paradoxical element in inspiration affords the widow the opportunity to develop new relationships in tandem with redefining the relationship with the deceased object in creative, nonpathological ways.

The word inspiration, derived from *inspirare* — to breathe on or into — originally had strict religious and mystical connotations. Witness Plato's famous remark that when the poet functions properly, he is divinely possessed — breathed into, as it were, by the gods. This notion of an outside object temporarily occupying the inspired's body or soul is also ritualistically prevalent in societies whose shamans develop extraordinary healing powers by working themselves up into a frenzy and becoming "possessed" by divine forces.

Apparent from the foregoing is that most therapists are reticent to examine an area which they believe is imbued with magical or mystical overtones. Others simply consign inspiration to the realms of art and/or serendipity and thereby relegate it to a non-psychological or extra-psychological domain.

The definition of inspiration as a breathing into is similar in some respects to that of absorption (Hymer, 1984; Searles, 1979). The object, whether viewed as animate, inanimate, or deistic, is believed by the inspired to be instrumental in the evocation of creative products. Creative products, moreover, are not confined to the *opera* of geniuses. Freud (1900/1953), as did Plato, observed that all of us are inspired in our dreams.

Thus, another reason why therapists may shy away from inspiration is that they commonly misconceive that only the few endowed with genius or madness can be said to possess inspiration. Although other therapists believe that inspiration exists in the general populace, they view its occurrence as so sporadic that it defies rational discourse and analysis.

The example that is often given to illustrate the link between inspiration and madness is that of the famous Delphic oracle in which the priestess supposedly entered into an abnormal trance prior to uttering her oracles. The Greeks believed that a vapor rising from a fissure in the ground was inhaled by the priestess and entered her womb. Hence we find the connection between breath, womb, life, and inspiration.

That the subject establishes an intense, fervent object relationship—whether real or imagined—is a major aspect of inspiration. For exegetic purposes, whether or not divine, mystical, or cosmic forces operate in inspiration is immaterial. Of psychological import is how the individual establishes an absorptive relationship with the object enabling him or her to transcend mundane experience and to create products or ideas which would not materialize in the absence of this unique relationship.

Blake claimed that some of his poetry came as if dictated to him without any premeditation. Handel secluded himself for 24 days in 1741 and wrote as if God's breath had infused his spirit. Asked about his emotions while composing *The Messiah*, Handel replied, "I did think I did see all Heaven before me, and the great God himself" (cited in Weinstock, 1968, p. 233).

At critical junctures during therapy several patients have described the infusion of inspiration as "new life being blown into me." Being in the presence of the empathic other, the patient can truly experience the calm and acceptance that engenders the receptivity needed to "grab hold of" an idea which appears suddenly in the absence of formulaic antecedents.

Since the breath, wind, and spirit are associated cross-culturally with the feminine (Jung, 1938), the nurturant mother in the person of the therapist can foster an atmosphere of non-anxious anticipation of the unknown. The patient's willingness to anticipate the unknown, in turn, heightens the possibilities for inspiration in therapy.

Yet inspiration does not inevitably accompany free association or any other standard therapeutic tool for that matter. For inspiration to play a part in therapy, patients must have a tolerance for paradox without panicking or seeking conventional solutions. Thus, the patient/therapist dyad which functions paradoxically as an "active receptacle" is most likely to welcome and be attuned to unusual emotions and ideation from within and from without.

To reiterate, in most conceptualizations of inspiration, we find the notion of the other (whether divine of secular) as instrumental in the evocation of creative products or ideas. Yet, one can conjecture whether the individual/patient is simply the passive receptacle by which an object expresses itself or whether the object serves as the inchoate encouraging and nurturing force which sets the creative process in motion. This active-passive dichotomy works against inspiration by ruling out the possibility of the individual employing both active and passive dimensions simultaneously.

Again, we can see the necessity for toleration of paradox in inspiration. The patient is fortified to receive the "breath" (influence) of an often unknown or unfamiliar object by feeling secure in the presence of the familiar, safe background object (Grotstein, 1981). This notion is similar to that of Winnicott's (1958/1965) capacity to be alone that eventuates from the infant's feeling comfortable in the presence of the mother.

Another inspirational object which may appear to be unfamiliar is the self as object (Bollas, 1982). Not infrequently, the patient draws upon his or her own inner resources and feels suffused with energy and creativity that appears to come from "out of the blue." Analysis of the origins of such inspiration frequently traces the object of such inspiration to an aspect of the patient's self.

Why therefore does the patient not initially realize or acknowledge this self-induced inspiration? For patients in which the grandiose self (Kohut, 1984) has incompletely developed or has been repressed, to acknowledge that inspiration emanates from the self is akin to bringing the grandiose self into prominence — an experience that in fantasy is often viewed with an admixture of dread, fascination, and desire. Still other patients enter therapy with a creative self that remains disavowed. Patients are often unaware of this aspect of self and learn to monitor and even to welcome it as therapy progresses.

While inspiration frequently happens quickly and unexpectedly, it does not necessarily follow that the end-product of inspiration is likewise produced in a frenzy of activity. It is true that a genius like Mozart thought out entire symphonies, quartets, and sonatas in his head. Indeed, Mozart once conceived a piano concerto in such haste that he just had enough time to write out the orchestral parts, but had to play the piano part "from memory." Beethoven, on the other hand, wrote down fragments and would work and rework them at times over years. His many drafts of the Fifth Symphony, for example, illustrate the many revisions enacted before the final product emerged. Beethoven's work style certainly did not reflect the frenzied speed believed by some to be an inevitable accompaniment to inspiration.

Mutatis mutandis, patients process and react to inspiration experienced in therapy with varying degrees of speed and closure. Many patients who have been in therapy for a considerable period of time often are more receptive and welcoming of the unusual in themselves and in others. My patient John, a 33-year-old designer, one day interrupted his morose soliloquy on the meaninglessness and hopelessness of life to comment on the sun streaming into the room. Suddenly, John brightened and uncharacteristically stated, "God is in this room. He's letting me know that no matter how bad things seem, there's always hope."

Three aspects of inspiration manifested themselves in the patient's comments:

1. The non-religious patient went beyond the givens of his own values and impressions to reach out to God as an inspirational object.
2. The patient's perception surprised him and was accompanied by intense energy and affect differing from his habitual mode of relating.
3. The patient was suddenly infused with hope as if new life had been breathed into him.

John was then able to productively work with this material in contrasting this sudden burst of hope with the hopelessness he had experienced in the presence of his depressed mother who "provided no rays of hope" and "made everything dark and heavy." The contrast in the light and dark imagery underscored John's need to go beyond his past and present objects (I was currently transferentially perceived as offering no hope) to a transcendent object that held forth the promise of hope and renewal.

Patients engaged in creative activities (artistic or scientific) extratherapeutically are often more attuned to sudden changes in their internal and external environment. As a result of drawing on their inner resources and utilizing them in a novel, transformational manner, such individuals (e.g., actors, artists, inventors) are trained to "seize the inspirational moment," whether from within or from without, to creatively transform their world. For such patients who routinely go beyond the habitual in their careers, we again see the importance of paradox in inspiration. With the unusual being somewhat routinized, these patients can often transfer this ability to draw on inspirational sources to therapy.

Another type of patient who engages in extratherapeutic activities, such as meditation or yoga, is more likely to be "actively receptive" (Shafii, 1973) to inspiration within therapy. Indeed, concentration on breathing is an essential component in many forms of meditation, just as the notion of "breathing into" is inherent in inspiration. In both inspiration and meditation, we find a cogent link between breathing – a basic life force – and receptivity to the novel.

Carrington and Ephron (1975) noted a release of blocked energy in one third of their meditating patients. These patients showed increased productivity, ideational fluency, and, in some instances, dissolution of writer's or artist's block. Following meditation, their patients were also found to be more open and spontaneous. Such freeing of inhibitions places the patient in a more receptive stance facilitating the evocation of the novel and the willingness to risk change – prerequisites for inspiration.

Meditation thereby can function as a catalyst in inspiration. Shafii (1973) observed that EEG studies of Yogi practitioners in India and of Zen masters in Japan revealed that after they were exposed to the same stimuli for 5 minutes they still reacted to these stimuli as though they were new and fresh. Paradox thus enters into meditation as well as into inspiration. Although meditation is a habitual, repetitive activity, it nonetheless results in the dehabituation of individuals to repetitive stimuli. Patients who perceive the familiar in a new way do not habituate to a status quo reality, and thereby find themselves more receptive to analogous inspirational forces which are thereby facilitated.

KLEIN: INTROJECTION, PROJECTION, AND REPARATION

In the Kleinian world, taking in the good object and identifying with it becomes life-enhancing and protective. These introjects can be seen as sources of inspiration. Good objects, in turn, can then be projected onto the world. How the deceased object was viewed in life and creatively redefined in death (Lopata, 1986) to a large extent determines whether the widow finds the self diminished via pathological mourning (Abraham, 1927) or enhanced by drawing on the deceased object (Klein, 1975) and thereby facilitating inspiration.

The good object or symbolic maternal equivalent (e.g., nature) is introjected as a source of fulfillment which, in part, fuels the individual/patient to produce *objets d'art*, free associations, and so forth. Conversely, when patients perceive the therapist as persecutory, they resist introjecting the object. They may indeed attempt to constrict any spontaneity in an effort to expel and to destroy the object who, via splitting, is now perceived as all bad.

Klein (1979) also conceptualized the rejected aspects of self and others as contributing to inspiration. "Though the rejected aspects of the self and of internalized objects contribute to instability, they are also at the source of inspiration in artistic productions and in various intellectual activities" (p. 245). The more the ego can synthesize and integrate diverse aspects of the self and of objects, the more riches it can draw upon for inspiration.

For inspiration to flourish rather than to disintegrate, it must be shared with others or with the collective other (the world). Thoughts, feelings, memories, and desires born out of inspiration remain sollipsistically strangulated unless they are brought forth and further worked through in the collective dialogue of therapy. To be receptive to inspiration is to then transform the initial spark — the core idea — into a product or process that can then be shared and given back in completed or "works-in-progress" form.

Patients who forget or resent interpretations may fear being intruded upon or penetrated. Others may block interpretations in an effort to maintain a defensive narcissistic self-sufficient stance (Modell, 1975). Since a major aspect of inspiration involves the individual's willingness to be infused with energy, excitement, or ideational and affective content from an object, the abovementioned patients' fears of taking in *anything* from the object diminish their capacity to draw on inspiration from objects other than themselves.

Further, since inspiration is associated with a life-giving force (Oxford English Dictionary, 1979), patients who feel deadened or indeed dead cannot take in or give out aspects of self or of objects. My patient Jean, a 41-year-old published poet, during periods of psychotic relapse experienced herself as dead and the world as hostile and annihilating. While able to utilize me as a good introject and to write poetry to and for me during nonpsychotic periods, Jean would shut down and disaffiliate herself from all objects of inspiration, especially myself, "God," and her own "poetic self."

Reparation is another factor that can enter into inspiration. Lee (1948) viewed inspired fantasies as expressing the intention to restore the damaged or destroyed object and to love it. These fantasies resulted in feelings of oneness with mother as her idealized image was projected onto the supernatural in inspiration.

Kris (1952) conceptualized inspiration as a desexualized, originally unconscious thought which was externalized and experienced as if it came from the outside. The Muse was seen by Kris and Lee as the projection of the idealized inspirational mother onto the supernatural. Jung (1938) likewise noted that inspiration was generally attributed to an archetypal feminine figure—the anima or mother-beloved.

Inspiration has sometimes been described as a gift from the gods or from the mother in Klein's secular world. The give-and-take between the self and objects, originating in the earliest bountiful mother-child interactions, results in the patient not only being infused with the bounty of objects, but also giving out and giving back to others or indeed to the world (viewed by Klein as maternal substitute objects) the outcome of such infusions.

OBJECT RELATIONS IN INSPIRATION

Inspired writers, painters, musicians, theologians, and mystics are often seen as "losing themselves" during periods of inspiration. In a previous article (Hymer, 1984), I defined absorption as the temporary loss of self through immersion in an object that eventuates in self-enhancement. Absorption results in an expansive self rather than in a regressed or undifferentiated self. Inspiration is not regressive, although it may provide reparative possibilities to archaic objects, but rather progressive. The progressive element pertains to the notion that inspirational objects are cognitively utilized in new, ingenious ways that were developmentally inaccessible to the infant's consciousness.

Gardner (1982) pointed out that inspiration includes the creator's affective as well as cognitive life. Einstein and Darwin were cited as examples of inspired individuals who had a strong, almost primordial tie to their subjects of creativity—nature. The object tie dated back to their childhoods and underwent transformation in the process of their scientific journeys.

These examples underscore the notion that experiences of absorption during the process of inspiration are progressive and transformational rather than regressive. Both Einstein and Darwin utilized and transformed these early object relationships into passionate cognitive/affective involvements in which the world—the collective other—was the beneficiary. Patients who had positive early experiences with objects likewise are often more receptive to influences from a variety of later inspirational objects without fearing manipulation, engulfment, or annihilation.

Inspirational objects can be subdivided into "divine"; Searles' (1979) inanimate objects (e.g., nature, music); secular (e.g., teachers, mentors, and therapists); and the self-as-object (Bollas, 1982). Inspiration has often been depicted as taking place under divine influence. The Scriptures were described as having been inspired by divine revelation. The inspired writer was here viewed as being the channel through which the deity revealed his will or teachings. In ancient Greece, Dionysus, the god of wine, was also the god of inspiration. In their orgies, worshipers believed themselves to enter into real union with the deity.

A strong affective tie to the deific object is evidenced in religious conceptions of inspiration. The experience of possession by a divine object enabling the inspired person to see and to communicate supernatural truth is a universal concept found in pagan cultures, Christianity, Eastern religions, and among preliterate peoples. The notion of "sanctioned madness" finds its greatest currency in theistic conceptualizations of inspiration. That the shaman is often considered to be a madman in many preliterate societies accords with Plato's theory of inspiration as divine madness.

The importance of paradox as a constituent of inspiration is again here manifested. In preliterate cultures, it is the "mad" shaman who is able to productively utilize his possession by divine objects to cure the "non-mad." The shaman who cannot save himself from the darker side of his own nature can nonetheless redeem others precisely because he has the courage to risk entering into a "mad," frenzied relationship with the divine.

We likewise draw inspiration from our relationship with inanimate objects such as music and nature. The aesthetic element in inspiration was early acknowledged by the Greeks and Romans whose epics were believed to have come into existence by the invocation of the Muses. Wordsworth, Coleridge, and Dickinson were frequently inspired to write some of their best poems by their lifelong relationship with nature.

Secular objects, such as teachers, mentors, and therapists, often serve as transitional way-stations for inspiration. Burton (1979-1980) viewed the mentor as a special facilitator in the domains of creative work and creative love. The therapist can serve as an inspirational source in and out of therapy. The therapist who is prepared to flexibly alternate between activity (questioning, commenting, and problem-solving facilitation) and passivity (serving as a background presence to mirror the patient's inspirational and creative flow) may well become an inspirational object.

The therapist's enthusiasm concerning a patient's creative project may itself create inspirational sparks which provide further input into the creative endeavor. As a result of the therapist's "being-with" the patient and showing a willingness to participate with the patient in creative problem-solving, the patient receives both the empathic mirroring (Kohut, 1977, 1984) and ego-psychological support and building to generate further inspiration in and out of therapy.

The therapist not only alternates between active and passive modes, but also engages in "active receptivity" to enhance the potential for inspiration. Optimally listening to the patient, for example, involves both passively taking in the material so that the unconscious of the patient resonates with that of the therapist (Langs, 1978; Reik, 1977) and actively processing that information to select and to transform it into interpretations or questions that generate further associations or the working-through of material.

Kohut's (1984) definition of empathy as "the capacity to think and feel oneself into the inner life of another person" (p. 82) again involves the active extension of oneself into another's being, along with the more passive, unobtrusive being-with that person. The therapist's active receptivity provides the patient with a model for a paradoxical way of being-with an object that is at the core of inspiration.

Regarding the transitory nature of mentoring and therapeutic relationships, it is precisely the knowledge that the patient/individual has that such relationships are transitory which often engenders the desire to "seize the moment" and to fruitfully avail oneself of the gifts that these relationships offer. Again, the notion of paradox becomes relevant. Knowing that his death was imminent, the composer Benjamin Britten continued to write some of his most inspired music. His lifelong relationship and commitment to music infused him with a creative life-force concomitant with the awareness of his impending death. Knowledge of the inevitable termination of a relationship can thereby help us revitalize that relationship as new life is breathed into it via inspiration.

Finally, individuals can be inspired by the self-as-object (Bollas, 1982). The widow is faced with the task of restructuring the self (Lopata, 1986). A cohesive self can serve as an inspirational source from within. The self can then reach out to others to provide additional sources for inspiration. Stroebe, Stroebe, Gergen and Gergen (1982) found that widows' perception that the situation was hopeless and out of control contributed to the stress of bereavement more than the spouse's death per se. Inspiration infuses the widow with hope as an antidote to despair.

Each of us has a sustained relationship with the various aspects of the self-representation (e.g., the self in personal, professional, and creative relationships). As such, there are times in which we can see and draw sustenance from our own self viewed reflectively, as did Britten. The ability to perceive, remember, and draw upon the self as an inspirational object can now help the individual utilize that self as an object from which he or she can receive inspiration and a sense of renewal and purpose.

My patient Jim, a gifted writer who had become depressed and underwent a creative slump, took little pleasure in reading the poetry and prose of writers whom he had hitherto greatly admired. In fact, he had virtually suspended all his reading and writing activities, and had taken to filling in his time by cleaning out his file cabinet.

One day he came upon a fragment of a half-written story he had begun many years before. Jim became absorbed in it, reading it as though it had been written by another. This unforeseen event in which he was able to somewhat objectify the self evoked the most uncharacteristic response. Jim dashed to his desk and started to frenetically scribble ideas that would propel the story forward. This chance encounter with a long-forgotten creative remnant was able to inspire the disconsolate patient. He began to breathe life into the forgotten story which simultaneously served to revitalize the self.

ACTIVE, PASSIVE, AND TRANSFORMATIONAL ELEMENTS IN INSPIRATION

Inspiration requires the coexistence of discipline and spontaneity, mindlessness and mindfulness, receptive waiting and active searching. Both the analytic and the receptive self work together to facilitate inspiration. Relaxing, listening to music, walking, and so on provide a quiet arena for the receptive self to harvest the fruits of the prepared, analytic mind. Pasteur's notion that chance favors the prepared mind here pertains. What appears to be a serendipitous thought or discovery in or out of therapy indeed derives both from flashes of quick impressions and from the slower, more painstaking analytic work which precedes and follows such flashes.

A notable example of the active and passive dimensions in inspiration is provided by Kekule's daydream in which he saw a snake swallow its tail. The inspiration yielded by the daydream was combined with years of mathematical calculations to give rise to the solution of the chemical problem of the benzene molecule being a ring rather than a chain of carbon atoms for which he won the Nobel prize.

The Buddha's quest again underscores the active and passive in inspiration. Buddha was inspired by both actively seeking enlightenment for 16 years and then ceasing to seek it. One night under the Bodhi tree he achieved enlightenment through meditation. Inspired, he "saw" what he called the "wheel of causation" producing suffering and the way to achieve freedom.

Inspiration for the Buddha involved both active searching and receptivity to inner and outer forces. Similarly, the analytic quest for enlightenment does not only proceed by formulaic prescriptions, but also involves spontaneity and receptivity to surprise elements which enter into a transformational experience.

The theological function of inspiration is redemption — "to make men wise unto salvation" (Encyclopedia Britannica). In therapy, inspiration can likewise help to save patients from the darkness of their own self-deception and disavowed selves. The self can thereby begin the process of transformation in the direction of relatedness and greater self-understanding. Such secular redemption was perhaps what Goethe had in mind when he uttered his alleged dying words, "More light."

Finally, the Egyptian myth of Horus and Osiris relates to the active, passive, and transformational elements in inspiration. Osiris in dying descends to the Underworld to become the inert, potential power of nature. He only remains passive until his son Horus, the new king, visits to tell him the old order has been reestablished. In one version Horus opens his father's mouth by touching it with an adzq. As a result of Horus' ministrations, Osiris can "send out his soul" or "set himself in motion" (Rundle, 1978, p. 122). Osiris is thereby transformed into a living soul.

Through the medium of another (Horus), Osiris becomes his original, enlivened self. So are patients, at times, "brought back from the dead" as it were in part through the infusion of hope by the therapist. The therapeutic process becomes the medium by which patients open their mouths (symbolic of breath, life, and communication) and hearts to be transformed in and by the process.

Osiris is the prototype of every soul who hopes to conquer death. Patients who are depressed, disillusioned, or demoralized routinely undergo death-like experiences. Revival requires the therapist, like Horus, serving as a facilitator breathing life back into the patient who has adopted a primarily passive state of being. Inspiration — the breathing of life into the patient in the form of renewed hope — offers the possibility of redemption through the joint efforts of the therapy pair.

The ancients thought of death as the essential prelude to life — the blending of active and passive elements. Whoever occupied the Underworld was seen as being in a state of becoming (not unlike Freud's notion of the unconscious being an active unconscious). The unconscious is not simply the dormant, passive repository of the repressed. As such, repressed material can be restored to consciousness and transformed in the process.

UNCONSCIOUS AND CONSCIOUS ELEMENTS IN INSPIRATION

Cocteau, (cited in Ghiselin, 1952, p. 82), speaking of the moment when the inspiration "takes hold" continued, "For it is at this moment that consciousness must take precedence over the unconscious and that it becomes necessary to find the means which permit the unformed work to take form." Inspiration, in order to be sustained, must involve conscious discipline. Further, as illustrated by Buddha's Enlightenment, the process which gives rise to inspiration involves a combination of conscious, sometimes painstaking search, along with a willingness to temporarily suspend consciousness via absorption.

Inspiration is more than just a reflection of the unconscious. The individual is also a cognitive creature who draws inspiration over time from a series of self-conscious problems and projects which he or she is determined to carry through to successful completion. Robert Louis Stevenson, for example, spent years looking for a story to fit his sense of man's double being when the plot of *The Strange Case of Dr. Jekyll and Mr. Hyde* was suddenly revealed to him in a dream. Both conscious cognitive effort and receptivity to the unconscious afforded him the inspiration necessary to write the celebrated tale.

Bowra (1955) noted the confluence of conscious and unconscious forces in inspiration when he wrote, "one of the peculiarities of inspiration is that it lays hold of the intellect and forces it to make its proper contribution" (p. 24). Inspiration involves both access to the unconscious and the harnessing of cognitive ego functions to carry through the incipient inspirational spark to completion.

The notion of inspiration emanating from the lower depths was popularized by Plato. "No man, when in his wits, attains prophetic truth and inspiration; but when he receives the inspired word, either his intelligence is enthralled with sleep, or he is demented by some distemper or possession" *Timaeus*, 71. Yet, even for Plato, this divine rapture is not a negation of a logical intellectual process, but rather a link to it. Bevan (1928) asserted that something resembling direct and ecstatic vision was for Plato the very foundation of the logical process. For Plato, the rational and irrational, the conscious and unconscious, were wedded in inspiration. For inspiration to be sustained, the initial spark had to be captured and rendered cohesive in an enduring form.

Inspiration is thus not simply a sudden impulse or flash that disappears once the conscious work commences, but is rather an ongoing process that facilitates and lends continuity to the conscious creative work. In therapy, patient and therapist weave back and forth between the initial inspirational spark which may have lent cohesion to a historical puzzle or may have evoked an isolated insight. Inspiration is most likely to eventuate and be sustained when the linkages between the unconscious and conscious are strengthened.

SPECIFIC THERAPEUTIC CONSIDERATIONS

Assagioli (1974) astutely observed, "But it is not necessary to ascertain where they originate. What *is* important is to *recognize* these . . . inspirations, to open oneself to them, and to welcome them" (p. 156). Inspiration has too often been narrowly relegated to the arts and to creative discoveries in the sciences. Yet therapy as both an art and a science can be both enlivened and furthered when the analytic pair are receptive to inspiration. Attunement between patient and therapist facilitates greater receptivity to the novel and to the unusual. Inspiration is thus fueled in part by empathy.

Inspiration as a life force can help propel the dispirited patient back into a more hopeful existence. Patients experience feelings of being trapped, disillusioned, or even dead from transferential or present-day relationships which stultify spontaneity or further growth in the therapeutic relationship.

Inspiration in therapy can arise from the following:

1. Aspects of the real relationship. The patient's knowledge (however derived) that the therapist writes, plays music, draws, or is an enthusiastic audience of such creative endeavors, often helps to breathe life into a patient's abandoned hobby or to infuse hope into a patient's deadened ideals.

   A patient once met me outside a movie theater that was showing a retrospective on Glenn Gould, the Canadian pianist. She later told me that this chance encounter sparked her latent love of music which, in turn, stimulated her to return to painting.

   The therapist's willingness to take risks with the patient in therapy infuses the more cautious patient with the conviction that taking risks and welcoming surprise — integral aspects of inspiration — have beneficial rather than catastrophic consequences. A very reticent, guarded patient told me that after a particular session in which he was able to confront his own fears regarding confrontation, he was "inspired" to confront his son and his boss in one week. That I was somewhat more directive and confrontational with this patient — a development he described as "out of character" for me — helped him muster his courage to face others.

   The therapist's willingness to "step out of character," to risk change and to perhaps surprise both herself and the patient, helped him face these disowned elements in himself. The introduction of these new aspects into the therapeutic relationship and the establishment of novel behaviors, such as confrontation in a habitually nonconfrontational patient, infused life into the patient's stultifying existence. This life-enhancing quality in inspiration can thereby profoundly influence the course of therapy.

2. Transferential-countertransferential dynamics. During therapy, objects are evoked whose ideals, aspirations, problems, and life paths now converge and resonate with those of the patient and therapist in and/or out of therapy. Such extratherapeutic objects may breathe life into the therapeutic process itself. These objects may at times serve to infuse or transfuse the patient with inspiration, and thereby propel the patient into future creative endeavors, rather than bog him or her down in the mire of the past.

When the therapist transferentially assumes idealized qualities, the therapist may be rendered a source of inspiration and resultant action by the patient. A schizophrenic patient would call me every day to sustain a lifeline symbolically represented by the umbilical telephone connection. She would often say during sessions, "You gave me a transfusion when I spoke to you on the telephone." After these calls, she was sporadically able to return to her considerable writing talent, describing her ideas as coming from "the right side of my head—out there."

She never took any credit for her creative endeavors, attributing her inspiration primarily to outside forces and, at times, to her relationship with me. This patient required "daily transfusions" in order to experience a sense of connectedness and purpose. The interpersonal connection inspired her to literally hold on to her life, even in the midst of turmoil, confusion, and a sense of futility and disintegration.

Inspired individuals may find themselves in a state of frenzied excitement while on the verge of a risky breakthrough in or out of therapy. Sustained excitement eventuates when inspiration provides the fodder for the patient to be able to realize and/or work-through a segment of his or her life.

Sudden flashes of inspiration, in the absence of the often arduous working-through process, can be quickly extinguished and thereby come to naught. The therapist, in turn, who fears novelty and dogmatically adheres to strict and "proper" technique, unconsciously sanctions the status quo position of the analytic couple. In so doing, the therapist colludes with the patient in nullifying the effect of any inspirational force that might spontaneously appear. The empathic therapist and patient, attuned to each other and welcoming of paradox and novelty, are most likely to experience inspiration as a catalyst in the overall therapeutic process.

REFERENCES

Abraham, K. (1949). A short study on the development of the libido viewed in the light of mental disorders. *Selected papers on psychoanalysis*. London: Hogarth Press. (Original work published 1924).

Arens, D. (1982). Widowhood and well-being: An examination of sex differences within a causal model. *International Journal of Aging and Human Development, 15*(1), 27-40.

Assagioli, R. (1974). *The act of will*. New York: Penguin Books.

Bevan, E. (1928). *Sibyls and seers, a survey of some ancient theories of revelation and inspiration*. London: G. Allen & Unwin.

Bollas, C. (1982). On the relation to the self as an object. *International Journal of Psychoanalysis, 63*(3), 347-359.

Bowlby, J. (1961). Processes of mourning. *International Journal of Psychoanalysis, 42*, 317-340.

Bowlby, J. (1982). Attachment and loss: Retrospect and prospect. *American Journal of Orthopsychiatry, 52*(4), 664-678.

Bowling, A. (1987). Mortality after bereavement. *Social Science and Medicine, 24*(2), 117-124.

Bowra, C. (1955). *Inspiration and poetry*. New York: Macmillan.

Burton, A. (1979-1980). The mentoring factor in the therapeutic relationship. *Psychoanalytic Review, 66*(4), 507-517.

Carrington, P., & Ephron, H. (1975). Meditation and psychoanalysis. *Journal of the American Academy of Psychoanalysis, 3*(1), 43-58.

Ferraro, K. (1985-1986). The effect of widowhood on the health status of older persons. *International Journal of Aging and Human Development, 21*(1), 9-25.

Freud, S. (1953). The interpretation of dreams. In J. Strachey (Ed. and Trans.), *The standard edition of the complete psychological works of Sigmund Freud* (Vols. 4 & 5). London: Hogarth Press. (Original work published 1900)

Freud, S. (1957). Mourning and melancholia. In J. Strachey (Ed. and Trans.), *The standard edition of the complete psychological works of Sigmund Freud* (Vol. 14, pp. 237-260). London: Hogarth Press. (Original work published 1917)

Freud, S. (1961). Civilization and its discontents. In J. Strachey (Ed. and Trans.), *The standard edition of the complete psychological works of Sigmund Freud* (Vol. 21, pp. 64-145). London: Hogarth Press. (Original work published 1930)

Gardner, H. (1982). *Art, mind and brain*. New York: Basic Books.

Ghiselin, B. (Ed.) (1952). *The creative process*. New York: Mentor.

Grotstein, J. (1981). *Splitting and projective identification*. New York: Jason Aronson.

Holmes, T., & Rahe, R. (1967). The social readjustment rating scale. *Journal of Psychosomatic Research*, *11*, 213-218.

Hymer, S. (1984). Absorption as a therapeutic agent. *Journal of Contemporary Psychotherapy*, *15*(1), 93-108.

Jacobson, E. (1964). *The self and the object world*. New York: International Universities Press.

Jones, E. (1964). The madonna's conception through the ear. In *Essays in applied psychoanalysis* (pp. 266-357). London: International Psychoanalytic Press. (Original work published 1923)

Jung, C. G. (1938). *Psychology and religion: West and east*. In *Collected works of C. G. Jung* (Vol. 11, pp. 5-640). Princeton, NJ: Princeton University Press.

Klass, D. (1987). John Bowlby's model of grief and the problem of identification. *Omega*, *18*(1), 13-32.

Klein, M. (1975). *Envy and gratitude and other works. 1946-1963* New York: Delta. .

Kohut, H. (1971). *The analysis of the self*. New York: International Universities Press.

Kohut, H. (1977). *The restoration of the self*. New York: International Universities Press.

Kohut, H. (1984). *How does analysis cure*? Chicago: University of Chicago Press.

Kris, E. (1952). *Psychoanalytic explorations in art*. New York: International Universities Press.

Langs, R. (1978). *Technique in transition*. New York: Jason Aronson.

Lee, H. B. (1948). Spirituality and beauty in artistic experience. *Psychoanalytic Quarterly*, *17*, 507-523.

Lindemann, E. (1944). Symptomology and the management of acute grief. *American Journal of Psychiatry*, *101*, 141-149.

Lopata, H. (1981). Widowhood and husband sanctification. *Journal of Marriage and the Family*, *43*(2), 439-450.

Lopata, H. (1986). Becoming and being a widow: Reconstruction of the self and support systems. *Journal of Geriatric Psychiatry*, *19*(2), 203-214.

Marris, P. (1975). *Loss and change*. New York: Anchor Books.

Modell, A. (1975). A narcissistic defence against affects and the illusion of self-sufficiency. *International Journal of Psychoanalysis*, *56*, 275-282.

Nietzsche, F. (1968) *Ecce homo*. In *Basic writings of Nietzsche* (pp. 655-772). New York: Modern Library. (Original work published 1908)

Oxford English Dictionary. (1979). Oxford: Oxford University Press.

Plato. *Timaeus* (H.D.P. Lee, Trans.). Baltimore: Penguin Books.

Reik, T. (1977). *Listening with the third ear*. New York: Jove/HBJ Books.

Rundle Clark, R. T. (1978). *Myth and symbol in ancient Egypt*. London: Thames & Hudson.

Searles, H. (1979). *Countertransference and related subjects. Selected writings*. New York: International Universities Press.

Shafii, M. (1973). Silence in the service of the ego: Psychoanalytic study of meditation. *International Journal of Psychoanalysis*, *54*(4), 431-443.

Stroebe, M., Stroebe, W., Gergen, K. & Gergen, M. (1981-1982). The broken heart: Reality or myth. *Omega, 12*(2), 87-106.

Volkan, V. (1981). *Linking objects and linking phenomena: A study of the forms, symptoms, metapsychology, and therapy of complicated mourning*. New York: International Universities Press.

Weinstock, H. (1968). *Handel* (2nd ed.). New York: Borzoi Books.

Windholz, M., Marmar, L., & Horowitz, M. (1985). A review of the research on conjugal bereavement: Impact on health and efficiency of intervention. *Comprehensive Psychiatry, 26*(5), 433-447.

Winnicott, D. (1965). The capacity to be alone. In *The maturational processes and the facilitating environment* (pp. 29-36). New York: International Universities Press. (Original work published 1958)

Widowhood:
Integrating Loss and Love

Ruth S. Farber

SUMMARY. Conceptualizations concerning the process, outcome, and timing of bereavement have evolved over the years. Outcomes which focus on the "resolution" of bereavement, or "severing" the ties with the deceased may not adequately reflect the widow or widower's internal experience. More current research suggests that spousal bereavement may be more prolonged than had been anticipated and the internalized attachment may continue indefinitely. The depth and richness of this connection to the deceased loved one needs to be appreciated. This paper discusses the effects of these newer perspectives on clinical practice, especially by helping people to be able to express their experience more fully before and after the death of a spouse.

The death of a spouse profoundly changes the life of the surviving partner. In addition to the massive personal and social reorganization that must transpire, the widow and widower have to cope with the great emotional pain of losing their beloved partner. The complexity of the bereavement process becomes compounded by internal and external prohibitions to discussing this experience. For the individual, it is hard to put some aspects of this experience into words and initially it is painful to do so. Interpersonally, discomfort

---

Ruth S. Farber, MSW, is a psychotherapist in private practice. Currently, she is in a doctoral program in Counseling Psychology at Temple University, Philadelphia. Previously, she received her Board Certified Diplomate in Clinical Social Work. Mrs. Farber's last publication was entitled "Integrated Treatment of the Dual-Career Couple." Address correspondence to the author at 730 Westview Street, Philadelphia, PA 19119.

The author wishes to thank James P. Smith, PhD, and Gerald R. Weeks, PhD, for their thoughtful comments on previous drafts of the paper.

39

exists in speaking frankly with the dying or about the dead. Historically some clinical/theoretical perspectives on bereavement implied that talking (or thinking) too much, or too long, about the deceased was aberrant. More recent research suggests that continued memories (or relationship to the deceased spouse) may be both normative and sustaining for many widows and widowers. This paper explores both clinical and conceptual beliefs about these features of bereavement. The focus will be on: (a) the value of facilitating more intimate fuller communication during final moments (when possible), and (b) the importance of having ways to describe and discuss the internalization of the loved one constructively, once death occurs.

Lynne Caine (1974) expresses her beliefs about the significance of talking about death and dying in her book about her experience entitled *Widow*.

> I wish I had known about the therapeutic value of talk when Martin was dying. Because today I would insist on talking. I would talk to him about death and terror and pain as well as love. It is what you don't see, don't talk about, that terrifies you . . . talking dispels the phantoms. In helping Martin, I would have helped myself. I would have learned to talk about my feelings. And after Martin died, I could have talked about him. And talked about him and talked about him. Until I finally knew that he was dead and I was alone — starting a new life. I would have emerged from grief sooner. And so would the children. (p. 116)

Caine came to these conclusions after a tumultuous and painful grieving experience which was eventually assisted by psychotherapy. She underscores the healing function of talking. So straightforward, yet so difficult — when talk concerns death.

We are all aware of death — the finiteness of our lives and our loved ones' lives, and at the same time we must also detach from these thoughts and put our energy into living. The awareness of the inevitability of death exists side by side with the automatic "wish to continue to live" (May & Yalom, 1984). Death brings up tremendous anxiety in all of us. Yalom (1980), an existentialist, suggests that the repression of the awareness of death definitely has an adaptive aspect; however, if the individual's defenses are built primarily on denial, complications occur. The anxiety around death affects both the individual and the relationship.

FINAL COMMUNICATION

On an interpersonal level, death is often a tabooed topic. Bowen (1978) explained that there are at least two processes that are occurring in a family when a death-threatening illness occurs. The first one is the individual's intrapsychic denial of death. The second is related to being part of a system in which mutual protection occurs. He believes that communication often becomes closed in couples when death is imminent. Although the individual may think he or she is protecting the other from becoming upset, Bowen suggested this is really an "automatic emotional reflex to protect self from the anxiety in the other person" (p. 322). This happens in families because of the strong emotional interdependence of each spouse and their subsequent sensitivity to each other. Caine (1974) poignantly describes this phenomenon, as her husband's awareness of his cancer began to unfold.

> I knew. He knew. He knew that I knew. I knew that he knew that I knew. And we didn't say a word to each other.
> It was so strange. It was as if our emotional wiring had gone awry and all communication had to be extrasensory. The knowledge was too enormously devastating to touch with words or even looks. (p.10)

Not all deaths allow time to talk or prepare. According to Glick, Weiss, and Parkes (1974) in their study of widows, anticipation of their husband's death (forewarning) was one of the most significant determinants of the adequacy and direction of the widow's recovery. As clinicians, how do we use this time and intervene in a sensitive way when death is impending? The following case demonstrates an example of this.

Sonya and Morris had been married over 40 years. In their first couple's session a struggle over Sonya's low appetite and social withdrawal ensued. It was the very tip of the iceberg. Sonya had metatastic breast cancer. It had been under control for a number of years, however, recently she had a reoccurrence which was unresponsive to the last treatment. She was going through a new more adversive treatment that resulted in minimal appetite and exhaustion. Morris pleaded with her to eat, to be more active and social. His anxiety about her behavior filled the content of each sentence in an angry complaining fashion. What was not said but felt was "I'm terrified this means I'm losing you."

Sonya intellectually appreciated Morris' caring and acknowledged that his encouragement had helped her in the past. However, this time she experienced him as harassing and resented him for the pressure she felt from him . . . to eat, to do her usual housework and stay social, despite the dreadful chemotherapy treatment she was experiencing.

In a subsequent individual session, Sonya revealed she had made peace with the likelihood of her death. She realized the odds were against her this time and was examining her willingness to go through painful treatment which severely compromised the limited time she had left.

Sonya had a few things she wanted to do before she died, such as visiting her grown children in their new homes that were located on the opposite coast. In the couple session she had been quite defensive and annoyed with Morris; however, in an individual session she revealed how worried she was about Morris. She worried about his emotional dependence as well as certain concrete tasks he would have to do on his own if she became sicker and died. She felt very thwarted in being able to discuss any of this with him since every time she tried, she reported that he would raise his voice and seemed unable to listen.

Although the setting allowed only a short-term intervention, Morris was given support to discuss the likely reality of Sonya's impending death (through his sorrow and tears). He depended on her greatly and had difficulty acknowledging that, as well as his love for her. He had to be helped to express thoughts and feelings he had never been taught to talk about. Sonya was helped to realize his loud affect was related to his anxiety (reframing), not anger at her. This helped her to be more sympathetic towards him.

Treatment opened up communication. Once this occurred Morris was more able to listen to Sonya, discuss her reality concerns in a more open manner, including her wish to visit her children (with backup plans if her health worsened during the travels). She felt more respected, which freed her limited energy to be devoted to the things she wanted to do with the time she had left. They began working more cooperatively as a couple. After Sonya's death, Morris expressed gratitude for the help and the more positive last months with her.

We speak of critical periods in growth and development. What could be more critical than one's last conversations with a loved one, one's life partner. So important, yet so difficult. Who is prepared? Who knows what to say; what not to say? What will allow acceptance of self and fate, forgiveness; what would convey premature giving up or abandonment? The answers are very difficult and inexact. Death needs to be addressed straightforwardly, without excessive euphemisms. The delicacy of the process needs to be respected, yet the therapist must be comfortable enough with these real issues to lend courage to the individuals to open up communication on an affective as well as intellectual level. The finality makes each word and feeling precious. Not only does this often help the dying one feel less alone, but for the surviving partner it can fortify the actual and internalized relationship, to buttress him or her for the tumultuous times ahead.

INTERNALIZATION OF THE LOVED ONE

This portion of the paper will examine the internalized relational reality for the widow and widower after their spouse's death. Relationships do not end like cutting a ribbon, in which each piece is completely disconnected from the other. According to Moss and Moss (1985), their work with elderly widows and widowers brought them to the following conclusion: "Having once been part of a couple, the survivor maintains that relationship or bond as a permanent factor in his or her sense of identity" (p. 203). On an individual level, inhibition in being able to deal with memories or talk about the deceased may contribute to a diminishing in the individual's sense of self or self-esteem.

Historically, views on the bereavement process emphasized the termination of the relationship with the deceased loved ones. According to Freud in this 1917 paper on Mourning and Melancholia:

Reality passes the verdict that the object no longer exists — upon each single one of the memories and hopes through which the libido was attached to the host object, and the ego, confronted as it were with the decision whether it will share this fate, is persuaded . . . in being able to *sever* the attachment to the non-existent object. (166)

Lindemann (1944), in his classic study of bereavement with 101 patients (including those survivors of the Coconut Grove Fire), not only emphasized the severing of ties to the dead, but established a time table for this process. He describes one result of successful "grief work" as the "emancipation from the bondage to the deceased . . . and the formation of new relationships" (p. 143). In addition, the time table he found for "grief work" with help of a psychiatrist, was a period of 4-6 weeks for "uncomplicated and undistorted grief reactions."

This view that energy/attachment must be withdrawn/decathected from the deceased before it could be reinvested in the living (as well as a finite timing of the process) prevailed in the literature for quite a while and was challenged by Goin, Burgoyne, and Goin (1979) in their article entitled "Timeless Attachment to a Dead Relative." They described two women in a case study, who were widowed at least 6 years. One had remarried, one had not. Both discussed the continued relationship with their deceased spouses. One woman (remarried) felt that her relationship with her dead spouse "gave her a sense of added fulfillment" because he had always been very supportive to her. She still felt his continued encouragement with her. The other woman also felt a permissiveness from her husband to do things, spend money on herself to make up for her suffering during her deceased spouse's illness. It is important to note both women had normal MMPI and the Beck Depression Scale showed absence of depression. Because of these findings of a relationship to the deceased in psychologically healthy women, these authors suggest this phenomenon should not be viewed as necessarily pathological.

Vaillant (1985) addresses this issue from both a conceptual and empirical perspective in an article entitled "Loss as Metaphor for Attachment."

Contrary to folklore and psychiatric myth, separation from and loss of those we love do not cause psychopathology. Rather failure to internalize those whom we have loved — or never having loved at all — causes psychopathology . . . We have no language for internalization and a very limited one for attachment. The discussion of grief, loss and separation provides patients and therapist alike a metaphor for discussing attachment and the people who live within us. (p. 59)

Although his article views treatment as helping the client find the lost loves within oneself, he does acknowledge the painfulness of highly ambivalent relationships in life or death (especially when the negative outweighs the positive). This is congruent with Freud's (1917) discussion of one of the differences between mourning and melancholia. He described the latter condition as demonstrating difficulty letting go of an introject of a person when there was a strong love-hate relationship.

Zisook and Shuchter (1985, 1986) have done extensive and comprehensive empirical research on spousal bereavement with a 4-year follow-up (after death of a spouse). They acknowledge that a conflictive relationship may contribute to a particularly difficult bereavement; however, in general they have concluded, "There is no prescription for how to grieve properly for a lost spouse, and no research validated guidepost for what is normal vs. deviant mourning" (1986, p. 288). They challenge the simplisticness and dichotomous terms with which bereavement has previously been associated, such as "resolved" or "unresolved." They found even in later adjustment (up to 4 years post death) that "an incomplete acceptance of the loss and a sense of continuing relationship with the deceased spouse are not uncommon concomitants of otherwise 'normal' widowhood" (1985, p. 98).

This last dimension, the continued relationship with a deceased spouse is described as a tenacious phenomenon in spousal bereavement (even in those with conflictual relationships). Even though the actual relationship has ended, some continued emotional attachment to the lost partner seems inevitable. The continuing of the relationship with the deceased does lessen over time, but does not disappear. This may occur in numerous ways. Zisook and Shuchter (1986) found that many widows and widowers had predominant thoughts of the deceased spouse, clear visual images of them, a sense of a continued presence, or even heard the deceased spouse's voice. (This last experience was the only one not present by 4 year follow up and was the least common of the above perceptual phenomenon.) In addition, personal possessions of the deceased spouse may be imbued with his or her spirit and become very significant for the survivor. The deceased spouse may be viewed as being located spatially in heaven or in the cemetery. Also, the conviction of the widow or widower of carrying out the wishes of the deceased as a living legacy may provide a sense of continuity. Lastly, dreams and memories of the deceased spouse alive or at younger times occur and are often quite welcome, "reflecting the simple wish that the spouse has returned to life" (Shuchter & Zisook, 1986, p. 300). The following vignette demonstrates an example of this phenomena.

Sadie was 76 years old. She had been married 42 years, and widowed 4½ years. She was a well-adjusted widow. She was active, had friends and good relations with her children and their children. Her only complaint, which she expressed with humor, was that she was a young woman (with a young mind) trapped in an old body, and was unable to travel as easily as she wished. When interviewed about the concept described in the paper—she was asked if she experienced a continued relationship with her deceased spouse. She said:

> Stu is always with me . . . I like him being with me . . . Just this morning as I was waking, it was as if he was lying beside me, my arm stretched out, I imagined his abdomen going up and down. I grabbed the rolled up quilt and felt united with him . . . When I dream of him I'm always happy—he is always alive.

She went on to describe how sustaining the relationship was for her. His thoughts and opinions were still with her and she could call on them if needed during every day. Although she felt that I may think this is morbid, she felt comforted that she would be beside him in the cemetery (double plot, double tombstone) someday.

Sadie's experience is congruent with the experience of Moss and Moss (1984-1985), who find the persistency of the tie with the deceased spouse in elderly widows and widowers as often a "nourishing link with the past." They believe that this symbolic interaction may fortify the ego by reminding them of past "caring, intimacy, family feeling, commitment and identity support" (p. 204). Instead of interfering with adjustment and establishing new roles (as somehow implied by early theories of bereavement), they believe it can facilitate the transition to the new world and new roles the widow or widower has to adapt to.

It is important for us as therapists to be aware of the normativeness of this phenomena, so that we may be better able to listen for these thoughts and affect in the context of adaptation, and provide opportunities for discussion within the therapeutic relationship. This must be done with care since initially there is also some pain evoked in remembering. Shuchter and Zisook (1986) discuss the mourners' need to "dose" the exposure to reminders of the deceased with their ability to tolerate the painful affect. Each individual varies in the timing and dosage he or she can take. However, this opening-up process is important to lift a layer of isolation off the already painful grieving experience.

Once the individual gains more comfort in talking about these issues, encouragement of opening dialogue with significant remaining others (family) of the widow or widower should be pursued. The "emotional shock waves" of the death of a significant family member are felt for many years by the entire family (Bowen, 1978). A sensitive discussion of the profound meaning of the loss of this unique family member may prove a valuable opportunity for connectedness for the entire family (Wright, 1985) at this time of reorganization when feelings of fragmentation of the family unit may occur.

CONCLUSION

This paper has focused on the importance of facilitating more *intimate communication* with the dying spouse, as well as working with the *internalization* of the positive aspects of the intimacy once the spouse has died. Contrary to past taboos in communication with the dying, as well as past inhibition and fears about too much thought, affect or talk about the dead, this author suggests that paradoxically the permission to be open with these components of bereavement/attachment, may help the dying process be less isolating and survival be somewhat fuller for the widow/widower and their families.

REFERENCES

Bowen, M. (1978). *Family therapy in clinical practice*. New York: Jason Aronson.

Caine, L. (1974). *Widow*. New York: Bantam Books.

Freud, S. (1917). Mourning and melancholia. Collected papers, Vol. IV. In E. Jones (Ed.), *The international psycho-analytic library No. 10*. New York: Basic Books.

Glick, I. O., Weiss, R. S., & Parkes, C. M. (1974). *The first year of bereavement*. New York: John Wiley and Son.

Goin, M. K., Burgoyne, R. W., & Goin, J. M. (1979). Timeless attachment to a dead relative. *American Journal of Psychiatry, 136*(7), 988-989.

Lindemann, E. (1944). Symptomatology and management of acute grief. *The American Journal of Psychiatry, 101*, 141-148.

Moss, M. S., & Moss, S. Z. (1984-1985). Some aspects of the elderly widow(er)'s persistent tie with the deceased spouse. *Omega, 15*(3), 195-206.

Shuchter, S. R., & Zisook, S. (1986). Treatment of spousal bereavement: A multidimensional approach. *Psychiatric Annals, 16*(5), 295-305.

Vaillant, G. E. (1985). Loss as a metaphor for attachment. *Journal of Psychoanalysis, 45*(1), 59-67.

Wright, S. (1985). An existential perspective on differentiation/fusion: Theoretical issues and clinical applications. *Journal of Marital and Family Therapy, 11*(1), 35-46.

Yalom, I. D. (1980). *Existential psychotherapy*. New York: Basic Books Inc.

Yalom, I. D., & May, R. (1984). Existential psychotherapy. In R. J. Corsini (Ed.), *Current psychotherapies* (pp. 354-391). Itasca, IL: F. E. Peacock Publishers.

Zisook, S., & Shuchter, S. R. (1985). Time course in spousal bereavement. *General Hospital Psychiatry, 7*, 95-100.

Zisook, S., & Shuchter, S. R. (1986). The first four years of widowhood. *Psychiatric Annals, 16*(5), 288-294.

When the Spouse Is Dead: The Alternative Approach of Experiential Psychotherapy

Alvin R. Mahrer
Terry M. Howard
Patricia A. Gervaize
Donald M. Boulet

SUMMARY. The purpose is (a) to show practitioners how to carry out experiential psychotherapy with patients whose spouses are dead, and (b) to defend the thesis that experiential psychotherapy is a viable alternative to approaches that comprise the field of bereavement counselling, grief therapy, mourning, death and dying.

There is a more or less established field of bereavement counseling, grief therapy, death and dying therapies. These therapies share a set of accepted truths, clinical axioms, assumptions and presumptions about (a) what their patients are like, the central features of these patients and the focus of therapeutic work; (b) the goals and optimal directions of change with these patients; and (c) the appropriate therapeutic methods and procedures, including the roles of the therapist and the helpful relationships with the patient. If you

Alvin R. Mahrer, PhD, is Professor of Psychology with the School of Psychology at the University of Ottawa. Terry M. Howard is in the doctoral program of the School of Psychology. Donald M. Boulet, PhD, is Director for the Centre for Psychological Services, University of Ottawa. Patricia A. Gervaize, PhD, is Associate Professor with the Department of Obstetrics and Gynecology of Ottawa Civic Hospital and the School of Medicine of the University of Ottawa. Address correspondence concerning this article to Alvin R. Mahrer, PhD, School of Psychology, University of Ottawa, Ottawa, Canada K1N 6N5.

are going to work with someone whose spouse is dead, here is an established approach.

Experiential psychotherapy offers a distinctive alternative. We decline virtually all of the accepted truths, clinical axioms, assumptions and presumptions in the field of bereavement counseling, grief therapy, death and dying. Accordingly, our aim is to show practitioners how to carry out experiential psychotherapy with these patients, to invite practitioners to choose the experiential alternative, and to join us in declining the accepted truths and practices of the traditional approaches in this field.

THE FOUR STEPS IN EACH EXPERIENTIAL SESSION WITH PATIENTS WHOSE SPOUSES ARE DEAD

Experiential psychotherapy is based upon its own existential-humanistic theory of psychology and psychiatry (Mahrer, 1989a), and is a comprehensive, intense, powerful approach that offers the ready and willing patient an opportunity to undergo radical and profound personality and behavior change in each session (Mahrer, 1978, 1985, 1986, 1989b, 1989c, 1989d; Mahrer & Gervaize, 1986). It is also distinguished from such other experiential therapies as the experiential family therapy of Carl Whitaker based on the work of the early "Atlanta group" (Malone, Whitaker, Warkentin, & Felder, 1969; Whitaker & Malone, 1969), from the updated and revised experiential therapy of the current Atlanta group (Malone, Malone, Kuckleburg, Cox, Barnett, & Barstow, 1982a, 1982b, 1982c), from Gendlin's experiential focusing therapy (1973, 1978) within a client-centered framework, the experiential family therapy of Kempler (1970) within a Gestalt framework, Kutzin's (1970) experiential therapy integrating structured fantasy and communications theory, Friedman's (1982) experiential therapy based upon Angyal, Rogers, and Gendlin, and from the other experiential psychotherapies.

The fundamental principle in our experiential psychotherapy is that each session offers the patient an opportunity to go through the same four steps. Patients whose spouses are dead go through the same four steps as all other patients. There are no special steps for patients that other approaches may label as bereavement or grief patients. We proceed through these four steps whether this is the initial session, the final session, or any intervening session whatsoever. There is no special intake or evaluation session (cf. Schwartz-Borden, 1986).

The office is relatively soundproofed. Chairs are large and comfortable, situated alongside each other a few feet apart. There is no smoking or drinking. Therapist's and patient's eyes are closed throughout the entire session which ends when both agree that the work is completed for this session, generally after an hour and a half to two hours or so.

What follows are the four steps in each session. These will then be further elaborated and contrasted with bereavement and grief therapies.

1. Attaining the Level of Strong Feeling and Accessing the Inner Experiencing

The purpose of the first step is to access an inner experiencing, to lift it closer to the surface so that it is sensed and felt. It does not matter whether this inner experiencing has anything to do with the spouse's death. It can be any nature and content whatsoever. What is uppermost is the accessing of an inner experiencing, typically one that is rarely felt by the patient for it is generally alien, deeper, and essentially inaccessible.

The way to access an inner deeper experiencing is through the crucible of strong feeling. Accordingly, the overall direction of the first step is toward attaining a level of strong feeling, whether the route is direct or circuitous, whether it takes a short time or a long time.

Each session begins by showing the ready and willing patient how to express any feeling whatsoever that is immediately present, or how to focus attention on whatever feelinged attentional center may be uppermost right now. From these natural beginning places, we move in the general direction of strong feeling, whether we work with the same continuing feeling or feelinged attentional center, or whether we proceed through a series of subsequent feelings and feelinged attentional centers. The process is wholly open and flexible, and is determined fully by the patient's readiness and willingness, as well as by whatever feelings and feelinged attentional centers occur next. Once we attain the level of strong feeling, an inner experiencing accesses, and the first step is completed.

2. Appreciating the Inner Experiencing

Whatever the nature and content of the accessed inner experiencing, the goal of the second step is "appreciate" this experiencing by (a) welcoming, receiving, and accepting it; and (b) lifting it out a bit, raising and opening it up, giving it some form and shape. The inner experiencing is thereby enabled to be a little closer and more present within the patient. Whatever its nature and content, whether it has anything to do with the spouse's death, the inner experiencing is now appreciated, more welcomed and present.

3. Being the Inner Experiencing
in Earlier Scenes

The goal of the third step is for the patient to undergo a radical and transformative disengagement from the ordinary personality and into the wholesale being of the inner experiencing. The opportunity and the challenge is to leave go of the very person the patient is, and to transform into the radically different person who is the inner experiencing, with its own distinctive thoughts and feelings, perceptions and outlook, personality and character, actions and behaviors.

The method is for the patient to be the inner experiencing within defined and explicit scenes from the past. These scenes and situations may have taken place at any time in the patient's life, from a few months ago to many years ago, from adolescence or childhood or infancy. Now the patient is truly being the inner experiencing in earlier scenes, and this opens the way for the final step.

4. Being-Behavior Change in the Prospective
Extratherapy World

The final step offers the patient the opportunity to be and behave as this new inner experiencing in the imminently future extratherapy world. The ultimate opportunity and challenge is for the patient to be and to behave as this new experiencing from now on, permanently, as a new personality. In any case, the final step provides the patient with a taste and sample of what it is like to be and to behave as this new experiencing in prospective scenes and situations in the imminent external world.

Patients whose spouses are dead are given the opportunity to go through these four steps in each experiential session, whether or not any of the content bears upon the spouse's death directly or indirectly, or not at all.

SOME FUNDAMENTAL DIFFERENCES

The balance of the article shows practitioners how and why to undertake these four steps with patients whose spouses are dead, and essentially to illuminate some fundamental differences between the experiential approach and the field of bereavement counseling, grief therapy, mourning, death and dying. Our thesis is that the experiential approach is a distinctly viable and preferred alternative. The traditional field includes a body of accepted truths, "facts," clinical axioms, assumptions and presumptions. The whole package is uniformly declined by the experiential approach. Accordingly, the experiential approach will be presented and contrasted with the traditional field in regard to (a) the central features of the patient and the focus of therapeutic work; (b) the goals and optimal directions of change; and (c) the therapeutic methods, and procedures, including the role of the therapist and desired relationships with the patient.

The Experiential Approach to the Central Features of the Patient and the Focus of Therapeutic Work

How do we arrive at some way of understanding this person in this session? How do we arrive at whatever is to be seen as the central features of this person, and the focus of therapeutic work in this session?

We begin each session with any feeling or feelinged attentional center that is present. It does not matter whether this is the initial session or any other session whatsoever. We begin with whatever

.

feeling is right here in the patient, present right now, or we begin with whatever feelinged attentional center is front and center on the patient's mind right now. It may be any feeling whatsoever. It may be any feelinged attentional center whatsoever. It may have some direct or indirect connection with the spouse's death. It may have nothing to do with the spouse's death. The patient is absolutely free to start with any feeling or feelinged attentional center at all.

Wherever we begin, there is complete freedom for the feeling to change to some other, and there is complete freedom for the attentional center to change to some other. The only important guideline is that the feeling gradually move in the direction of strong feeling.

The central feature and focus of work in this session is the inner experiencing that emerges when the patient attains the level of strong feeling. Once we arrive at a level of strong feeling, the therapist listens for the nature of the inner deeper experiencing that is accessed, that is present at this strong level of feeling. This inner deeper experiencing is the central feature of the patient and is the focus of all the work in this session.

Nothing else serves as the central feature of the patient. Nothing else serves as the focus of therapeutic work. All we can do is to grasp the nature of this precious inner deeper experiencing as faithfully as we can. We may grasp this inner deeper experiencing with words such as standing up for oneself, being tough and certain, being strong and defiant. Or we may grasp it as the experiencing of closeness and oneness, intimacy and bonding, being one with. These words point toward the nature of the inner deeper experiencing, and this experiencing constitutes the central feature of this patient as well as the focus of the therapeutic work in the balance of the session.

The inner deeper experiencing may or may not have any connection with the spouse's death. When the patient reaches the level of strong feeling, the patient may be feeling or attending to some aspect connected to the spouse's death, or the patient may be feeling and attending to something entirely unrelated. Likewise, the nature of the inner deeper experiencing may be connected with the spouse's death, or it may have no connection whatsoever. We simply accept and use whatever inner, deeper experiencing is present when the feeling level is strong.

Even if the patient is attending to some aspect connected with the spouse's death, all we prize is the nature of the accessed inner deeper experiencing. Accordingly, we have no list of experiencings that "these patients" are expected to have, no "theory" of "their psychodynamics" or inner personality processes. We do not hold that the spouse's death is uppermost and that such patients have predefined kinds of feelings or symptoms or reactions or anything at all.

Within and across each session, there is wholesale flexibility for any experiencing, feeling, or feelinged attentional center. In each session, we begin with any feeling or feelinged attentional center. As we move toward the level of strong feeling, the initial feeling may continue or it may give way to some other feeling. Similarly, an initial attentional center may remain or it may be replaced with a progression of other feelinged attentional centers. In the same way, we accept and use whatever inner experiencing occurs at the level of strong feeling. Within each session there is wholesale flexibility until we arrive at whatever inner experiencing occurs at the level of strong feeling.

This same wholesale flexibility pertains to the next session, and to all subsequent sessions. Regardless of where we began or what was achieved in the prior session, the present one opens with any feeling or feelinged attentional center that is present, and we accept any progression of any feeling or feelinged attentional center on our way toward strong feeling. Once we attain the level of strong feeling, we accept any inner experiencing that occurs.

Declined Approaches to the Central Features of the Patient and the Focus of Therapeutic Work

The experiential approach declines a body of accepted truths, "facts," clinical axioms, assumptions and presuppositions with regard to the central features of the patient and the focus of therapeutic work.

The patient is classified as falling in a given category with predefined characteristics of what patients in that category are like. The central features and focus of therapeutic work are already predefined and predetermined by the category into which the patient is placed. The patient is classified as a bereavement case, a widow, undergoing grief, coping with loss. Such a classification predefines the central features of the patient and the focus of therapeutic work. Once the patient is labeled as a widow or coping with grief, the therapist has a good idea of what the patient is like. The category includes a predefined description of the patient's personality characteristics, symptoms, psychodynamics, the kinds of stresses, prognosis of treatment, present and future feelings and thoughts and problems. The category is powerful. Classify the patient as falling in the category and you have predefined what "these patients" are like. We decline the use of such classifications and categories.

Death of the spouse places high levels of "stress" on the patient. We decline the general truth that the death of the spouse is automatically a central feature in the patient's world, and that it is automatically a high-stress life event. Most approaches, on the other hand, presume that the death of the spouse is something that releases a great deal of 'stress' on the patient (Barrett, 1979; Dohrenwend & Dohrenwend, 1974; Maddison & Viola, 1968; Parkes, 1972), and that this stress is the central feature in all or most of these patients.

Furthermore, it is generally accepted that certain factors determine how serious the stress is to be. For example, the stress is to be extreme when the death is unexpected (Crosby & Jose, 1983; Hyde, 1985; Silverman, 1981), when relationships with the spouse were paramount and long-lasting (Buchanan, 1974). This accepted picture of personality is one in which there is a supposed reservoir of resources for coping with stress so that these resources are depleted to the extent that there are other stresses (Crosby & Jose, 1983; McCubbin et al., 1980). None of this is part of the experiential approach.

The patient has characteristic feelings, reactions, and symptoms connected to the death of the spouse. We decline the general truth that patients whose spouses are dead are supposed to have a prescribed set of feelings, reactions, and symptoms such as loss, threat, insecurity, grief, loneliness, numbing aloneness, despair, devastation, depression, alienation, alcoholism, drug abuse, antisocial behavior, loss of sexuality and loss of identity (Barrett, 1979; Buchanan, 1974; Crosby & Jose, 1983; Frieze et al., 1978; Lopata,

1969; Parkes, 1965; Peterson & Briley, 1977; Rohrbaugh, 1979; Schoenberg, 1970; Uroda, 1977). Likewise, we do not accept that the patient's central features will include such characteristic bodily "symptoms" as weight loss, sleeplessness, shortness of breath, rheumatism, choking, a "need" for sighing, lack of muscular strength, exhaustion, digestive difficulties, asthma, bronchitis, chest pains, ulcers, swollen feet, hair loss, skin irritations, headaches, and dizziness (Lindemann, 1944; Marris, 1958; Parkes, 1972).

Nor do we accept the general truth that the patient has characteristic feelings and reactions because of what "society" believes and expects. For example, the widow "who cannot go along with society's reluctance to acknowledge her grief and loss and who continues to show it, begins to wonder not what is wrong with society but what is wrong with her" (Silverman, 1981, p. 17). This may be an apt description of some patients in some sessions of some therapies, but it is not accepted by the experiential approach as a transcendent truth.

Once you classify the patient as, for example, a bereavement case, then it is typically held that the patient has characteristic feelings, reactions, and symptoms, and these are then accepted as the focus of therapeutic work. Whether, for example, the patient shows grief, the presumption is that there is grief, and "the grief work *will* be done. Sooner or later, correctly or incorrectly, completely or incompletely, in a clear or distorted manner, it will be done" (Hodge, 1973). The therapist presumes that there is painful loss and grief, and the therapist therefore presses for their expression and acceptance: "If the client does not accept the pain of his or her loss, the other grief work cannot proceed. The worker must continuously 'persuade' the client to accept the grief . . ." (Schwartz-Borden, 1986, p. 501). The experiential approach declines the generally accepted truth that the patient will have such a package of characteristic feelings, reactions, and symptoms.

Certain factors determine the nature and extent of the patient's feelings, reactions, and symptoms connected to the death of the spouse. By virtue of our declining the presumed truth of a set of characteristic feelings, reactions, and symptoms, we thereby disclaim the whole array of factors that are held as determinants. For example, some approaches hold that the effect of the death is a function of the patient's belief in God and an afterlife (Buchanan, 1974), or whether the death was quick and unexpected or the result of a long and drawn out illness (Crosby & Jose, 1983; Hyde 1985), or the amount of unexpressed and unresolved feeling between the spouses (Tobin, 1971), or whether the patient is young or old. "The very elderly woman seems psychologically better prepared for her husband's death" (Heyman & Gianturco, 1973; Hyde, 1985, p. 181; Rohrbaugh, 1979). On the other hand, the spouse's death is also held as easier on patients who are younger (Bequaert, 1976), and female: "It seems that the death of a spouse is harder on men than it is on women" (Hyde, 1985, p. 178; also cf. Bock & Webber, 1972; Spreitzer et al., 1975; Strobe & Strobe, 1983).

The patient will go through a predefined series of stages of reactions to the spouse's death. We decline the general truth that patients go through a series of stages; we decline the supposed nature and content of the stages, and we decline the time the stages are expected to comprise. Most approaches hold that the patient will proceed through a defined series of stages. It may be Kubler-Ross's (1969) five stages: denial, anger, bargaining, depression, and acceptance. It may be Parkes' (1970) six stages: shock and numbness, yearning and intense mourning, anger and protest, disorganization, mitigation of the pain, and identification. Or it may be some other rendering of the number and nature of stages (Bowlby, 1961; Clark, 1982; Clinebell, 1962; Marris, 1974; Uroda, 1977; Weiss, 1976).

These approaches accept that therapeutic work starts with whatever is conceived to be the initial stage, whether this is supposed to be denial, shock or numbness, self-grieving, anger, fear of facing a radically changed world, the realization of their loss, or anything else (e.g., Buchanan, 1974; Silverman, 1981).

It is also accepted that these stages take a certain length of time to run their course. Most versions hold that the stages take a year or so. On the other hand, some hold that it only takes about 6 weeks for a "normal grief reaction" to run its course (Switzer, 1970), while, at the other extreme, some hold that even the normal grieving process may take upwards of 2 to 4 years to go through the stages (Maddison & Viola, 1968; Parkes, 1972; Schoenberg et al., 1975). We decline the whole package of presumed stages.

The patient's state and reactions may be classified as "pathological" or "normal." We also decline a category system in which the therapist diagnoses or labels the patient's overall state or the reactions to the death as pathological (morbid, acute, abnormal, ill, emotionally sick, neurotic, or psychotic) or as normal or even healthy (Adler et al., 1975; Lindemann, 1944; Silverman, 1981; Switzer, 1970, 1972; Volkan, 1975). Most approaches think in terms of normality and pathology, and either casually or formally assign the patient to one or the other. This picture generally includes a model in which there is a certain degree of "stress" and a reservoir of "resources" to "cope" with the stress (Silverman, 1981). If you categorize the state of reactions as pathological, these approaches label the person as a "pathological mourner" or an "unresolved grief reaction," and administer a special program designed to treat the pathological state or reaction (Melges & De-Maso, 1980; Volkan, 1975).

The Experiential Approach to the Goal and Optimal Direction of Change in this Session

The first step of this session enabled the patient to attain a level of strong feeling, and to access or lift up some deeper inner experiencing. The goal of this session, the optimal direction of change, is for the patient to be and to behave as this experiencing in the imminent extratherapy world.

The aim is for the inner, deeper experiencing to be gentle, open and available, on good relations with everything else that is the patient, to occur in its good and friendly form. We call this 'integration.' The aim is for this inner, deeper experiencing to come into the operating domain, to be a part of what the patient is, to be connected with actual new ways of behaving, to open into the world which the patient constructs and lives in. We call this 'actualization.' Ideally, the goal and optimal direction of change is for the patient to be able to be this integrated and actualized experiencing, to be a radically new and different person who is this experiencing, and to be this new person from this moment on.

This goal and optimal direction of change in this session may or may not have anything to do with the death of the spouse. Usually it does. It may not.

Goals and Directions of Change Declined by the Experiential Approach

Once you classify the patient as a bereavement case or in the grieving process or coping with loss, then your therapeutic goals are already largely predetermined. Once you believe that the death of the spouse places extremely high levels of stress on the patient, you are constrained to certain therapeutic goals. Your goals are generally predetermined once you see the patient as falling in a class with characteristic feelings, reactions, and symptoms connected to the death of the spouse, especially when you are constrained to accept that certain factors determine the nature and extent of these feelings, reactions, and symptoms. Once you accept that patients go through defined stages of reactions to the spouse's death, your goals are largely set in place. We decline this whole package of presumptions and the connected goals and directions of change.

Working through the process of grief and loss. One of the most popular goals is working through whatever the approach accepts as the stages of grief, loss, and mourning. The patient is to achieve "resolution of the grieving process and ultimate accommodation and adjustment to the catastrophe" (Crosby & Jose, 1983, p. 82). With grief and loss as the central features, the aim is to proceed through the stages in order to attain "(a) freedom from bondage to the deceased, (b) readjustment to social environment, and (c) formation of new relationships" (Peterson & Briley, 1977, p. 32; cf. Buchanan, 1974; Schuchter, 1986; Silverman, 1981; Volkan, 1975).

Recovery from other negative effects of the death. The goal is recovery from all the other personal and universal negative effects of the death (Anderson, 1965; Buchanan, 1974; Clark, 1982; Schoenberg, 1970; Silverman, 1981). These include recovery from all the stress, loneliness, depression, and despair. Patients are to learn to understand and accept their negative emotional reactions to the death. They are to recover from feelings of threat and insecurity, alienation and fearfulness. They are to recover from physical symptoms such as weight loss, exhaustion, ulcers, headaches, digestive problems, and sleeplessness.

Attaining a healthy, mature adjustment. The goal is to attain whatever the approach holds as healthy, mature adjustment. This generally includes developing new relationships, creating new personal lives, accentuating virtues, getting on with their lives, being physically healthy (Buchanan, 1974; Clark, 1982; Peterson & Briley, 1977; Schuchter, 1986).

THERAPEUTIC METHODS USED IN EXPERIENTIAL PSYCHOTHERAPY

Each session goes through the same four steps whether or not the patient is a person whose spouse is dead. The methods used in these steps are the same for every patient. There are no special steps or methods for patients whose spouses are dead.

The first step enables the patient to attain a level of strong feeling and thereby to access whatever inner experiencing is present. We begin with any feeling that is here right now or with whatever feelinged attentional center is here right now. We accept whatever the patient presents, whether or not the feelings have anything to do with the spouse's death, and whether or not the attentional center has anything to do with the spouse's death. Likewise, when we arrive at the level of strong feeling, we accept whatever inner experiencing is accessed, whether or not it has anything to do with the spouse's death.

Once we start with any feeling or feelinged attentional center, the methods are designed to let the feeling show and grow, to open up and become stronger. Once the feelings are at least moderate, the patient is shown how to go from a moderate to a strong level. All the methods of the first step are designed to attain the level of strong feeling in order to access the inner experiencing.

The purpose of the second step is to appreciate whatever inner experiencing is accessed. We use methods of listening for and identifying this inner experiencing, naming and describing it, welcoming and accepting it, and lifting it up and expressing it.

The purpose of the third step is for the very heart and identity of the patient to disengage from the ordinary continuing personality and to enter wholesale into the very being of the inner experiencing. This is accomplished within the context of earlier life scenes and situations. Our methods enable the patient to identify an earlier scene or situation, to enter into the inner experiencing, and to be this experiencing within the context of the earlier life scene or situation.

The purpose of the fourth and final step is for the patient to gain a taste and sample of what it is like to be this inner experiencing in the context of the extratherapy world, to be and behave as this new experiencing in the imminent future world. Our methods are especially designed to achieve this being-behavioral change.

There are no special methods for patients whose spouses are dead. Perhaps the only distinguishing feature is that in some sessions the starting point may consist of feelings or feelinged attentional centers dealing with the spouse's death. Nevertheless, the steps and methods are the same whether or not the patient's spouse is dead.

In carrying out this therapy, the experiential therapist carries out three functions or roles. One is that of instruction-giver. The therapist tells the patient what to do and how to do it for each step. Second, when the patient talks, the therapist allows the patient's words to be as if they were coming in and through the therapist. This is called 'experiential listening,' and it enables the therapist to grasp the immediate feeling and inner experiencing. Third, the therapist undergoes the process of therapeutic experiencing right along with the patient. Together, these comprise how the therapist is with the patient. There is no other prescribed therapeutic role or relationship.

Therapeutic Methods Declined
by Experiential Psychotherapy

Many other approaches use special methods for patients whose spouses are dead. We do not.

Going through the stages of mourning and grief. The patient is to be helped through each of the stages of mourning and grief (Clark, 1982; Frieze et al., 1978; Gorer, 1965; Marris, 1958); "the task of the therapist is to facilitate the grief process" (Simos, 1977, p.

340). If there is difficulty in proceeding through the stages or if there is a pathological block, then special methods are called for, methods such as identifying the obstacles, removing them through guided imagery, and then re-grieving (Melges & DeMaso, 1980).

Giving vent to negative feelings and emotions. The patient is to open up and express the negative feelings and emotions presumably connected to the spouse's death: e.g., anger, hurt, loss, guilt, bitterness, chaos and confusion; "nothing helps so much as to let our feelings pour out in a veritable flood" (Peterson & Briley, 1977, p. 34). Use any expressive method, including the Gestalt two-chair technique (Tobin, 1971). The aim is both to give vent to these negative feelings and emotions, and also to avoid the deleterious effects of containing them, bottling up and repressing them (Buchanan, 1974; Peterson & Briley, 1977; Schoenberg, 1970; Schwartz, Borden, 1986; Schuchter, 1986; Simos, 1977; Switzer, 1970). In our initial step, the aim is to access the inner experiencing rather than to give vent to and express negative feelings.

Accepting the status and feelings of bereavement. The methods are designed to lessen the pain and to accept the status and feelings of the bereaved state. If the patient is in a state of isolation and withdrawal, the therapist is to help the patient accept the state, and then "quietly encourage the individual toward less isolated activities" (Clark, 1982, p. 53). The patient "has to accept the pain of the bereavement. He has to review his relationships with the deceased and has to become acquainted with the alterations in his own modes of emotional reaction" (Lindemann, 1944, p. 141). Acceptance occurs as the patient gains insight and understanding of the feelings of bereavement, and learns "to differentiate clearly between anger, sorrow, and the other emotional responses of grief" (Clark, 1982, p. 55).

Acceptance includes being shown and reassured that the new, strange, perhaps frightening and alien feelings and reactions are normal and will pass in time (Peterson & Briley, 1977). "Probably the most frequent comment the author makes in grief work is 'Your reaction is part of grief, and normal'" (Simos, 1977, p. 341). While the therapist is to be alert to cases where the reactions are abnormal and pathological, most patients are to accept that they are proceeding through the normal stages of bereavement (Simos,

1977). In many cases, there "was no 'special' counseling needed, just someone to help him understand what was going on in his own life and to keep check from time to time to be certain that progress was being made" (Switzer, 1970, p. 185).

The patient is to accept that it may take a long time to recover from the effects of the death. "Perhaps the most important first step is to recognize that she will feel miserable for some indeterminate period of time and that she will simply have to endure that misery. Knowing that this is normal and inevitable can be very helpful" (Silverman, 1981, p. 47). In this connection the patient is to accept that it is unwise to make any substantial changes or decisions for a year or so following the death of the spouse (Buchanan, 1974). It is also helpful to promote acceptance by being in bereavement groups, and also by reading books and articles about bereavement, overcoming and accepting the negative feelings, and the expected stages of the grief process. All of these methods are declined in experiential therapy.

Resolving ties with the deceased. The therapist is to help the patient resolve ties to the deceased. "Cutting the ties to the deceased is an essential function of grief work. Make no mistake. If the ties are not cut, the grief process has not been completed" (Peterson & Briley, 1977, pp. 59-51; cf. Tobin, 1971; Schwartz-Borden, 1986; Weiss, 1950). This may entail repeatedly retelling the events surrounding the death and its aftermath, describing these in detail until the grief and distress are reduced (Mawson, Marks, Ramm, & Stern, 1981), the reality of the death is validated (Buchanan, 1974), the ties are resolved (Peterson & Briley, 1977), and she is free of clinging to the role of wife (Silverman, 1981).

On the other hand, it may be beneficial to foster other ways of constructively resolving these ties. "The widow does not want to cut herself off from the past even if it were possible to do so. Instead, she needs to find constructive ways to remember. Her memories become important for they are a means of honoring the dead and of building continuity between the past and the future" (Silverman, 1981, p. 51). This constructive preservation of the ties is also emphasized by some psychoanalytic approaches where patients may need reassurance that the loss does not prejudice the original parental love and acceptance of the infant (Klein, 1940).

If the ties to the deceased are too powerful, then special methods are called for to resolve these pathological bonds. For example, the therapist may invoke a program of re-grief therapy including such methods as interpretation, loosening of contacts with the deceased, detailed description of the events of the death, and reevaluation of the reality of the actual death (Volkan, 1975).

Using special therapist roles to attract, retain and relate to these patients. In most approaches, therapists are adept at justifying and carrying out special roles that attract and retain patients whose spouses are dead, and that allow therapists to fulfill these special roles.

One common role is that of an acknowledged specialist in grief therapy, bereavement counseling, grief resolution therapy, re-grief therapy, death and dying counseling. Such specialization is open to psychiatrists, social workers, psychologists, counselors, physicians, funeral directors, pastoral counselors and others. Often these specialists also provide special support groups, bereavement therapy groups, self-help groups, and the like. By means of such specialization the therapist is both elevated above and distinguished from the ordinary therapist.

On the other hand, ordinary therapists can cloak themselves in a role that can compete with these specialists. This role includes emphasizing that bereavement may only be symptomatic of a larger clinical picture that these therapists are especially trained to understand and treat, that there may be deeper pathological components that they are especially equipped to deal with, that medication and hospitalization might be called for. Emphasize that only these therapists are trained to deal with the acute problems, the serious depressions and suicidal aspects, the deeper psychodynamics and pathological components.

Another common therapist role is that of the professional helper who provides what the patient "needs" throughout the entire course of the bereavement process. This is reinforced by the belief that there are stages and phases to the entire bereavement process which may require professional help for about a year or more. This belief can be extended even further by framing the belief as requiring help at least 3 or 4 months prior to the death of the spouse (Adler et al., 1975). By believing that the spouse "needs therapy," you can thereby justify contacting the spouse and suggesting the value and need for entering therapy (cf. Battin et al., 1975).

The plight of the patient invites, and many therapists expressly welcome, the role of manager. Someone is to fulfill the role of manager of the patient's exploded world, and many therapists are quietly eager to justify such a role. They arrange for a family friend or grown child to live with the patient, or for the patient to live with a sister or friend (Buchanan, 1974). The therapist decides when and how the patient is to have helpful contact with other persons and groups. "As a practitioner working with widows you have to sort out when you can be helpful and when it would be of value to involve your clients with other widows" (Silverman, 1981, p. 56). Life decisions are to be funneled into and discussed in therapy. In fulfilling the role of manager, the therapist must win the competition with such other contenders as the family physician, the priest, the capable sibling, the uncle and aunt, the funeral director, bereavement counselor, lawyer, family friend, self-help group leader, and the grown child.

Many favorite therapist roles are conjointly worked out by patient and therapist, and revolve around whatever patient feature is emphasized. Patients are labeled as having problems featuring loneliness and withdrawal, or bottled up negative feelings, or being sexually dried up, or giving up, or being at loose ends and unraveling. Each of these featured problems is fitted to a particular therapist role. Accordingly the therapist is the close friend and companion who dispels the loneliness and walks with the patient out of her withdrawal. The therapist is the one who opens the gates to the bottled up awful feelings. The therapist fulfills the role of the rekindler of the dried up sexuality. The therapist is the one who lifts up the patient who is worn out and has given up, and offers light and hope and rebirth. The therapist offers strength and solid secure reality to the patient who is at loose ends and unraveled.

Therapists and patients establish these mutual roles inadvertantly and essentially outside awareness. Yet these roles have a powerful determining effect on what transpires session after session, month after month, for these roles tend to lock in both therapist and patient. The changes that occur tend to be those that feed and sustain these therapist and patient roles. Symmetrically, whole avenues of possible changes are thereby set aside as outside the boundaries of these roles.

CONCLUSIONS

1. In experiential psychotherapy, all patients are invited in each session to go through four steps of therapeutic change. This includes patients whose spouse is dead as well as all other patients. In other words, there is no special labeling of the patient as a bereavement case and no special therapeutic programs or procedures.
2. Each experiential session offers the patient the opportunity of undergoing profound depth and breadth of personality and behavioral change, whether or not these changes relate to the death of the spouse.
3. Experiential psychotherapy differs basically and fundamentally from virtually all bereavement or grief therapies with regard to essentially all of their accepted truths, "facts," clinical axioms, assumptions and presumptions, especially as they relate to (a) the presumed central features of the patient and focus of therapeutic work, (b) the goals and optimal directions of change, and (c) the therapeutic methods, including the role of the therapist and relationships with the patient.
4. We invite therapists to consider and try out experiential psychotherapy with patients whose spouses are dead, as well as with patients whose spouses are not dead. We also offer experiential psychotherapy as a powerful and effective alternative to the field of bereavement counseling, grief therapy, death and dying.

REFERENCES

Allen, G., Beiser, M., Cole, R., Johnston, L., & Krant, M.J. (1975). Approaches to intervention with dying patients and their families: A case discussion. In B. Schoenberg, I. Gerber, A. Wiener, A.H. Kutscher, D. Paretz, & A.C. Carr (Eds.). *Bereavement: Its psychosocial aspects* (pp. 281-293). New York: Columbia University Press.

Anderson, B.B. (1965). Bereavement as a subject of cross-cultural inquiry: An American sample. *Anthropological Quarterly, 38,* 181-200.

Barrett, C.J. (1979). Women in widowhood. In J.H. Williams (Ed.), *Psychology of women*, (pp. 496-506). New York: Norton.

Battin, D., Arkin, A.M., Gerber, I., & Wiener, A. (1975). Coping with vulnerability among the aged bereaved. In B. Schoenberg, I. Gerber, A. Wiener, A.H. Kutscher, D. Peretz, & A.C. Carr (Eds.). *Bereavement: Its psychosocial aspects* (pp. 294-309). New York: Columbia University Press.

Bequaert, L.H. (1976). *Single women, alone and together*. Boston: Beacon Press.

Bock, E.W. & Webber, I. (1972). Suicide among the elderly: Isolating widowhood and mitigating alternatives. *Journal of Marriage and the Family, 34,* 24-31.

Bowlby, J. (1961). Processes of mourning. *International Journal of Psychoanalysis, 42,* 317-340.

Buchanan, R.L. (1974). The widow and widower. In E.A. Grollman (Ed.). *Concerning death: A practical guide for the living* (pp. 182-211). Boston: Beacon Press.

Clark, A. (1982). Grief and Gestalt therapy. *The Gestalt Journal, 5,* 49-63.

Clinebell, H. (1966). *Basic types of pastoral counseling*, Nashville, TN: Abingdon.

Crosby, J.F.. & Jose, N.L. (1983). Death: Family adjustment to loss. In C.R. Figley & H.I. McCubbin (Eds.). *Stress and the family. Vol. 2: Coping with catastrophe* (pp. 75-89). New York: Brunner/Mazel.

Dorenwend, B.S., & Dorenwend, B.P. (Eds.). *Stressful life events: Their nature and effects*. New York: Wiley.

Friedman, N. (1982). *Experiential therapy and focusing*. New York: Half Court.

Frieze, I.H., Parsons, J.E., Johnson, P.B., Rubler, D.N., & Zellman, G.L. (1978). *Women and sex roles: A social psychological perspective*. New York: Norton.

Gendlin, E.T. (1973). Experiential psychotherapy. In R. Corsini (Ed.). *Current psychotherapies* (pp. 317-352). Itasca, Illinois: Peacock.

Gorer, G. (1965). *Death, grief, and mourning*. New York: Doubleday.

Heyman, D.K., & Glanturco, D.T. (1973). Long term adaptation by the elderly to bereavement. *Journal of Gerontology, 28,* 359-362.

Hodge, J. (1972). They that mourn. *Journal of Religion and Health, 3,* 229-234.

Hyde, J.S. (1985). *Half the human experience: The psychology of women*. Lexington, MA: D.C. Heath.

Kempler, W. (1970). Experiential psychotherapy with families. In J. Fagan & I.L. Shepherd (Eds.), *Gestalt therapy now* (pp. 150-161). New York: Harper and Row.

Klein, M. (1940). Mourning and its relation to manic-depressive states. *International Journal of Psychoanalysis, 21,* 126-162.

Kubler-Ross, E. (1969). *On death and dying*. New York: Macmillan.

Kutzin, A. (1970). Paradoxical experiential psychotherapy. *Journal of Contemporary Psychotherapy, 11,* 131-153.

Lindemann, E. (1944). Symptomatology and management of acute grief. *American Journal of Psychiatry, 101,* 125-158.

Lopata, H.Z. (1969). Loneliness: Forms and components. *Social Problems, 17*, 248-261.

Madison, D., & Viola, A. (1968). The health of widows in the year following bereavement. *Journal of Psychosomatic Research, 12*, 297-304.

Mahrer, A.R. (1978). Sequence and consequence in the experiential psychotherapies. In C. Cooper & C. Alderfer (Eds.), *Advances in experiential social processes* (pp. 39-45). New York: Wiley.

Mahrer, A.R. (1985). *Psychotherapeutic change: An alternative approach to meaning and measurement*. New York: Norton.

Mahrer, A.R. (1986). *Therapeutic experiencing: The process of change*. New York: Norton.

Mahrer, A.R. (1989a). *Experiencing: A humanistic theory of psychology and psychiatry*. Ottawa: University of Ottawa Press. (Original work published 1978)

Mahrer, A.R. (1989b). *Experiential psychotherapy: Basic practices*. Ottawa: University of Ottawa Press. (Original work published 1983)

Mahrer, A.R. (1989c). *The integration of psychotherapies: A guide for practicing therapists*. New York: Human Sciences Press.

Mahrer, A.R. (1989d). *How to do experiential psychotherapy: A manual for practitioners*. Ottawa: University of Ottawa Press.

Mahrer, A.R., & Gervaize, P.A. (1986). The steps and methods in experiential psychotherapy sessions. In P.A. Keller & L.G. Ritt (Eds.). *Innovations in clinical practice: A source book* (pp. 59-69). Sarasota, FL: Professional Resource Exchange.

Malone, K., Malone, T., Kuckleburg, R., Cox, C., Barnett, J., & Barstow, D. (1982a). Experiential psychotherapy: Basic principles, part I. *Pilgrimage, 10*, 25-47.

Malone, K., Malone, T., Kuckleburg, R., Cox, C., Barnett, J., Barstow, D. (1982b). Experiential psychotherapy: Basic principles, part II. *Pilgrimage, 10*, 102-123.

Malone, K., Malone, T., Kuckleburg, R., Cox, C., Barnett, J., & Barstow, D. (1982c). Experiential psychotherapy: Basic principles, part III. *Pilgrimage, 10*, 152-168.

Malone, T.P., Whitaker, C.A., Warkentin, J., & Felder, R.E. (1961). Rational and nonrational psychotherapy. *American Journal of Psychotherapy, 15*, 212-220.

Marris, P. (1958). *Widows and their families*. London: Routledge and Kegan Paul.

Marris, P. (1974). *Loss and change*. New York: Pantheon Books.

Mawson, D., Marks, I.M., Ramm, L., & Stern, R.S. (1981). Guided mourning for morbid grief: A controlled study. *British Journal of Psychiatry, 138*, 185-193.

McCubbin, H.I., Joy, C.B., Cauble, A.E., Comeau, J.K., Patterson, J.M., & Needle, R.H. (1980). Family stress and coping: A decade review. *Journal of Marriage and the Family, 42*, 855-871.

Melges, F.T., & DeMaso, D.R. (1980). Grief-resolution therapy: Reliving, revising, and revisiting. *American Journal of Psychotherapy, 34*, 51-61.

Parkes, C.M. (1964). The effects of bereavement on physical and mental health — A study of the medical records of widows. *British Medical Journal, 2*, 274-279.

Parkes, C.M. (1970). The first year of bereavement. *Psychiatry, 33*, 444-467.

Parkes, C.M. (1972). *Bereavement: Studies of grief in adult life*. New York: International University Press.

Peterson, J.A. & Briley, M.P. (1977). *Widows and widowhood*. New York: Association Press.

Rohrbaugh, J.B. (1979). *Women: Psychology's puzzle*. New York: Basic Books.

Schoenberg, B. (Ed.). (1970). *Loss and grief: Psychological management in medical practice*. New York: Columbia University Press.

Schoenberg, B., Gerber, I., Wiener, A., Kutscher, A.H., Peretz, D., & Carr, A.C. (Eds.). (1975). *Bereavement: Its psychosocial aspects*. New York: Columbia University Press.

Schwartz-Borden, G. (1986). Grief work: Prevention and information. *Social Casework, 67*, 499-505.

Schuchter, S.R. (1986). *Dimensions of grief: Adjusting to the death of a spouse*. San Francisco, California: Jossey-Bass.

Silverman, P.R. (1981). *Helping women cope with grief*. Beverly Hills, CA: Sage.

Simos, B.G. (1977). Grief therapy to facilitate healthy restitution. *Social Casework, 58*, 337-342.

Spreitzer, E., Snyder, E.F., & Larson, D. (1975). Age, marital status, and labor force participation as related to life satisfaction. *Sex Roles, 1*, 235-247.

Stroebe, M.S. & Strobe, W. (1983). Who suffers more? Sex differences in health risks of the widowed. *Psychological Bulletin, 93*, 279-301.

Switzer, D.K. (1970). *The dynamics of grief*. Nashville: Abingdon Press.

Switzer, D.K. (1972). Repressed affect and memory reactive to grief: A case fragment. *Omega, 3*, 121-126.

Tobin, S.A. (1971). Saying goodbye in Gestalt therapy. *Psychotherapy: Theory, Research and Practice, 8*, 150-155.

Uroda, S.F. (1977). Counseling the bereaved. *Counseling and Values, 21*, 185-191.

Volkan, V.D. (1975). "Re-grief" therapy. In B. Schoenberg, I. Gerber, A. Wiener, A.H. Kutscher, D. Peretz, & A.C. Carr (Eds.). *Bereavement: Its psychosocial aspects* (pp. 33-350). New York: Columbia University Press.

Weiss, E. (1950). *Principles of psychodynamics*. New York: Grune & Stratton.

Weiss, R. (1976). Transition states and other stressful situations: Their nature and programs for their management. In G. Caplan & M. Killilea (Eds.). *Support systems and mutual help*. New York: Grune & Stratton.

Whitaker, C.A., & Malone, T.P. (1969). Experiential or nonrational psychotherapy. In W. Sahakian (Ed.). *Psychotherapy and counseling: Studies in techniques* (pp. 416-431). Chicago: Rand McNally.

Psychotherapist and Widower

Roy Persons

SUMMARY. The sudden death of a young spouse is a tragic loss and its impact is pervasive. The article deals with the grieving process of a psychotherapist whose wife was murdered.

For all of my adult life I have been a psychotherapist. My life's commitment is to my own unfolding and evolving and to assist others in the excitement, pain, and struggle of their journey to a more fully developed personhood. I am a master guide. I don't do therapy. I am a therapist. Being therapeutic is the essence of my being. It has been both a calling and quest that I have been very dedicated to for more than 25 years. I feel fulfilled and blessed as a therapist. As I enjoy my work, I make meaningful contributions to others. In being a therapist, I feel alive, vital, and connected most of the time. It has not been easy.

Through the years I have been in individual psychotherapy, group psychotherapy, done postdoctoral training for several years that involved working on me, and have been to an untold number of workshops that involve personal growth. No person is complete. We all are in process and have work to do on ourselves. The nature of the work on myself that I was doing, have done, am doing, and will be doing, dramatically changed on July 27, 1967. As I write that date I am crying. Carol Emrick Persons was murdered on that day.

Carol was 26 years old and a graduate student in clinical psychol-

---

Roy Persons received his PhD in clinical psychology from Ohio State University and has been in practice for more than 20 years. He has been the Chair of the Psychology program with Union Graduate School. He spends half his time as a painter and is completing his PhD in art. Address correspondence to Roy Persons, 1420 W. Busch Blvd., Tampa, FL 33612.

71

ogy completing her internship at the University of Florida Medical School. We had been married for 4 years when she was killed. Like many widowers and widows I probably overidealize our relationship. Yet my internal truth is that we had a loving, growing, passionate (in the full sense of the word), and intimate relationship. Our relationship was not just based upon our love and caring for each other but, in addition, was based upon values, pursuits, and commitments that were beyond our relationship. We were both committed to a life of service. Our relationship enhanced and was enhanced by our commitments beyond ourselves. I loved Carol for not only how she was with me, but also how she was in the world.

Carol was warm, tender and tough, powerful and soft, nonconformist and conformist, timid and confident. She laughed a lot, and was fun to be with, and she was also quiet and self-contained. At 5'10" tall, Carol was a statuesque and classic beauty. She was excited about becoming a child psychologist and her involvement with her Ph.D. studies led to her having a 4.0 grade average at Ohio State University. She had the energy of youth and the depth of an old soul.

On July 27, 1967, Carol just did not come home. I did not have a clue where she was and for a week or so the police would not investigate because they said that she just probably ran away with another man. In fact, I found our car that she drove that day, but that offered no clues to her whereabouts. The police finally agreed to start looking for her after I consented to take a lie detector test. Some days I searched fields and the swamp areas between our house and Gainesville. On other days I withdrew and isolated myself in our house. Her body was not discovered for about 6 months. The 6 months of not knowing what had happened to Carol was almost more than I could bear. The *Columbus Dispatch* ran a headline that said that her disappearance was the result of amnesia. I suppose that their fantasy conclusion helped them sell more papers, but their imagined reason for her disappearance only brought her family and me more suffering.

After 6 weeks of looking for Carol, I left Gainesville, Florida, and went back to Ohio State University to work at the College of Medicine and write my dissertation. It was wrenching for me to leave not knowing what had happened to Carol, but I could not take any more and in my heart I knew that she was dead. It had already been a devastating year with my father unexpectedly dying at the young age of 55 and my sister's baby dying. I handled my fear, pain, and grief by overworking at the medical school and on my dissertation. Overwork is still one of my coping mechanisms. I also got into individual and group psychotherapy. The individual therapy was helpful. The group therapy, which was with my classmates at OSU was worse than no help at all. My classmates were our friends and talking about her disappearance, what might have happened to her, and my pain was too much for the group. My memory is that my efforts were deflected by the group. The therapist was also a friend of Carol's and it was probably difficult for him too. Other graduate students tended to avoid me. I believe my pain, their liking of Carol, and their own confusion lead to my isolation. I believe that all widows and widowers experience some degree of emotional abandonment. Some friends just do not know what to say or do, and death is so difficult for many people to deal with.

In January of 1968 Carol's body was found. Willie Rivers, who had murdered her, led the police to her body. I flew down to Gainesville and stayed with a friend during the trial. Rivers was rightfully convicted. The evidence was indisputable. Willie Rivers was sentenced to die in Florida's electric chair. I was unalterably opposed to this sentence and published a letter to the editor to that effect at the conclusion of his trial:

> My wife, Carol Persons, was murdered by Willie Rivers. She was a good and beautiful person, and I loved her very much. That heinous act robbed her of her chance to have a full and productive life, and robbed us of the opportunity to continue the meaningful relationship that we had developed over the past four years. Her life was precious, as is all life. Despite my feelings of anger, disgust, pity and nausea toward Rivers, I do not believe that his life should be taken. I would have been willing to testify in court that I or Carol would not have wanted him to be sent to his death, but this testimony would not have been legal.
>
> Do not misunderstand, I am not criticizing the jurors, nor do I think that they made a mistake. All of the evidence unmistak-

ably proved that Willie Rivers murdered Carol Persons. The jury made the only choice that was possible under the existing law. The jury is not mistaken, but the law is. Nobody has the right to take a human life, and this includes the State of Florida.

If a life sentence in prison really meant life in prison, the jury's choice would have been easier. However, if he were given life, he could be released in a few short years to endanger the lives of others. These laws need to be changed not only to preserve the dignity of human life, but also to have a more humane manner to protect those of us in society who do not want to harm others.

Carol's death was a real tragedy to her and those of use who loved her so dearly. Her life as a person and as a psychologist represented an attempt to create better interpersonal relations among people and to promote understanding. Therefore, it is even more tragic that her death will, by sentencing Willie Rivers to his death, reinforce and perpetrate feelings of vengeance, hate, and further human evil. The laws should be changed.

Ultimately the death penalty for Rivers was overturned.

Another publication by so-called liberal/radical people came out at about the same time. These blind and self-serving people at the university who had more of an axe to grind than they had information, published and circulated a pamphlet charging the entire process with racism. The pamphlet asked such questions as: "Where was the husband the night of the murder?"; "Was their marriage in trouble?"; "Did he have another lover that he wanted to be with?" The whole pamphlet continued in a very disgusting display by these self-declared radicals. These supposed correctors of human injustice were in fact fanning the flames of racism and creating even more evil by their gross pamphlet. Carol Persons was murdered by Willie Rivers and he was the product of a racist society. Until we can change our society there will continue to be many innocent victims—both black and white. The pamphlet was not in the direction of helping deal with a problem, but was a product of personal and collective psychopathology that increased negativity in the world. Carol and I both had been involved in liberal causes and this slanderous pamphlet felt like a double betrayal.

There is a principle involved in my mentioning the police refusing to look for Carol's body because she must have run away with another man, in mentioning the indignity of my having to take a lie detector test before they would investigate her disappearance, the demeaning and totally concocted amnesia headline on the front page of the Columbus Dispatch, and in mentioning the vicious lies in the pamphlet. The principle is that people often are insensitive or worse around death. While my illustrations are more dramatic than most, I have not met a grieving person who has not had to deal with insensitivity while attempting to cope with the trauma of death. I remember seeing a local politician going around glad-handing everybody at my father's funeral. In my experience in working with grieving in psychotherapy, people tend to be more insensitive or cruel when someone has been murdered, or the death was suicide, or the person died unexpectedly, or was very young. My father's funeral should not have been an occasion for Pete to advance himself politically and it is this type of insensitivity that most people experience at the time that they are most vulnerable. It is important that the therapist inquire into any additional possible hurt or anger surrounding the death.

Willie Rivers, an 18-year-old high school dropout, abducted Carol Persons at the Gainesville shopping Mall when she was putting the groceries in our car. He pointed a gun at her and made her drive him to a deserted area. There, I am told, he had her strip, and she began to run rather than be raped. He shot her through the head and killed her. He was convicted of first degree murder and sentenced to die in the electric chair at Raiford Prison (where I had conducted research) in Florida.

When I left Gainesville and returned to Columbus, Ohio, I did not fully enter the grieving process. I believed that Carol was dead, but all that was factually known was that she was missing. Inside I knew that she was dead, but I did not fully engage the grieving process because of all the uncertainty and because of my hoping for a miracle. I did do some grieving, especially in therapy, but mostly I was numbing myself. I felt isolated from former friends, hid in my work, and was terribly lonely and afraid. No! I was terrified about what might have happened to Carol, but I did not let myself feel it very often. I kept busy and finished my dissertation in record time. My therapist loved me and nurtured me, for which I feel grateful. I certainly needed it. In retrospect I do not believe that he confronted me enough and made me go through as much of the grieving as I needed. Perhaps he decided that because of my isolation and isolating, I needed support most of all and could not handle some of the heavier grief work. Perhaps he too was uncomfortable with the grief work. He knew Carol and perhaps it was easier on him to be emotionally supportive to me rather than both of us dealing with her murder. Or perhaps what happened in therapy was right for that time. I am simply not in a position to evaluate.

I know that I did have most all of the experiences that Elizabeth Kubler-Ross discusses. My process was distorted by the delay in grieving and from my numbing myself. I certainly experienced denial. I was hoping and praying for the miracle of Carol's return even though I *knew* that first night when she did not come home that she was dead. I don't remember going through bargaining, but I do remember feeling lots of "if only's" . . . if I would have only gone to the grocery store with her . . . if I would have only been a better husband . . . if we had only taken the internships in Wisconsin . . . And so on and on. I do remember being angry. Angry at Carol for getting into the car in the first place. Angry that this brilliant woman could not figure her way out of the situation without getting killed. Angry that she ran and did not let him rape her rather than killing her. I remember doing some Gestalt work in therapy and saying to Carol, "Why did you let him kill you! We could have dealt with the rape," and so on. Of course, this was all crazy, but I needed to do it. But mostly I was just angry because I felt abandoned, and I missed her terribly.

I was angry with Willie Rivers. I was rageful at Willie Rivers. I was angry with the police. I was angry with our racist country that helps create the Willie Rivers. But mostly I was just angry for the senselessness of the most beautiful person that I had ever known being destroyed and was angry at the fear and suffering that she had to experience out of no fault of her own. Of course, I was angry that she was so mercilessly snatched from my life.

During those months of not knowing, but knowing, I imagined

bribing the police (it would not have taken much of a bribe) to beat him once they caught him. I imagined some inmate friends at Raiford mutilating him if he were sent there. Certainly that later would have been very easy to arrange. In fact, my inmate research assistant offered to have Rivers killed, but I stopped it. Fortunately I was able to work out letting go of most of that anger. As bizarre as it may seem, I found myself feeling compassionate for Willie Rivers' mother when I saw her in court because she was facing the loss of her son, as I was trying to deal with my loss.

I cried on and off for months — until I had no more tears. Crying seemed unpredictable. I never knew what would prompt it. Mostly it was being reminded of things that we did together, places that we had been, talking with her family or mine, or other associations. But sometimes I could just be driving the car and begin crying. In workshops I said good-bye to her, remembered the positives that she had given, and owned what of her I would hold dear to me. But the wounds were deep.

When someone dies, I believe that friends and acquaintances have expectations about when a person ought to be over the loss. Their expectation is, in part, based on their own discomfort. I certainly felt the pressure from myself and others to hurry up and be over Carol's death. I experienced the external pressure in a variety of ways from people directly stating that I needed to be over it, to deflecting any conversation, to well meaning attempts to fix me up with someone new. I believe that a major problem for most grieving people is the internal and external pressure to hurry up and be over the grief.

Gestalt therapy had taught me that I needed to complete the emotional trauma with Carol. I knew that I needed to avoid a premature closure of that gestalt by cutting short the grieving process. I was, however, not prepared for my own self-admonitions. When years later I found myself grieving I would be critical and say to myself that I *should* be over Carol's death and it was a sign of an incomplete gestalt to still be upset many years later. It took me some time to understand that it is important to honor, respect, and welcome our tears as our teachers. Pandora's death 10 years after Carol's death brought tears to me and a missed day at work to pay homage to the connection between Carol, our kitten and me. The tears and day off were honoring the continuing letting go process.

Some years ago, I wrote an article (Persons, 1975) describing a concept of temporary closure in gestalt therapy. The concept involved acknowledging the importance of fully grieving to the point of completion with the understanding that occasionally a person will reexperience grieving. When death, especially in youth, takes a loved one the best that we can hope for is temporary closure – to cry all of our tears and to know that we will cry and grieve from time to time all of our lives when significant losses occur. It is important not to accept internal or external pressure to end the grieving or to accept an introject that in future years a person should be done with the pain and sadness.

I have now learned that for the survivor, there is not one date of death but many. Carol Persons did not just die on July 27, 1967, but she has also died when our cat died, when I break a piece of our china, when I see her parents, when I dispose of things that we owned together, and so on it goes. Each one of these events is a letting go of what was, a reminder of what was, a reminder of what will never be, and a reminder of our fragility. Each of these psychic events ushers an opportunity for tears, reflection, valuing, and growing in depth. I now welcome my tears and letting go as a part of my deepening.

In addition to overworking after Carol's death, I attempted to deal with my pain by trying to find somebody new. I thought that trying to start over was better than wallowing. There is another factor that propels a person, me included, to look for another mate after they have lost a great love. The factor for me was that I had never experienced life so wonderfully and wished to experience that depth of living again. I did marry again and too soon. Marilyn and I were together for eight and a half years. Just as people who have lost a great love have a great desire to achieve it again, they also have a great fear of being deeply hurt. I believe that my contribution to Marilyn's and my relationship ending was my fear of being deeply hurt again that put up barriers that prevented Marilyn and me from achieving that great depth that we both wanted. Marilyn divorced me and I believe that she did so because I never allowed great intimacy. Again I felt abandoned.

In the 15 years since my divorce from Marilyn I have had several passionate, powerful, deep, and meaningful relationships. They have significantly enriched my life and I believe that I contributed to my companions' lives. I have troubled myself however, that these relationships, as important as they have been, have not been lifelong commitments. I have frightened myself that I am too scarred from the past, that my expectations are too high, that I pick the wrong people, or that I am too afraid of deep intimacy to maintain a lifelong relationship. I have felt ashamed or embarrassed that I have not been successful in creating an ongoing loving relationship.

I have tried to comfort myself by acknowledging that most people are having trouble maintaining loving relationships, and my failure is no different in kind than what seems to be a cultural phenomenon. In another attempt to gain relief from my sense of failure, I have told myself that it is only an assumption that a long relationship with one person is more meaningful and desirable than is a series of meaningful relationships over a life span. The bottom line is that I was still seeking release mechanisms for my feelings of hurt and failure. The process of learning to lighten up and be less demanding was correct, but not the full story.

Recently, one of my clients, who is also a psychotherapist, was being hard on herself for never having developed a deep loving relationship after her husband's suicide. She believes that she has been so wounded by the tragic experience in her life that she has been unable to open herself to risk that kind of vulnerability again. I suspect that the same is true of me as well. For many of us who still carry scars, it may be more difficult to establish and maintain a loving intimate relationship. As I help my client, friend, colleague to a more compassionate, accepting experience of her scarring, I know that a compassionate acceptance coming from a personal knowing is the healing and growing path. Yes, I am scarred, and that accepting and knowing can temper and guide. Another factor with us scarred people is that we have too great expectations and desires. I believe that accepting my scarring and keeping my expectations-desires and fears in my awareness will enhance my chances of developing a loving relationship.

I know that in the last 15 years my eagerness for another deeply meaningful relationship has led me to be impatient when I was in a relationship that fell short of my vision for what a relationship should be. I believe that my impatience led to a certain demandingness in attitude or disappointment in the relationship when the relationship was not up to snuff. Impatience, demandingness, and disappointment is not the soil that flowers a blooming relationship.

As I come to accept these character traits with compassion and forgiveness that come with the scarring territory, I believe that I am in a better position to help create a new loving relationship. My belief is that these difficulties and learning challenges I have experienced may also speak to the experiences of many of you. As I continue my quest, I hope that my personal sharing may aid you on your quest.

However, my life will still be meaningful and successful if I never develop the relationship that I imagine that would be so fulfilling. I have a good loving relationship with my son, Scott. I put lots of love, energy, and thought into working with clients and students. I do develop meaningful relationships in my work. I deeply share myself as a psychotherapist and artist. Being a painter and a psychotherapist is a privileged life for which I am grateful and which I celebrate.

I also want to acknowledge that it is not only people who have suffered the loss of great loves that are scarred. We are all scarred. Who can live through these times and not be fearful, skeptical, or impatient? Hopefully, with awareness, acceptance, and compassionate acknowledgment I/you will be better able to be a loving companion. I am no longer looking for Carol or a relationship similar to ours. I am looking to help nurture a new loving relationship through all of the various stages of learning, challenges, and growing. As I begin a new relationship I hope to be aware of all that is involved in nurturing a new relationship. We'll see!

REFERENCE

Persons, R. W. (1975) Closure and a thirty year recurring dream. *Pilgrimage, 1,* 9-11.

Separation, Widowhood, and Divorce

Gladys Natchez

SUMMARY. Widowhood is akin to separation or divorce. The traumas usually are difficult to overcome although, strangely enough, when the relationship between the partners is strained it is sometimes a blessing. Talking with friends, counselors, social workers, therapists and the like can alleviate the wounds and hasten recovery.

After 35 years I asked for a separation from my husband. He was a decent man, but we were miles apart in interests and ways of life so when the children were all grown, (the youngest was 21) I wanted to retrieve some parts of myself that had lain dormant. I also wanted to explore new vistas. I saw no need to divorce, but I did move from the suburbs to the city. My husband was a successful businessman and I was a college professor as well as a psychotherapist so we postponed any financial settlement until much later on the agenda.

My husband was furious when I left and there was no contact between us save for his storming the door trying to get into my newly rented apartment. Of course I just ignored the histrionics. For the first two weeks I felt euphoric and free. Then reality set in. What had I done? Did I really want to be alone? Did I really need a man? Could I go it by myself? I was scared, but adamant that I would stick it out.

Finally my husband stopped trying to contact me, but he did manage to slander me in the village we had lived in. He was vindic-

Gladys Natchez, PhD, is Professor Emerita from the City College of the City University of New York, is in private practice of psychotherapy and is the author of many books and articles. Address correspondence to the author at 263 West End Ave., New York, NY 10023.

81

tive; he told people I was cheating on him. Then he tried to commit suicide several times. When I told him that he was using emotional blackmail and that I would not fall for his ruses he desisted. In fact he soon moved to Florida and not long afterward he got a Mexican divorce which he sent me in Spanish. Later, I was absolutely stunned that he remarried. The nerve of him! I hadn't yet found someone *I* wanted to live with. Was this really final? I must say I felt weird. It seemed like the equivalent of widowhood. I wondered whether my decision to be alone made any sense.

What surprised me most was the reaction of my three children. Despite their grown-up ages they were horrified at our divorce. All of them complained. With which parent are we supposed to live when we come home from college? Who is this "other woman" with our father? With which parent are we supposed to spend the holidays? What is all this? Of course they calmed down, but it was sad. What *were* all of us supposed to do?

Since I was alone for the first time in years I was ostensibly a widow or a divorcee – I didn't know which felt most predominant. As a therapist my experience with widows and divorcees was fairly extensive. Many of them fell apart when their husbands died or left them, but just as many blossomed, The ones who had enough courage to admit it said that after a reasonable mourning period they almost had to hide their high spirits. They experienced a type of freedom that they never had before. Those wives whose husbands had discouraged them from working, felt liberated and many of them sought work. Most of them enjoyed working but even more they liked that no one was restricting them about money or anything else and they proceeded living the way they found best. Those who were fortunate enough to be financially well off obviously had an easier time with practical problems. However they often became as angry and or depressed as those who struggled with finances.

In therapy, those who were able to mourn deeply seemed to find it easier to take up their life after a brief period. I found that those with good marriages often found suitable mates or companions within a reaonable amount of time, whereas those with poor marriages usually needed extensive treatment to rebuild their own lives. The ones who had been most symbiotic and dependent were usually depressed, but interestingly enough, as soon as they were able to venture into the world again, they found new ways of living. One woman who had been utterly dependent began asserting herself. In an amazingly short time she became a leader among her friends, was fairly self sufficient, and found she was a "new woman." I met many single women with a similar pattern.

The women who grieved extensively became increasingly morose and withdrawn. Friends who tried to help them often found them detached and removed. Sometimes this resulted in their becoming even more isolated. Some women remained in this stance for a long period; others sought help and many soon began to live again.

One ploy I discovered amazed me — sometimes widows seemed to fake mourning, perhaps to gain attention. They may have had husbands who were disinterested, withholding, unresponsive, or even generous and loving, yet the idea of being alone was so frightening that these widows sometimes put all their energy into weeping and feeling sorry for themselves. Secondary gain was often rampant.

Another woman whom I knew slightly told me that she was widowed at 26. She said all her friends thought it was horrible, but she felt that it might be better to be widowed at 26 when she could find someone else to share her life than it was if he had died much later. That seemed wise enough, but then she went on to say that she felt the emptiness acutely. She said she might be able to change her life but she didn't have the energy for it yet. Slowly, slowly, however, she began to realize that her life could indeed augur independence and freedom ahead. The prognosis seemed favorable.

During these difficult times of crisis it is important for people to talk about their problems with others. Besides therapists, they can contact counselors, religious leaders, social workers, or other understanding people including family and friends so that their grief can be softened and finally healed. I found that the more the aggrieved ones could talk about their feelings of anger, the more they could recover. I never stopped marveling at how these women often became strong, viable, and adjusted to living alone after allowing themselves to open up to their emotions.

As to my own reaction, I didn't know whether I felt like a widow or a divorcee and I was fairly disconcerted for a while. Depression and loneliness set in despite my good friends and my full life. Gradually, however, I began to recover from my initial fright by involving myself in workshops that I attended or gave. I found congenial friends in my new milieu. Interestingly enough most of them were single.

You see, I had to drop many of my married friends. I found that being single in a group of "marrieds" was a no win game. Often my female friends were jealous if they felt their husbands were paying too much attention to me. To my amazement wives told me how angry they felt. One woman said to me directly that I wittingly aroused so much sympathy in her husband that he began acting like a golden savior. She also inferred that he was ready to have an affair with me and that some of the other wives felt likewise. Another blamed me for having made her husband feel so anguished by my situation that he was more attentive to me than to his wife. Of course the innuendo for these women was that sexuality would rear its ugly head. Actually they were not far off the track because I did have passes made at me by their mates! Not that I didn't like it, but I assure you, I did not get entangled with any of their husbands.

In addition, there was the situation of going out to dinner with couples. It became embarrassing when the bill came and they refused my contribution to the check. I felt awkward and annoyed. If we went to theater the same thing happened. I could have had them all for dinner as reciprocity or used similar antics but I didn't like the tit-for-tat. It just seemed peculiar and for whatever reason I didn't like the kind of undercurrent which I sensed from the women. To be frank, I must say that I enjoyed the sense of flirting from the men, but I knew that going with couples became too distressing and so I gradually stopped being with them. Many of my patients encountered similar experiences.

A year or so after my former husband got married he became ill and had to go to the hospital. For some reason that appeared sensible to me at the time, I went to visit him (was it duty that I felt?) When I arrived at the hospital, his wife was in the room. It was the first time I had seen her. She was kind enough to say she was going out for a cigarette.

My ex-husband was in bed of course and watching the baseball game. He didn't even look up. I said, "Can we turn off the television and talk?'' He didn't answer, but merely pushed the off button without looking at me. I proceeded with a monologue saying something like: "I'm sorry I hurt you. I'm glad you seem happy with your wife. I just came to see if there was anything I might do for you or that we might want to discuss together." I really struggled to make sense, but I was talking to a stone wall. Finally I said: "That's all I have to say. Do you want to respond to anything?" After a long pause, all he said was: "Can I turn on the television now?" Whew! I felt slapped in the face. When I recovered I realized how true he was to himself. He had no wish or reason to talk with me; he wanted to watch the game. That's just the way he was. Besides being hurt, I couldn't help admiring his authenticity and I felt sad, but resigned.

After a few years I remarried. I was 56 and amazed to be head over heels in love. I loved this man's humanness, his humor, his insight with me and others. I loved his brilliance and his knowledge. Even more, he called a spade a spade and was very exciting.

We had about 2 great years together and then he became emotionally and physically ill. These were days of nightmare for me. He would yell in terror in his sleep; he began getting senile and couldn't take care of himself physically or mentally. He went into tantrums and could hardly sleep. I had to get attendants for him around the clock. It was heartrending. In the meantime my eldest son, who was married with two little children and who lived out of town, was diagnosed with stomach cancer and was very ill in the hospital. I commuted between the two sick men as best I could. Finally my husband died and a year later my son. It was a horror. It also was so sad that they both had to spend their last years in torment—to say nothing of my torment. So widowhood and loss for me was horror and bereavement. I must say there was some relief in their deaths because they were so ill. But the stark facts were almost too hard to bear. I denied hurts in order to tolerate the heavy situation. I had hoped for so much happiness in my life only to experience tragedy and sorrow.

It took me two and a half hard and weary years to come to myself. The thing that triggered me back to sanity was the motto:

"Living well is the best revenge."[1] For some reason it inspired my creativity and helped to give me the strength to go on. Not that I could dispel the numbness I felt, but there seemed to be a glimmer of hope. I managed to get the strength to go on with my life. As Lady Bird Johnson (cited in Caine, 1974) once said, "Grief carries its own anesthesia" (p. 90).

Being able to deny the tragedy of my two dearly loved ones was a godsend and I indulged in it for at least a year. Gradually I substituted anger for denial. I railed in my pillow at night. I neglected my friends. I remained a solitary wreck. I really don't know how long it took me to become somewhat human, but it felt like years.

Soon my family began bugging me to marry again. That was the last thing I wanted to do. Being divorced and widowed and experiencing the death of my beloved son was just too much. I had to be firm and tell them I would pick my own mate; they didn't have to do it for me even though I knew they were trying to be of help. It seemed my family couldn't bear my being single. I was the youngest sister in my family and perhaps they were fearful of being widowed themselves. If I could find a mate, then they might not be so alarmed.

I discovered another facet about being alone. It seems that widows often lose their identity when they are "single." Society turns away from death and illness and often I didn't know how to react to the stigma of the so-called "single life." In Konrad Lorenz's book (1966) *On Aggression*, he mentions that the moment a partner of a goose is gone, it loses all courage and flees from the rest of the geese. When members of the colony know of the "lonely goose", that goose rapidly sinks to the lowest step in the ranking order. This phenomenon partially parallels us singles.

It is well known that single women have a more difficult time finding a mate than single men. Since women outnumber them, particularly in latter years, it is sometimes far harder for them to find a suitable man. Magazines that include personal ads for mates

---

1. In a New Yorker cartoon, Nov. 7, 1988, p. 7, two portly older men, wearing tuxedos are sitting in plush comfortable armchairs. One says to the other, "Forget living well, The best revenge is revenge." I laugh, but I like the original motto better.

state that there are an overwhelming number of women who advertise for a man in contrast to the other way round. On the other hand, it is usually harder for men who have household responsibilities and young children to deal with such matters. many men find they are often dependent on family, friends, or hired help, for instance, to carry on their practical life. Although a widow also may need such assistance, she is usually more familiar with the everyday routine of home maintenance and children. Even if she works, it is probably somewhat easier for her to settle the practical aspects of homemaking.

In another vein, women have not yet gained equal financial status with men. Although the situation has vastly improved, the majority of women receive lower wages and if the widow is not financially independent and has to work she also needs the aid of others just the way the men do. Obviously both parties need to struggle through a multitude of hardships while putting together a new life-style whether it be money, interests, security, adventure, or all the other elements that signify a viable life.

Fortunately I had a great many plusses to handle my own loneliness as a widow. I had enough money, family, and friends. It is interesting that I think mostly of my first husband. After all, we raised our children together; we led a life together. I become a bit ashamed (but not too much really) that with all these assets I have hibernated and mourned for so long. However, it takes what it takes.

Widowhood, separation, and divorce are traumatic wounds that need time and healing. In fact the word, *widow* comes from the Sanskrit word that means empty. I most certainly felt empty for a while and am fortunate that I had enough strength to continue my life and expand my horizons. I write articles; I have my work as a psychotherapist; I create video and book projects; I garden; I even cook. Finally, I enjoy my independence and have become accustomed to living alone.

To my surprise, I find that since my first husband died, I grow fonder and fonder of him. My grown children have had the same experience. I suppose time obliterates faults and fosters endearment. However, I do not have these feelings for my second husband even though I had been wildly in love with him. As I reminisce I find I was really infatuated, determined to win "my prize man" and live happily ever after.

As I look back at my life I know I could never make it without enjoyable work, exciting interests, and good friends, particularly the special close friend I have now. We are sympatico, have many congenial interests and love the warmth and fun of spending time together. We are usually available for each other and yet we enjoy our independence. The most joy is that I know someone who cares for me and vice versa.

Freud, of course, always claimed that love and work were the major ingredients that mattered in the world and that's certainly true. Perhaps other significant aspects, include having a more or less congenial family and friends, loving a special person, having work and substantial interests that are satisfying, and being able to handle "singlehood," marriage, and other important relationships. A life with those kinds of components can help to mend us — whether we are widowed, separated, or divorced.

REFERENCES

Caine, L. (1974). Widow. New York: Willima Morrow & Co.
Lorenz, K. (1966). On Aggression. New York: Harcourt, Brace.

The Loss Unit:
Reflections on Widowhood

Daphne Barnes

SUMMARY. Spousal bereavement is a common, severe loss which brings with it a threat to both psychological and physical health. It is not always resolved successfully, a significant proportion of widows need professional help with grief work. Certain factors predispose to morbid grief, personality style, previous psychiatric illness, nature of the death, prior relationship to the deceased, perceived social support system, and so on. Grief therapy is beneficial to those with bereavement difficulties. An outline of the grief therapy used by the author is described.

Mourning is treated as if it were a weakness, a self-indulgence, a reprehensible bad habit instead of a psychological necessity. We do not burn our widows, we pity and avoid them.

—Geoffrey Gorer (1965, p.161)

Bereavement is usually felt as a distressing painful process which results not only in psychological distress but also in bodily dysfunction and changes in social functioning. Loss may exacerbate preexisting disease, precipitate new disease, or produce life threatening

---

Dr. Barnes is Assistant Professor of Psychiatry in the Faculty of Medicine, at the University of Calgary, Calgary, Alberta, Canada. She directs a multidisciplinary loss unit at the Calgary General Hospital and serves as professional advisor to various bereavement support groups within the city of Calgary. Address correspondence to the author at Calgary General Hospital, Bow Valley Centre, 841 Centre Ave. East, Calgary, Alberta T2E 0A1, Canada.

89

behaviors, for example, excess alcohol intake, substance abuse, suicidal behavior. Frequently the grieving process has a restorative healing function but in a significant proportion "grief goes wrong," typically with the onset of a depressive illness or morbid grief (Parkes & Weiss, 1985).

This is more likely in the Western world where formalized rituals for mourning have been lost and extended family support is the exception. Approximately 20-30% of major losses can be expected to lead to problems for which professional help may be required (Raphael, 1983). Ten percent of adult Canadian women are widowed at any one time and widows outnumber widowers in a ratio of 4:1. Although widowhood is traditionally associated with older age groups, in fact 20% of all new widows in any one year are under the age of 45. Fifteen to 25% widows and widowers suffer poor psychological and physical health for up to 13 months or more following the death of a partner (Clayton, 1974). Widowhood is also an important and widespread role change which often occurs together with the influences of increasing age.

LITERATURE REVIEW

The Huli people of Papua, New Guinea, mourn following culturally determined patterns which are very different between sexes. Women are expected to express emotions while men are discouraged from doing so. In a follow up study of 4 years following spousal bereavement it was discovered that widowers showed an excess mortality but widows displayed no such tendency (Frankel & Smith, 1982). This raises the interesting hypothesis that there is a relationship between mourning practices and mortality. Indeed, Maddison and Walker (1967) identified two factors which were related strongly to a "bad outcome": the discouragement of emotional expression and also the discouragement of the mourner's wish to review the past relationship. Parkes (1970) reported that widows under 65 consulted physicians in the first year of widowhood three times more than the expected rate, physical symptoms were prominent (Clayton, 1973), the use of sedatives was seven times the expected rate (Parkes, 1964), they spent more time in bed and in hospitals than non-widowed women of the same age (Parkes & Brown, 1972). Although it is similar to other life events, conjugal bereavement involves an irreversible, usually unpreventable event which shatters long term attachment bonds necessitating new roles and status. Stress research indicates that not only is the type of stress of importance to outcome but also the victim's perception of the stress (Paykel, 1976), indeed the power to influence normal bereavement seems to lie in the meaning of the loss to the bereaved rather than the type of the loss. Those widows who experience a sudden death are more likely to have difficulties with grief and to evaluate their adjustment as poor. Factors cited as important in adjustment to loss include demographic, the nature of the relationship, type of death, initial response to bereavement, social support network, past response to losses, past medical and psychiatric history as well as personality style and other ongoing life stresses. The literature is confusing, conflictual, and complex. A study by Zisook, Shuchter, and Lyons (1987) was consistent with most others and concluded that older widows and widowers handle the stress relatively well but that younger people were more at risk to the negative consequences of spousal loss. Women were found to suffer great drops in income whereas the financial status of most men remained stable. Poorer marital relationships were linked to "poorer" grief outcome, in particular relationships described as clinging or ambivalent were related to poor adjustment. In most studies men seem to have worse adjustment than women although this was not found in the Zisook study.

Health-care-seeking behavior may represent an attempt to gain support and the bereaved may substitute somatic complaints for distress of loss. The health status before loss is the most important determinant of physician visits and hospital use, it may be that those with previous health problems further somatize distress, while healthy people are at increased risk of increasing alcohol use. Shakespeare, in *Macbeth*, wrote: "Give sorrow words, the grief that does not speak whispers to the oerfraught heart and bids it break." What the poet tells us, the pathologist often confirms. The excess mortality found in epidemiologic studies seems to largely relate to cardiovascular events in accordance with the model of sudden and rapid death during psychological stress described by Engel (1971). Raphael (1977) found preventive interventions in early bereavement to be effective, subjects being selected on risk factors — a high degree of perceived lack of support, a highly ambivalent marital relationship and concurrent life stressors. At follow up 13 months post-bereavement, Raphael found 77% to be improved compared with 41% in the untreated control group. In the same study she also concluded that the morbidity rates were significantly lowered in the intervention group, this was especially noticeable in those who perceived their social network to be unsupportive. Sixty-one widows who sought help for grief gone wrong were randomly assigned to either brief dynamic psychotherapy with experienced clinicians or mutual self-help group treatment by non-clinicians. Both groups were associated with a reduction in symptoms as well as improvement in social and work functioning. Women in the brief psychotherapy group showed a greater decline in one measure of general symptoms and there was greater attrition in the group treatment condition.

When two subgroups who had completed the majority of sessions were compared, treatments were found to be equally effective (Marmar, Horowitz, Weiss, Wilner & Kaltreider, 1988). Gerber, Weiner, and Battin (1975) compared brief psychotherapy with no treatment controls in elderly widows and those receiving psychotherapy were found to use less psychotropic medications and few medical services, but did not differ in their experience of medical illnesses. The relationship of dispositional and process variable to outcome was studied in 52 bereaved given time limited dynamic psychotherapy. Outcome was found to be generally good for symptom relief and in relationship and work functioning. On the whole, symptoms improved more than did social and occupational functioning. Motivation for dynamic therapy and developmental level of the self-concept were significantly related to outcome. The findings suggested that more exploratory actions were more suited to the highly motivated and/or better organized patients and less suitable for patients with lower levels of motivation or organization of self-concept. More supportive interventions were better for patients at lower dispositional levels and less therapeutic for patients at higher levels. What emerged as the most consistent prediction of good outcome was the patient's perception of the therapist-offered relationship (Horowitz, Marmar, Weiss, DeWitt, & Rosenbaum, 1984). A review of intervention studies revealed mixed results. It seems that when the target group is preselected on predictors for poor outcome, then intervention seems beneficial for physical and psychological health. In contrast, studies of interventions with early treatment of unselected patients or those with low distress levels have not demonstrated a beneficial effect to treatment (Marmar et al., 1988).

By the end of 4 years, the majority of widows and widowers were relatively well adjusted, financially secure, and without dramatic increases in illnesses or depression. However, despite this the majority did not feel, even after 4 years, that they had made what they could call an excellent adjustment (Zisook et al., 1987) and 2% continued to rate their adjustment as fair to poor after 4 years (Zisook & Shuchter, 1986). Thus, the loss of a spouse through death appears to leave for some at least a permanent mark. Silverman (1970) commented "You don't get over it—you get used to it."

THE LOSS UNIT

There has been a recent resurgence of interest in the care of the dying and the family following a loss. Losses are not always as a result of the death of a family member. We grieve the loss of a limb, a breast, a pet, our fertility, a home, a job, a marriage, a "dream," and so on. There are a number of groups who fill a need for specific losses, or specific groups such as widows, parents of a dead child, mothers of babies who succumb to SIDS, and others. However, loss units are not so common, the mandate for our service being to offer help to all people grieving a loss independent of the type of loss. The unit has now been running for 4 years and consists of both inpatient and outpatient services. It is run on multidisciplinary grounds with representatives from several disciplines. The "core" team consists of a psychiatrist, nursing staff, a psychologist, a social worker, an occupational therapist, and a minister. In keeping with this the types of therapies offered are varied, including grief psychotherapy, family therapy, marital therapy, stress management, cognitive therapy, group psychotherapy, drug treatment, occupational therapy, and spiritual counseling.

The unit functions as a referral source for numerous community agencies within the province and is designed to fill the need of people suffering from morbid grief, not normal bereavement. Whereas acute grief is easy to detect, morbid grief may be well camouflaged and resist detection for years. Since the inauguration of the unit a grief register has been kept. An initial assessment interview is carried out by the psychiatrist on referral. This is conducted in a semistructured format including details of the loss, the grief process and previous experience of loss, as well as a routine psychiatric history and mental state. At this point the first record is made in the grief register with details of the loss, previous losses, and demographic details being made. Following discharge from the unit, the entry into the register is completed with bereavement diagnosis, psychiatric diagnosis, length of care, compliance, and types of therapies employed being recorded. Knowledge of response to previous losses is a clue to capacity and coping skills and it is therefore important to take a full loss history to assess such skills and to ascertain whether there are previous unresolved losses. There are various clues to morbid grief, minor events trigger intense grief, the person cannot talk of loss without fresh grief years after, the patient keeps returning to the theme of loss when inappropriate, the surroundings are mummified ("Queen Victoria Syndrome"), identification symptoms occur, the patient excludes all family and friends associated with the loss. Anniversary responses may be extreme, phobias and exaggerated health seeking behavior may occur involving the same type of illness that killed the deceased. Once the assessment interview has been completed an appropriate "plan" for grief work can be formulated.

The presence of unresolved previous losses is important to acknowledge and if present a hierarchy of losses needs to be formulated with the patient. This hierarchy is based on the meaning of each loss for the patient and is not necessarily in temporal order. It is important to start grief work with the "easiest" loss first and work up the hierarchy to the "hardest" loss last—this may or may not be the loss which initiated referral. This avoids flooding the patient with emotional overload and confusion between the losses which often leads to inappropriate response in the psychotherapeutic relationship. It also gives the patient a model for working through loss once an "easier" loss is successfully grieved, usually making the "harder" losses less of an "insurmountable" prospect.

WIDOWS

In the first 3 years the unit saw 173 patients. Of these, 124 patients experienced loss as a result of a death. From this 124 patients, 21 women had an "index" referral loss of the death of a husband. The mean age of the widows was 56 years but with a broad range of 32 to 78. The patient status of the widows was almost divided equally between inpatient and outpatient with 11 women remaining as outpatients and 10 patients requiring a period of inpatient care. This is unusual for the unit as the majority are outpatients—it seems that both caregivers, family and patients allowed things to deteriorate to such a state that a period of inpatient care was required for "crisis" intervention. The length of stay with the loss unit is short with a mean of three months (range 1-12 months)—the patient who remained in therapy for one year had a considerable number of other unresolved losses. If inpatient care is required this is usually a short crisis admission of one to two weeks.

The mean time from the death to the first contact with the unit is 9 months for widows, which is much shorter than with other types of index losses where the mean time between loss and contact is 22 months. This may represent the profound social role change of widowhood which precludes long periods of denial and repression. The cause of death of the husbands is illustrated in Table 1, and as can be seen shows a preponderance of sudden, unexpected deaths which is in keeping with the literature on morbid grief.

Table 1.

Cause of Death　n = 21

Murder	=	1　(5%)
Epileptic Seizure	=	1　(5%)
Postoperative	=	2 (10%)
Suicide	=	4 (19%)
Cancer	=	5 (25%)
Cardiac	=	8 (38%)

*　*　*

Expected	=	8 (38%)
Sudden death	=	13 (62%)

One woman was addicted to both prescribed tranquilizers and alcohol on admission to the unit, both addictions following the death of her husband. One woman had experienced four major losses in 6 months (grief overload) and another was living with the ashes of her husband in her bedroom. One woman was experiencing severe identification symptoms and had seen numerous physicians resulting in a "mountain" of normal test results prior to contact with the unit. As already described, all referrals are assessed using a semistructured interview resulting in a psychiatric diagnosis and a grief assessment. The results of these are shown in Tables 2 and 3.

Table 2.

Psychiatric Diagnosis:　n = 21

5 patients had Major Depression　　　　(24%)
2 patients had Substance Abuse　　　　(10%)
3 patients fulfilled D.S.M.III criterion
　　for personality disorder

All the patients with major depression had presented in "crisis" requiring a period of inpatient care usually because of concern over suicide potential.

Likewise, the two patients with addiction difficulties were first seen in the emergency department of the hospital where they presented in crisis following overdoses, and they too required a period of inpatient care to detoxify and to initiate grief work. The diagnosis of a personality disorder was not associated with the need for "crisis" intervention on an inpatient basis and all three patients with a diagnosis on Axis II were outpatients.

Table 3.

Grief Diagnosis n = 21

Morbid Grief   = 18 (86%)
Normal Bereavement   =   3 (14%)

Nine patients (43%) had unresolved previous losses, these nine woman had a total of 31 unresolved previous losses which gives a mean of 3.4 per woman (this excludes the index loss which led to referral). The length of time they had been experiencing difficulty with loss was quite long with a mean of 10 years but with a range of 1 to 30 years. The type of unresolved previous loss was varied and included such losses as death of a child, death of a pet, death of a parent, death of a friend, and so on. The types of therapy employed for the widow group was varied and broad. Five were given tricyclic antidepressants for major depression but the rest were kept drug free. The types of psychotherapy employed are listed in Table 4.

Table 4.

Type of Psychotherapy Used n = 21

Grief Therapy   = 18 (86%)
Grief Counselling   =   3 (14%)
Family Therapy   =   4 (19%)
Stress Management   =   5 (24%)
Assertive/Cognitive   =   4 (19%)
Group Psychotherapy =   5 (24%)

Compliance with treatment plans was assessed and 57% were compliant with 43% showing various degrees of non-compliance.

When compliance was related to patient status an interesting observation resulted. Of the inpatients only 30% were compliant compared to 82% of outpatients, 70% of inpatients displayed noncompliance in comparison to only 18% of outpatients. It may well be that the same factors of avoidance and denial lead to crisis in widowhood and to noncompliance with treatment. With regard to outcome, 61% were improved by contact with the unit, not surprisingly when compliance is taken into account the picture changes somewhat. Seventy-five percent of compliant patients improved compared to only 33% of patients displaying any degree of noncompliance. Only 25% of compliant patients were not changed compared to 67% of noncompliant clients. Certain themes and expressed concerns were frequently noted amongst the widows. A considerable number had had to move house as a result of a decline in finances and several had had to find a job or to increase their working hours. Living alone, the quietness of the house, loneliness, and the loss of "couple" friends were mentioned commonly. Some widows cut short the days by going to bed early, and a number found mornings in an "empty" house particularly difficult. For some, cooking and shopping for one represented a big chore. The bureaucracy, form filling and red tape of death was frightening for most as was the generally perceived attitude of unhelpfulness of officials. A significant number mentioned they felt officials saw them as stupid and incompetent, and they felt they were ignored and dismissed. One woman has subsequently set about the task of writing a booklet for new widows to help them through the maze of forms, bureaucracy, agencies, and so on in the hope that no one else will have to face the enormous barriers she felt.

Many were aware that people chose to avoid them in their grief and therefore decided to restrict talking about their husband and their grief so as to avoid further isolation and loneliness. A number were aware that it was taking them longer in grief than others in the family and often perceived this as their fault and again chose to minimize their difficulties to family members, fearing rejection or being thought of as "crazy" or "unstable." The majority of older widows expected to live largely alone as they were aware of the ratio of widows to widowers and therefore did not expect to remarry. Young widows were often fearful of being single and having to contemplate dating again when the rules of dating had often changed enormously since their last experience, many had also been left with small children which compounded the difficulties.

GRIEF THERAPY

Roy and Jane Nichols (1975) suggest that "in death and grief, we do not need as much protection from painful experiences as we need the boldness to face them. We do not need as much tranquilization from pain, as we need the strength to conquer it" (p.96). Grief is a process, not a state, consisting of working through the "tasks" of mourning. Although these tasks are the same for all of us, the process is given "a color" dependent upon the intrinsic uniqueness of each personality. These tasks are to accept the reality of the loss, to be prepared to experience the pain of grief, to readjust to an environment in which the lost object is missing, and finally to reallocate emotional energy into another relationship. The time required is highly variable and, provided progress is being made, largely unimportant. However, if the process is "stuck" then clearly intervention is indicated.

The individual grief therapy carried out on the unit is a brief, dynamic form of psychotherapy, often with some behavior modification added. During the initial assessment interview it is established that the bereavement process is stuck and often the area of difficulty can be ascertained. For many of those with morbid grief the actual acceptance of finality of loss is a major problem and many place the dead in a kind of "limbo" land between life and death, often still maintaining activities which involve their dead husband. For some widows, although they can accept the fact of their husband's death and can grieve, it is safer to be in a state of permanent grief, much like a sick role, than to progress through mourning and accept a cessation with the implicit awareness that they are now alone and have total responsibility for their lives. Often an interesting discordance between intellectual and emotional experience is noted: the widows, being well aware intellectually they had seen their husbands in the coffin, were certain that they had buried him; however emotionally they were unable to accept this, pretending that it was all a hoax, a "sham," and that their husband would return from his business trip if they only waited long enough. All these widows had insight and were well aware of the avoidance of the pain of grief but seemingly needed the control of the emotional intensity of the full grief process. The contract negotiated with the widows initially is for 8-10 sessions of 50 minutes duration at weekly intervals. At the end of this number, the therapy is reassessed by both partners. The basic framework of the grief therapy is built around the concept of tasks for mourning, the main focus being on the area which is compromised and stuck.

The first session focuses on the relationship prior to death and sets the scene for making the loss real. The patient is requested to describe her husband, both his good points and his bad ones, together with a history of their relationship. She is asked to recall one good memory and one bad, to adopt a balanced view of the deceased rather than to foster idolization of the dead. The first session usually also provides sufficient time to allow the widow to describe the terminal illness or event. This is encouraged to be "here and now" and the widow is requested to provide details of the last conversation, information given by caregivers, the appearance of her husband, quality of terminal care, and so on. In this way the loss/death is brought afresh into the therapy session. It is important to establish whether there was any "unfinished" business between spouses prior to death as it seems that this is a very powerful force mitigating against acceptance of death. If it is clear that the loss has not been accepted and/or that there were unfinished issues then a useful technique has been found to be the writing of a letter to the deceased finishing the relationship, and saying a final good-bye. This letter is usually discussed in the session but is written in between sessions by the patient. It is then brought to the next session where it is read sometimes to a "third" chair; very often the widows take the letter to the grave or other "significant" venue and read the letter to their husband, symbolically closing the relationship. The second session usually focuses on viewing the body after death, the funeral arrangements, cremation, and so on. Again the focus is "here and now" with encouragement and validation of emotions.

Sometimes it has been found that the widows have difficulty in recalling the funeral/cremation, often because they have been given minor tranquilizers or a "shot of brandy" prior to the ceremony. If this occurs they are asked to contact family/friends to fill in the gaps. Sometimes they wish to visit the grave or to scatter the ashes which may have been hoarded for years. How well they completed these tasks is brought to the next session. It has been found that a considerable element of affirmation, validation, and education needs to be included as most widows are unaware of normal bereavement; for example, many believe they are going crazy if they experience pseudohallucinations of the bereaved or a "sense of presence" and many fear talking about their experiences. They are relieved and reassured when the therapist describes normal bereavement and validates their experiences as being appropriate and within the normal. The strength of emotions particularly around anniversaries can frighten a lot of the widows, they seem to be totally unprepared for the normal "roller coaster" experience of grief with its ebb and flow. Photographs or treasured possessions can be used to further heighten the reality of loss and to facilitate the sharing of memories and emotions, especially when denial and avoidance are a particular problem. Once the loss has been accepted the next main focus of sessions is centered on the pain of grief, usually with a discussion of anger and guilt in particular. Widows often consider the pain of grief as an unjust punishment, feeling anger toward the dead person, caregivers, and sometimes family; this is not usually socially acceptable, resulting in social isolation, loneliness, and insecurity.

It is important to give the widow permission for the expression of negative emotions such as anger. In the session there is a focus on to whom and for what anger is felt, once again it has been found that putting this in "black and white" is very helpful for most. Each person to whom anger is felt, including the dead husband if applicable, is then worked through in the session enabling resolution and forgiveness. The same basic principle is carried out with guilt which is reality tested and gradually resolved in a session or two as applicable. "Was everything done that could be done?" is usually a very important question for most of the bereaved and usually needs at least to be posed in the therapy. Some widows need a medical explanation at least as to what happened and at times it is important to bring the autopsy report or medical records into the session. It is our experience that the Medical Examiner's office and police will provide any details if required and requested.

Widowhood involves the change from a "we" to an "I" and there is a loss of essential nurturing and practical "supplies" from a partner. These needs must be fulfilled in a different way and by other persons. The making of new relationships, the strengthening of old ones, and the ability to ask for fulfillment of needs is a major task for widows, as is the change of self-concept from married to widowed. Many bereaved find, to begin with at least, they need up to seven or eight relationships to complete the gap left by a spouse. In the session it is helpful to discuss what the spouse "gave to them" and how these needs are now going to be supplied. Most widows fear asking for support and are usually surprised when their requests meet with an affirmative response.

If appropriate, it is important to raise the issue of remarriage, dating, and sexual relationship—these are powerful producers of guilt. Toward the end of the therapy it is necessary to fantasize about stopping grieving and the loss of the therapy and therapist, as these can be very powerful issues.

SOCIETY AND WIDOWHOOD

The widow often finds herself in conflict with society and its expectations concerning the mourning process. On the whole, society and caregivers alike are poorly educated about grief and sometimes behave and respond as if it were a state—not a process—that is miraculously cured one day; hence if the widow returns to work she is expected to be 100% well with no ebbs and flows and no anniversary reactions. The usual length of time allotted by society is pitifully too short. Silverman (1976) warned that the final adjustment even in normal grieving requires about 2 years which is rather longer than was indicated by the research of earlier pioneers such as Lindemann. The importance of social support as an intervening variable between a major life event and a stressful outcome has been demonstrated in a number of studies (Andrews, Tennant, & Hewson, 1978). Unfortunately friendships centering on the marital dyad are not usually continued after the death of a spouse and there is often a lack of fit between the social and psychological needs of the individual in crisis and the individual's social support network. Maddison and Walker (1967) reported that 20 subjects identified as having a bad outcome perceived their environment as failing to meet their needs and as actively unhelpful.

If her income is reduced, as is often the case, the widow may suffer financial hardship which results in a move to a smaller house; this adds to a second loss and further stress. Her grown children may move further away and former supports fade after the acute phase. Many widows as well as their friends and relatives view widowhood as something of a stigma (Silverman, 1976). Indeed some societies shun the widow physically and separate from her for a time. Often the widow is not fully accepted in her group (Vachon, 1976) or her acceptance may be tentative, ambivalent, or full of pity. In order to avoid their own painful associations friends and family may withdraw from her at a time when her need for emotional support is most imperative.

In conclusion I make no apologies for reiterating the words of Geoffrey Gorer (1965), "Mourning is treated as if it were a weakness, a self-indulgence, a reprehensible bad habit instead of a psychological necessity. We do not burn our widows, we pity and avoid them."

REFERENCES

Andrews, G., Tennant, C., & Hewson, D.M., et al. (1978). Life event stress, social support, coping style and risk of psychological impairment. *Journal of Nervous and Mental Disease, 166,* 307-316

Clayton, P.J. (1973). The clinical morbidity of the first year of bereavement: A review. *Comprehensive Psychiatry, 14,* 151-157.

Clayton, P.J. (1974). Mortality and morbidity in the first year of widowhood. *Archives of General Psychiatry, 30,* 747-750.

Engel, G. (1971). Sudden and rapid death during psychological stress. *Annals of Internal Medicine, 74,* 771-798.

Frankel, S., & Smith, D. (1982). Conjugal bereavement amongst the Huli people of Papua, New Guinea. *British Journal of Psychiatry, 141,* 302-305.

Gerber, I., Weiner, A., Battin, D., et al. (1975). Grief therapy to the aged bereaved. In *Bereavement: Its psychological aspects* (pp.105). B. Schoenberg, I. Gerber, A. Weiner, et al. (Eds.), York: Columbia University Press

Gorer, G. (1965). Death, grief and mourning in contemporary Britain. London: Cresset.

Maddison, D.C., & Walker, W.L. (1967). Factors affecting the outcome of conjugal bereavement. *British Journal of Psychiatry, 133,* 1057-1067.

Marmar, C., Horowitz, M., Weiss, D., Wilner, N., & Kaltreider, N. (1988). A controlled trial of brief psychotherapy and mutual help group treatment of conjugal bereavement. *American Journal of Psychiatry, 145,* 203-209.

Nichols, R., & Nichols, J. (1975). Funerals: A time for grief and growth. In E. Kubler-Ross, (Ed.). *Death, the final stage* (pp.96). Englewood Cliffs, NJ.: Prentice Hall.

Parkes, C.M. (1964). Effects of bereavement on physical and mental health. A study of the medical records of widows. *Psychosomatic Medicine, 32,* 449-461.

Parkes, C.M. (1970). The first year of bereavement. *Psychiatry, 33,* 444-467.

Parkes, C.M., & Brown, R.J. (1972). Health after bereavement: A controlled study of young Boston widows and widowers. *Psychosomatic Medicine, 32,* 449-461.

Parkes, C.M., & Weiss, R.S. (1985). Recovery from bereavement. New York: Basic Books.

Paykel, E.S. (1976). Life, stress, depression and suicide. *Journal of Human Stress, 2,* 3-12.

Raphael, B. (1983). *The anatomy of bereavement.* New York: Basic Books.

Silverman, P.R. (1970). The widow as caregiver in a program of preventive intervention with other widows. *Mental Hygiene, 54,* 540-547.

Silverman, P.R. (1976). The widow as caregiver in a program of preventive intervention with other widows. In G. Caplan and A. Killelie, Eds., *Support systems and mutual help* (pp.233-243). New York: Grune & Stratton.

Vachon, M.L.S. (1976). Grief and bereavement following the death of a spouse. *Canadian Psychiatric Association Journal, 21,* 35-44.

Zisook, S., & Shuchter, S. (1986). First four years of widowhood. *Psychiatric Annals, 16,* 288.

Zisook, S., Shuchter, S., & Lyons, L. (1987). Predictors of psychological reactions during the early stages of widowhood. *Psychiatric Clinics of North America, 10,* (3), 355-368.

Treating the Widowed Client
with Rational-Emotive Therapy (RET)

Albert Ellis

SUMMARY. Widows frequently become not only appropriately sad and grieving when they lose their husbands but also often make themselves inappropriately and self-defeatingly depressed. They do so by almost always irrationally demanding that the sad events of their life consequent to widowhood absolutely *should* not, *must* not exist and that it is *awful* (more than bad) when they do. Rational-emotive therapy (RET) shows widows, as in the case presented here, how they can discover, uproot, and act against their depression-creating beliefs.

Rational-Emotive Therapy (RET), unlike many other popular psychotherapies, has always tried to clearly distinguish between clients' appropriate and their inappropriate negative feelings and does *not* favor the elimination of *all* their painful emotions (Ellis, 1962, 1973a, 1977, 1988; Ellis & Becker, 1982; Ellis & Dryden, 1987; Ellis & Harper, 1975). It does not endorse the extreme Zen Buddhist goals of detachment or Nirvana (desirelessness) (Suzuki, 1956), nor even the more moderate goals of calmness and serenity in the face of adversity (Maultsby, 1982).

In regard to widowed clients in particular, RET encourages them to experience feelings, and often intense feelings, of loss, sadness, sorrow, frustration, concern, and grief when a loved partner dies. This is because, usually, they *have* suffered a great loss and it would be inappropriate — and self-defeating — if they felt nothing

Albert Ellis, PhD, is Founder and President of the Institute for Rational-Emotive Therapy in New York City and is the author of over 600 articles and 50 books on psychotherapy and sex and family therapy. Address correspondence to the author at Institute for Rational-Emotive Therapy, 45 East 65th St., New York, NY 10021.

105

and did nothing about it. When we lose friends, position, or money, we *want* to do something to rectify our losses; and if we did not feel badly about them, how would we be *motivated* to rectify them? Our feeling calm, serene, detached, or indifferent would hardly help!

Nor would our feeling intensely depressed, panicked, and angry do us much good. For we would then usually sit on our rumps, stew instead of do, and act (if at all) in a frantic, disorganized manner.

Take the case of Sarah, a 68-year-old widow who had lived with a very competent and caring husband for 42 years and who had suddenly lost him when he had a heart attack 8 months prior to her seeking therapy. At first, she felt surprisingly numb and uncaring, even though she had always had a good relationship with her husband. She didn't object to that feeling, because it was self-protective. But she did virtually nothing, and balked at making the funeral arrangements, and her son and her close friends became so shocked and critical that she became guilty and frantic about losing their love.

Then, encouraged by a widow's group to vent her "real" feelings, Sarah became very angry. The group, quoting Kubler-Ross (1969), told her that she was doing very well, but her bosses at the art gallery where she worked took a dim view of her irritability with the customers and threatened to fire her in spite of her 20 prior years of good service.

Finally, hit by the realization that her husband was no longer around to take care of all her financial matters, and that her son had too many family problems of his own to give her much help, Sarah became severely depressed. She then did less than ever to take care of herself, lived alone in a highly disorganized apartment, stayed home practically all the time she was not working, and barely could drag herself out of bed each weekday morning. She almost quit working several times, but withdrew her resignations when she realized, once again, that if she lost her job income she could not maintain her standard of living, including the Park Avenue apartment she and her husband had lived in for over 30 years.

Sarah already knew the ABCs of RET and some of her main irrational beliefs when she began therapy, because she had read *A New Guide To Rational Living* (Ellis & Harper, 1975), *How To Stubbornly Refuse To Make Yourself Miserable About Anything— Yes, Anything!* (Ellis, 1988), and *Feeling Good* (Burns, 1980) before she saw me. As I have long claimed, however, insight, even insight into what you are telling yourself to make yourself depressed, is not enough. Only work and practice—yes, work and practice—to change these beliefs will do the trick.

Quite a job I had on my hands—to encourage the severely depressed Sarah to change! Like most depressives, she had the secondary disturbance of self-downing *about* her depression. This stemmed from her rational idea, "I wish I were not depressed! How annoying and uncomfortable this crummy feeling is!" But also, and much more importantly, she depressed herself about her depression, by the rational belief, "I *should not, must not* foolishly make myself depressed! What an idiot I am for doing this to myself! Now that I am *creating* my depression, I hardly *deserve* to have a good life and *should* be punished for being so dumb!"

When we ferreted out her self-denigrating idea about depressing herself (which was easy), we had a hard time, Sarah and I, joining forces to get her to give it up. For while she *weakly* agreed, "Yes, I agree that that's nonsense," she still very *strongly* believed that it was true. So I gave her the homework assignment of devising and repeating to herself several *forceful* self-statements to combat her feelings of worthlessness and undeservingness.

At first, she complained that this exercise was too hard for her to do, but when I (forcefully!) insisted that it was indeed hard but not *too hard*, she said, "Yes, I guess I have to agree. Hard really isn't *too* hard." She then came up with these strong self-statements: "Even if I do assininely work at depressing myself, I'm never a rotten, undeserving *person*! Only a fallible, screwed up *human*, who can get off my ass and stop making myself depressed—if I really work at stopping my nonsense and at *not* indulging in these damned depressing thoughts!"

After forcefully repeating and thinking through this anti-defaming philosophy, Sarah was able to go back to the irrational ideas that she was using to create her depression. First, she was making herself appropriately sad and loss-stricken, by telling herself, "It is very unfortunate to be without my husband, when he took care of me so well for all these years of our marriage. I hardly know how to do *anything* since he insisted on doing practically everything for me. My banking, my taxes, my heavy shopping—almost *everything*. So that I never learned to do them for myself. I see—I *now* see—that he was wrong to take over my main problems the way he did. And I was wrong, dead wrong, to let him! How stupid I was to let him!

These rational beliefs—which in RET we would not try to get Sarah to change—made her feel *appropriately* regretful and sad. Additionally, however, she was also irrationally telling herself, "How could I have been so stupid! I should have known that my copping out like that would get me into trouble. And it now has! What an idiot I was! Now I can't do *anything* to take care of myself! How awful! I *need* Harry to make my life bearable. I can't be happy at all now that he's gone!" With these ideas, she felt severely inadequate and depressed (Ellis, 1987).

Following the usual RET procedures, I helped Sarah clarify these self-defeating beliefs—and to actively dispute them. She asked herself, "Why *should* I have known that copping out like that would get me into trouble?" and answered, "No reason why I should! It would have been nice if I did realize this long ago. But I didn't. Too bad!"

She disputed, "Am I really an idiot for acting as I did and making myself so dependent on Harry?" She answered, "No, that was stupid *behavior* but it hardly makes me a totally *stupid person*. And demanding that I should have known what I did not then know only makes me act *more* stupidly!"

Sarah questioned herself, "Do I really *need* Harry to make my life bearable? Can't I be happy *at all* now that he's gone?" She answered herself, "No, I *want* him very much, and feel very badly without him. But I don't *have* to have what I want and I still can have *some* pleasure without him."

As she actively disputed her grandiose *commands* that she always act intelligently and that Harry *had* to come back and relieve her of practical problems and make her life easy and happy, Sarah continued to grieve over her formidable loss but became much less depressed. She also used several RET emotive methods of working through the grieving process. She used rational-emotive imagery (Maultsby, 1971; Maultsby & Ellis, 1974) to first make herself severely depressed (by vividly imagining that she would never be able to care for herself when husbandless) and then practicing only feeling very disappointed and frustrated but not depressed. She very forcefully told herself coping statements, such as, "I *can* take care of myself and can even *enjoy* doing so!'' She worked on her feelings of shame and used RET shame-attacking exercises (Ellis, 1969, 1973b) to ask friends and relatives to give her some support instead of shamefully avoiding asking for any help. She also forced herself to do several enjoyable pursuits, such as taking art classes and going dancing, even though some of her friends frowned on her doing so shortly after her husband's death.

Sarah also utilized several of RET's behavioral methods, especially in vivo desensitization of her irrational fears. She had let her husband take over and practically run her life because she was terribly afraid to fail at financial matters and to pursue high-level employment (especially college teaching). Spurred by my encouraging her to take risks and, for the first time in her life, to *refuse* to put herself down when she failed, she began to do her own financial investing, to buy a condominium, and to teach a poetry course at a junior college. The more risk-taking she did, the more she saw that she could fend for herself and that she didn't have to berate herself when some of her projects failed. Within a year after her husband's death, she became, as she put it, ''five times as self-sufficient as I ever was while he was living.'' What Bandura (1986) would call her self-efficacy startlingly increased and propelled her to do many more things (such as traveling to Mexico alone) which she had been terrified to do previously.

Although Sarah, when she was no longer depressed nor depressed about her depression, still sadly thought about her deceased husband on many occasions, and had a rough time becoming close to any other man, she learned during her 7 months of rational-emotive therapy (consisting of 19 half-hour sessions) to be much more of the person she had always wanted to be and had never been during the 42 years of her marriage. As she remarked during one of our last sessions, ''It is tragic that Harry had to die and, by doing so, sort of, uh, forced me to stand on my own two feet. But by his loss practically forcing me to try and to work at RET, I have gained much more, in some ways, than I ever did by his love and help when he was alive. I hate to say this, but in several important respects, I actually gained by his death. How strange, to have been propelled to change by such a sad event!''

''Yes,'' I said. ''But remember what Epictetus, one of the fathers of RET, noted over two thousand years ago: 'It's not the things that happen that change us, but our *view* of them.' "

"I'm glad you reminded me," Sarah declared. "Yes, it's really my *view* of Harry's death, or RET, and of myself that has made me undepressed."

"Yes — and your work at changing your view."

"Yes, you're right. My work."

I haven't had any additional sessions with Sarah for the last 3 years. But she comes several times a year to my regular Friday Night Workshop at the Institute for Rational-Emotive Therapy in New York, to observe me give live demonstrations of RET with public volunteers. From what she tells me, she still misses Harry and thinks of him sadly on anniversary days and certain other occasions. But she is no longer depressed and for the most part leads an exceptionally busy, independent, and often happy life.

Widowhood and bereavement are a very common aspect of modern life. As many clinicians and researchers have shown, widows frequently become not only appropriately sad and grieving but also what RET calls inappropriately depressed (Averill & Nunley, 1988; Laudenslager, 1988; Parkes, 1988; Weiss, 1988). Not that they have to, because a good number of them do not slide into depression. Those who do, I contend, almost always create for themselves irrational, self-defeating ideas (Ellis, 1987, 1988). As the case just presented shows, these can be discovered, uprooted, and acted against by effective psychotherapy. By the therapist's understanding and fully accepting the bereaved widow's emotional state? Yes, of course. But also by both the therapist and the widowed client persistently using two other nonmagical ingredients: work and practice. Yes, work. Yes, practice!

REFERENCES

Averill, J.R., & Nunley, E.P. (1988). Grief as an emotion and as a disease: A social-constructionist perspective. *Journal of Social Issues, 44*(3), 79-96.

Bandura, A. (1986). *Social foundations of thought and action: A social cognitive theory.* Englewood Cliffs, NJ: Prentice-Hall.

Burns, D.D. (1980). *Feeling good: The new mood therapy.* New York: Morrow.

Ellis, A. (1962). *Reason and emotion in psychotherapy.* Secaucus, NJ: Lyle Stuart.

Ellis, A. (1969). A weekend of rational encounter. *Rational Living, 4*(2), 1-8.

Ellis, A. (1973a). *Humanistic psychotherapy: The rational-emotive approach*. New York: McGraw-Hill.

Ellis, A. (1973b). *How to stubbornly refuse to be ashamed of anything*. Cassette recording. New York: Institute for Rational-Emotive Therapy.

Ellis, A. (1977). *Anger—how to live with and without it*. Secaucus, NJ: Citadel Press.

Ellis, A. (1987). A sadly neglected cognitive element in depression. *Cognitive Therapy and Research, 11*, 121-146.

Ellis, A. (1988). *How to stubbornly refuse to make yourself miserable about anything—yes, anything!* Secaucus, NJ: Lyle Stuart.

Ellis, A., & Becker, I. (1982). *A guide to personal happiness*. North Hollywood, CA: Wilshire Books.

Ellis, A., & Dryden, W. (1987). *The practice of rational-emotive therapy*. New York: Springer.

Ellis, A., & Harper, R.A. (1975). *A new guide to rational living*. North Hollywood, CA: Wilshire Books.

Kubler-Ross, E. (1969). *On death and dying*. New York: Macmillan.

Laudenslager, M.L. (1988). The psychobiology of loss: Lessons from human and nonhuman primates. *Journal of Social Issues, 44*(3), 19-36.

Maultsby, M.C., Jr. (1971). Rational emotive imagery. *Rational Living, 6*(1), 24-27.

Maultsby, M.C., Jr. (1984). *Rational behavior therapy*. Englewood Cliffs, NJ: Prentice-Hall.

Maultsby, M.C., Jr., & Ellis, A. (1974). *Technique for using rational-emotive imagery*. New York: Institute for Rational-Emotive Therapy.

Parkes, C.M. (1988). Bereavement as a psychosocial transition: Processes of adaptation to change. *Journal of Social Issues. 44*(3), 53-66.

Suzuki, D.T. (1956). *Zen Buddhism*. New York: Doubleday Anchor Books.

Weiss, R.S. (1988). Loss and recovery. *Journal of Social Issues, 44*(3), 37-52.

An Agenda
for Treating Widowed Parents

Betty C. Buchsbaum

SUMMARY. The agenda for treating widowed parents refers to the basic adult responses required by bereaved children in order to cope with their loss. The adult's caretaking functions examined in this paper include providing a stable environment for the family, explaining the facts and circumstances of a parent's death, understanding the child's developmental capacities for mourning, assisting the child in tolerating and expressing grief, and facilitating the transition to new relationships that may occur at the end of mourning. A child's ability to comprehend, adapt to, and mourn a parent's death is contingent on the empathic and enlightened support of a loved adult. The complexities inherent in implementing the suggested guidelines are highlighted by published autobiographical vignettes and clinical data.

Widowed parents of young children constitute a population predictably in need of guidance and support. Whatever the circumstances of a spouse's death, the confrontation of the loss, the sense of isolation, and the fears of facing the tasks of parenthood alone can be overwhelming. For those individuals who have significant relationships with available family members or friends, people who can share the practical tasks of child care and provide emotional

---

Betty C. Buchsbaum, PhD, is Director of Psychology Intern Training at the Center for Preventive Psychiatry in White Plains, NY; Clinical Assistant Professor with the Department of Psychiatry at Albert Einstein College of Medicine; and Adjunct Assistant Professor of Psychology in Psychiatry at Cornell University Medical College, Department of Psychiatry, Cornell University Medical College and Westchester Division, The New York Hospital. Address correspondence to the author at 515 Greenhaven Road, Rye, NY 10580.

113

understanding as well, consultation with a therapist may be unnecessary. For many, however, Lynn Caine's (1974) experience is pertinent. "The people one might turn to naturally — priests and ministers, other widows, friends, family, — cannot or do not want to cope with the wild, angry, desperate . . . talk of the grieving widow" (p. 115). Nor, as she noted, is the knowledge and objectivity of the professional something one can expect from friends and relatives.

In this paper, I will outline the ways in which parent consultation and guidance can assist a bereaved spouse in the effort to provide continuity and sensitivity in meeting the needs of a grieving child. In addition to elucidating the ways in which parents can support their children's response to loss, I will also illustrate from published autobiographies and clinical material the difficulties encountered in this process. I hope, thus, to underscore the complexities, the well-intentioned but often misguided efforts, as well as the intuitively "right" responses demonstrated by surviving caretakers. The suggestions made here can be applied to patients who ask a therapist for help. The issues addressed in this paper refer only to that segment of the therapeutic task involving the needs of a bereaved child. The clinical judgment and skill required in this work can be appreciated when one considers the wide range of strengths and weaknesses presented by each family a therapist encounters. When emotional problems predate a parent's death, or when the defensive reactions of either the parent or child are destructive to the mourning process, psychotherapy for the parent and/or child would be suggested. Parent guidance appears to be desirable even in the absence of psychological problems in order to provide significant preventive care for family members. Furman (1974) notes that through parent counseling soon after a bereavement, "the attendant and subsequent circumstances of the death may be ameliorated so that the child has an optimum chance of utilizing his capacities for mourning" (p. 294). Lynn Caine wishes she "had known the therapeutic value of talk when Martin (her husband) was dying . . . I would have emerged from grief sooner. And so would the children" (p. 116).

Hummer and Samuels (1988) recommended that assessing a bereaved spouse's capacity to respond appropriately to a child constitutes the first phase of a clinical evaluation. The following parental functions are considered to be essential in helping a bereaved child cope with the death of a parent:

1. Providing a stable environment for the family.
2. Explaining the facts and circumstances of a parent's death in a realistic, clear manner.
3. Understanding the child's developmental capacities for mourning with reference to both cognitive and affective aspects.
4. Modulating tension and mood states; encouraging the experience of the affects of grief as well as fostering progressive development.
5. Assisting the child in dealing with new relationships that may occur at the end of the mourning period.

The adequacy in performing these parental functions profoundly impacts on the child's ability to comprehend, to adapt to, and to mourn the death of a parent. In focusing on these tasks, the therapist contributes to the widowed parent's self-image as an effective individual whose family deserves the care and attention that the parent can provide.

MAINTAINING FAMILY STABILITY

A parent's need to make real life changes, such as those involved in moving out of the community, or even altering the composition of a household, serves both to deplete the parent and to further undermine a child's sense of security. Though often unavoidable, the widowed parent should be informed about the negative impact the uprooting experience can have. The mourning process of a young child cannot be accomplished easily if the predictable people and places in his or her life have suddenly vanished. When moves are necessary, explanation, support, and sustained connections to familiar people, places, and events should be provided.

Eileen Simpson (1987) described the fate of her family life following her mother's death when she was 11 months old. At the age of three she and her sister were placed in a convent by their father. Before this, she writes, "our father kept us with one grandmother, then the other. We did not flourish" (p. 22).[1] Placement outside of New York was recommended by a doctor. "So that we would have country air, we were boarded with a series of families in Staten Island and New Jersey. Each, before long, talked about separating us for the sake of convenience; or, equally distressing to my father, hinted at adoption. He decided it would be better to give us to the nuns" (p. 22). Simpson attributes her strength and psychic survival to the fact that she and her sister were together, serving as constant companions to each other. Later, when she was seven, her father died; Simpson and her sister experienced more dislocations, ultimately living with relatives who continued a pattern of shifts and changes. Continuity of care and stability of environment were goals not easily realized during Eileen Simpson's childhood.

The therapeutic work reported by Buchsbaum and Bethea (in press) reflects the effort made to reduce the number of separations imposed on two young siblings following their mother's death. Bobby, 2-1/2 years, and Nancy, 5 years, were referred for treatment at the time their mother was hospitalized. Since their parents had been separated, the children were living with their mother, aunt, and grandmother. Following their mother's death, Bobby was moved to his father's home while Nancy remained with her grandmother. During the first month of their separation, the children often requested joint therapy sessions, seeming to need the contact they had been deprived of at home. With the therapist's encouragement, the children were reunited in their father's household where, in time, the paternal grandmother joined them. Unfortunately, changes in living arrangements did occur again. By this time, however, their father had gained increased awareness regarding the effect of these disruptions. Efforts on his part to enable the children to remain together were more or less successful. The children's tendency to cling to familiar relatives subsided within the first few months. And Bobby's school adjustment, which had been impeded by the need to remain close to his grandmother, improved. As the family became educated in the issues relevant to the children, they worked together more cooperatively, using the therapist as a mediator as well as a source of support and guidance.

EXPLAINING THE FACTS AND CIRCUMSTANCES OF THE DEATH IN A REALISTIC, CLEAR MANNER

The importance of helping children to understand the general concept of death as well as to know the specific facts about how their own parents died is stressed by Bowlby (1980). He states, "The two crucial items of information . . . a child needs to know are first that the dead parent will never return and secondly that his body is buried in the ground or burned to ashes" (p. 271). A study of bereaved families by Becker and Margolin (1967), found that informing children about the disposal of the body is often postponed. The authors conclude that there was a "marked tendency for adults to insulate their young from the painful aspects of loss; they tended to promote avoidance and denial of the finality of death and of feelings in relation to it" (p. 757). Becker and Margolin report, further, that "when adequate preparation is given young children, the shared experiences of memorial observances and visits to the cemetery (serve to) further comprehension of death and facilitate the normal process of mourning" (p. 757). In assisting the parent in the task of communicating information to a child, Bowlby points up the need for the therapist to aid the bereaved parent's expression of such emotions as grief and anger in order to succeed. When a parent can explain the events and consequences of the death to a child, the recognition of irretrievable loss and the associated affects can be confronted. The surviving parent's participation in this process with the child permits a sharing of affects, offers a model to the child, and mitigates against the isolation inherent in the mourning work.

Two autobiographical excerpts portray the incomplete responses that only serve to deepen the loneliness and fears of the bereaved child.

Eileen Simpson (1987) writes,

> Our relatives . . . were enlightened enough to see that Marie and I attended our father's funeral. Perhaps if we had remained with them in the days that followed, they would have even talked to us about his death. Probably not, however. They were too stunned by the loss of a brother so young to talk about him, and also could hardly bear to look at us when they

thought what full orphanhood would mean in our lives. And in
theirs. Even later, when I asked questions about either parent's
death, they answered them shyly, reluctantly, as if to say, You
really don't want to be reminded of those events do you? What
I now know . . . I learned piecemeal, a bit from this aunt, a bit
from that uncle:
   "Ptomaine poisoning."
   "Yes, but from what?"
   "Shellfish."
   "What kind?"
   "So many questions? Clams. Beware of clams."
   Another said
   "Oysters. One shouldn't eat oysters in the summer." It was
a long time before I dared eat either, in any season. (p. 16)

In *Memories of a Catholic Girlhood* Mary McCarthy (1963) described how she discovered the signs and signals of her parents'
deaths from influenza. In her paternal grandparents' house, she (6
years) and her three younger brothers

were shut out from the knowledge of what had happened so
close to us, just out of our hearing—a scandal of the gravest
character, a coming and going of priests and undertakers and
coffins. (Mamma and Daddy they assured us, had gone to get
well in the hospital)—we became aware, even as we woke
from our fevers, that everything, including ourselves, was different . . . The behavior of the people around us, abrupt, care-
less, and preoccupied, apprised us without any ceremony of
our diminished importance. Our value had paled, and a new
image of ourselves—the image, if we had guessed it, of the
orphan—was already forming in our minds. We had not
known we were spoiled, but now this word, entering our vocabulary for the first time, served to define the change for us
and to herald a new order . . . Our new instructors (grandparents and members of their household) could hardly be blamed
for a certain impatience with our parents who had been so
lacking in foresight. It was to everyone's interest, decidedly,
that we should forget the past—the quicker, the better—and a

steady disparagement of our habits . . . prepared us to accept a loss that was, in any case, irreparable. Like all children we wished to conform . . . We no longer demanded our due and the wish to see our parents weakened. Soon we ceased to speak of it, and thus, without tears or tantrums, we came to know they were dead.

Why no one, least of all our grandmother, to whose repertory the subject seems so congenial, took the trouble to tell us, it is impossible now to know . . . Perhaps really she feared our tears, which might rain on her like reproaches, since the family policy at the time was predicated on our virtual insentience, an assumption that allowed them to proceed with us as if with pieces of furniture. (p. 37-39)

Staying on with her grandparents for a short while after her brothers had been sent off to another house, McCarthy believed that she

thought they (her brothers) were dead, but their fate did not greatly concern me; my heart had grown numb. I considered myself clever to have guessed the truth about my parents, like a child who proudly discovers that there is no Santa Claus, but I would not speak of that knowledge or even react to it privately for I wished to have nothing to do with it; I would not cooperate in this loss. Those weeks in my grandmother's house come back to me very obscurely, surrounded by blackness, like a mourning card: the dark well of the staircase, where I seem to have been endlessly loitering, waiting to see Mama when she would come home from the hospital, and then simply loitering with no purpose whatever. (p. 39)

Even when information is not deliberately withheld, the agony of not knowing the complete details of a death, not having closure, can be intense. Laurie Marshall (Krementz, 1981)[2] said that she was afraid to talk about what really happened to her father who had been killed in a plane crash.

They still haven't found out what made the plane crash . . . I think that she (mother) might know something more that I'd like to know, but I'm kind of afraid to ask her because I don't know what she'll do, or what she'll say. Not knowing what happened is terrible. It's like you're in suspense all the time and you just want to get the facts so that you won't have to think about it again. (pp. 2-3)

Bethea (Buchsbaum & Bethea, in press), working with Nancy and Bobby, made every effort to provide them with as much direct knowledge of ongoing events as possible. Mr. P. was encouraged to bring his children to visit their mother in the hospital, knowing that she was dying. The children were informed when she died and about the cause of her death. Though the therapist recommended that the children attend the funeral, Mr. P. was unable to comply. He recalled how upset he had been when, as a child, he had attended his grandfather's funeral.

Instead, the children were present at the wake and several months later were taken to the cemetery . . . Following consultation with Mr. P . . . the therapist explained the notion of death (to Bobby and Nancy) in naturalistic terms, confirming the fact that their mother would not return. This approach was . . . ultimately accepted by the family. Nevertheless, five months later, the children were observed by Mr. P. to be "speaking to their mother." Worried that his children thought their mother was still alive, he told them that she had gone away.

When Mr. P. was told that now the children might be misled into awaiting their mother's return, he spoke with them again about the finality of her death.

Explaining their mother's death to Bobby and Nancy was . . . not a simple procedure. Each relevant member of the family . . . was consulted in order to explain the confusions that incomplete and purely religious explanations would create for the children. In spite of their stated approval and cooperation, communications about death fluctuated from naturalistic to religious and evasive formulations. A kind of continuous monitoring of adults' responses to the children was required to sustain a consistent and coherent approach to the subject.

Along with the information relayed concerning the facts of a parent's death, sensitivity and awareness are required in handling associated affects and anxieties. In addition to answering the question of why a parent died, Koocher (1983) points out the need to attend to other issues, such as,

> Will that happen to me (or someone else I care about)? Did I have anything to do with it? Who will take care of me (if the deceased was one of the child's caretakers)? While these questions may not be specifically articulated by the child, they are almost always a part of the underlying anxiety that accompanies a prolonged grief reaction. (p. 1282)

Fantasies and fears of a young child regarding the appearance of the dead parent require attention. A 6-year-old reported to the author his regret at not having viewed his father's body. He confided that only later did he realize that his father had not looked like a skeleton. Another boy of seven said that when, at 5 years of age, he had seen his father's corpse, he had been relieved to find that "it was not all bones."

The child's capacity to test reality, validated by the caretaking adult, strengthens self-esteem, avoids confusion, and frees cognitive abilities to cope with other more relevant concerns.

UNDERSTANDING THE CHILD'S DEVELOPMENTAL CAPACITIES FOR MOURNING

Articulating to the parent the interactions of behaviors associated with both mourning and development constitutes a critical task. The ways in which children respond to bereavement at different ages can be annoying, demanding, perplexing, and even frightening to the uninformed adult. Kaffman, Elizur, and Gluckson (1987) reported a variety of disturbed reactions of children between 2 and 10 years of age whose fathers had died during the October 1973 war in Israel. They described the clinging preschooler beset by fears of separation from the surviving mother, regressing in areas in which mastery had been well established, such as bladder control, frequently denying the fact of a father's death. Latency-age children appeared indifferent to the death, were quiet and withdrawn, and ignored references to the subject. They coped with the trauma less directly than did the younger children: "through reading sad books, writing, painting and games related to the 'forbidden' subject" (p. 68).

The memories and feelings of young children, expressed in play, may be quite direct and unmodulated, while older children are more reserved and defended in expressing sadness. For example, a third grader, Stephen Jayne recalled:

> I stayed home from school for two weeks and when I went back I wasn't crying anymore. My friends said, 'It doesn't seem like you're very sad your father died. It doesn't seem like you miss him.' I did feel sad, but I just didn't want to cry in front of them. (Krementz, 1981, p. 39)

For the prelatency child, Furman (1974) emphasizes the role of the parent in helping the child recognize, verbalize, and tolerate affects. She observes that "it was a necessary part of the mourning process . . . that the surviving love object accept . . . verbal expressions of anger and, in some instances, acknowledge the objective reality of their (the child's) cause for complaint" (p. 56). Also, most children she worked with "needed a loved person who could either share their grief or empathize with them" (p. 57).

Furman also points to the importance of memories of the deceased parents in enabling the child to mourn. How the surviving parent can assist in providing age-relevant parental descriptions to the child is suggested by a preliminary study of bereaved children's memories of a deceased parent. In exploring the organization of children's recall, the regular progression from the 3-year-old to the adolescent was noted. With a death occurring in early childhood, different kinds of information about the parent would be required at each stage of the child's development. The study suggests that the preschooler would seek information about the activities that were shared by the child and parent. At about 7 years the child can assimilate descriptions of the parent's physical appearance, and the kind of work he did. The 9- or 10-year-old comprehends and is interested in knowing about the hobbies, habits, likes, and dislikes of the parents. At adolescence a more integrated picture of the deceased can emerge and a wide range of data regarding the parent's history, values, and attitudes is relevant and sought after (Buchsbaum, 1987). Nick Davis, 15-years-old when reporting his reactions to his mother's death, states,

> I like it when people tell me stories and I get to know . . . (my mother) better. I love finding out more about what she was like, because I was only nine when she died and I didn't know her that well. I mean, I knew her as a mother, not as a person. (Krementz, 1981, p. 26)

Eileen Simpson (1987) describes how her maternal relatives helped her learn more about her mother.

> It was Uncle Charlie and Aunt Hilda who blew a little life into our mother's statue. They had known her so intimately, they called her by a nickname we had never heard before. To them she was "Molly" . . . On rainy days we were allowed to play with our mother's table silver, . . . her Art Nouveau dresser set with brushes she used on her "glorious chestnut hair" that went down to her waist, a pair of black-and-white China spaniels she had used for doorstops. (p. 80)

The sisters also learned more about the details of their mother's illness and, finally, her death. It was

> during these holidays that for the first time I could imagine, if dimly, that she had an earthly existence. Tentatively Marie and I began to use the word "mother" not to signify a nun, but the woman who bore us. Playing in the attic we'd say, "Pass me Mother's mirror . . ." the word sounded theatrical as if we were playacting, but I felt I had a right to use it, and every time I did it stirred me deeply. (p. 83)

This welcome change, occurring at about 10 or 11 years, contrasted with Simpson's early efforts to visualize her mother when she was in the convent. "When I tried to picture my mother, my mind was like a blank screen. In the end, I settled on a double exposure photograph Daddy had on his dresser at home" (p. 28).

In working with Bobby and Nancy, the need to help the children sort out and differentiate memories from expectations and yearning became evident.

> Nancy asked one week after she was told of her mother's death—could she visit her mother in the hospital? This one inquiry effectively condensed her wish to see her mother, . . . the recent recollection of a visit to her and Nancy's uncertainty about the consequences of death. These meanings were clarified by the therapist. (Buchsbaum & Bethea)

When the surviving parent can learn from the therapist what a child is really asking and how to provide the information sought, the shared knowledge can further strengthen the bonds between two very different mourners.

MONITORING AND MODULATING A CHILD'S EXPOSURE TO STIMULATION

Monitoring and modulating the degree of stimulation associated with the events of and reactions to the death constitutes another task of the widowed parent. Children can withdraw in fear when witnessing adults who are emotionally overwrought. Yet they require a model as well as companionship in experiencing the range of affects associated with mourning. At each developmental stage different emotional concerns become pivotal. With the therapist's assistance, the parent can recognize key vulnerabilities and protect the child from too glaring an exposure to them. To illustrate, the preschooler reacts to the death of one parent with the fear of losing the other. Separations and changes take on an intensely disruptive meaning. During latency, separations can be tolerated somewhat better, but fear of illness, concerns about money, feelings of guilt and anger directed at the surviving parent may reflect mourning reactions. The adolescent often responds with exaggerated independence and seeming detachment.

A 15-year-old, whose mother died after his parents were divorced stated:

> I have to work things out for myself. That's why I like being alone — just to think. If I can't solve a problem by myself, I don't feel I've solved anything. I keep my own counsel . . . I don't cry often. When I do cry it's about stupid little inconsequential things, but that's a way of letting out my tears about my mother . . . I suppose my mother's death has probably made me more independent. I just have to rely on myself more. (Krementz, 1981, p. 101)

Sylvia Plath's (1971)[3] autobiographical novel describes how the grief of a 9-year-old was finally released in young adulthood. The absence of her mother's participation and support in acknowledging the reactions to her father's death is revealed as she describes a visit to his grave.

> I thought it odd that in all the time my father had been buried in this graveyard none of us had ever visited him. My mother hadn't let us come to his funeral because we were only children then, and he had died in the hospital. So the graveyard and even his death had always seemed unreal to me.
>
> I had a great yearning, lately, to pay my father back for all the years of neglect, and start tending his grave. I had always been my father's favorite, and it seemed fitting I should take on a mourning my mother had never bothered with. Arriving at his gravestone . . . my legs folded under me, and I sat down in the sopping grass. I couldn't understand why I was crying so hard.
>
> Then I remembered that I had never cried for my father's death.
>
> My mother hadn't cried either . . .
>
> I laid my face to the smooth face of the marble and howled my loss into the cold salt rain. (pp. 186-189)

Through the treatment of Bobby and Nancy, Mr. P. had gained an understanding and acceptance of his children's varying affective responses to their mother's death. This achievement was marked when, at the end of the first year of bereavement, Bobby asked to visit his mother's grave. Mr. P. arranged a family visit to the cemetery, further validating his son's needs and offering the supportive presence of others who could share his yearning.

ASSISTING IN THE LAST PHASE OF MOURNING

It is essential to inform a bereaved spouse of the prolonged period entailed in childhood mourning. Kaffman (1987), Raphael (1983), and Furman (1974) all reveal the difficulties that remain after the first year of mourning. The widowed parents may themselves recognize continued or reawakened mourning reactions on anniversaries, family events, or when involved in a new relationship. Children, too, continue to mourn. Evidence of childhood bereavement reactions 12 to 18 months after the death were "lessened resiliency, a propensity for separation problems, preoccupation with illness, death-related altered or lowered self-esteem, uncertainty about the future and worry about growing up" (Samuels, 1988, p. 22). "Almost all of the children (in the Barr-Harris study) indicated that the death of the parent continues to be an active issue for them many years later" (p. 23). Kaffman (1987) found that a decline in grief reactions among the children he studied did not occur until 3 1/2 years after the loss.

Often, an asynchronous pattern of mourning in adult and child affects varying degrees of readiness for new relationships. The parent may be sufficiently free of the attachment to the dead spouse to permit for the possibility of remarriage, while the child, still working on disengagement, may feel threatened by the presence of a strange adult in the household. Furman (1974) observes that

> One of the hardest phases is the end of mourning when a new love object is sought and the child needs to accommodate within him the new relationship alongside the remaining residual cathexis of the deceased-parent image . . . Our younger

patients were sometimes ready for a new parent before one was available, or they were offered a new parent before they were ready to accept one. (p. 25)

Lynn Caine's daughter, 3 years after her father's death, was still searching for someone to fill the gap left by him. "She yearns for a father. Even now, at eight, she still asks every man who comes to the house, "May I call you Daddy? I wish you were my Daddy" (p.164).

Russell Baker, 6 years old when his father died and 14 years when his mother remarried, expressed a less receptive attitude toward the man his mother dated and then married. At the dating stage, Baker (1982) writes, "It never occurred to me that Herb was courting. I would have been alarmed if I'd thought so. Wasn't I long established as the 'man of the family'? A competitor was inconceivable" (p. 209).

When, later, Baker was surprised by his mother's announcement of her marriage to Herb, he "was too stunned to speak . . . I had liked Herb well enough as an affable visitor, dropping in occasionally with ice-cream treats, but now my heart closed against him." Russell describes how he greeted his new rival:

The day Herb moved into Lombard Street with us I set out on one of those campaigns of silent resistance of which only adolescents and high-spirited nations are capable. I gave no spoken sign of my dislike. I was too cunning for that. My policy was to ignore him as completely as possible. Without saying a word that could possibly offend him, I would let him know that as far as I was concerned, he did not exist . . .

My technique was aimed at withering his soul without giving him the slightest excuse for a refreshing outburst of violence . . .

He not only tolerated me with saintly patience, he also tried to befriend me . . . Herb's patience with me was superhuman . . . Maybe he just understood how deep a boy's unhappiness could be . . . Much later when I was older and I grew to like and respect him, we never talked about those adolescent tortures I inflicted on him, and I never raised the subject or tried to apologize . . . He was never much good at talk like that. (pp. 225-226)

Younger children, feeling more needy and yet resentful, express negative attitudes in a less conscious manner. Five-year-old Susan was joyous and welcoming toward her father's fiancee 2 years after her mother's death. Yet once the new family moved to a different house and Susan's new mother was clearly an established family member, Susan developed such stomachaches that she could barely eat her meals. The therapist's suggestions to increase Susan's autonomy regarding choice of menu and amounts to be eaten were followed. As Susan's stepmother felt more adequate, even when Susan did not finish a meal, and when Susan felt more in charge, the stomachaches disappeared.

Raphael (1983) observes the inner struggles accompanying a child's response to a parent's remarriage.

> The child often longs for the regularity and security of a full family life again, yet may enjoy special privileges when he has only one parent . . . and become used to this situation . . . There may be initial rejection of the new parent and a renewal of loyalty and grief for the one who has been lost. If these further levels of grief can be supported sympathetically, then there is much to suggest that he may establish new and rewarding bonds. (p. 125)

Before concluding, I wish to reiterate the fact that parent guidance may not always suffice in dealing with a child's bereavement response. When the surviving parent lacks sufficient external support, exhibits maladaptive defenses against the emotions of mourning, or relates inappropriately to a child, further therapy for the parent is indicated. Conditions placing the child at risk also include "pre-traumatic variables such as the child's previous emotional state, the availability of family, marital status of the parents and prolonged separations from one of the parents" (Kaffman, 1987, p. 69). Kaffman reported that access to a surrogate father, the mother's coping skills, as well as the quality of the mother-child relationship affected the child's behavior.

It is thus part of the therapist's function to assess the factors which would indicate the need for more intensive therapy. Both Furman (1974) and Kaffman (1987) advocate early intervention in the treatment of children at risk to prevent the crystallization of severe pathology at a later time.

CONCLUSION

I have attempted to outline some of the significant areas of guidance required by a bereaved parent. The illustrations presented reflect the pain, confusion, and despair experienced by children; reactions which are often unexpressed and, so, go unobserved. As the children's feelings are recognized and supported their sense of security reinforced, questions answered, and confusions sorted out by the surviving parent, barriers to the work of mourning are diminished. In spite of the lingering marks of their loss, these children can recover and go on to form new and gratifying relationships.

Special preventive and therapeutic opportunities are available in this work. The support and insights offered enhance the parent's own capacity to mourn. In addition, increased coping skills and the consequent sense of competence relieve the inner depletion often associated with widowhood. Finally, as the child gains an understanding ally in the parent, the family bonds grow sturdier and more gratifying.

In the last pages of her book Lynn Caine (1974) writes:

> Things are better now. I tell myself the worst is over . . . The children are a responsibility . . . But they are also my bridge to a more stable world . . . Perhaps I would never have come to know and love my children quite as much as I do if Martin had not died. (p. 177)

NOTES

1. From *Orphans Real & Imaginary* by Eileen Simpson. Copyright 1987 by Weidenfeld & Nicholson, Publishers, Inc. Reprinted by arrangement with Weidenfeld & Nicolson, Publishers, Inc.

2. From *How It Feels When A Parent Dies* by J. Krementz. Copyright 1981 by Knopf, Publishers, Inc. Reprinted by arrangement with Knopf, Publishers, Inc.

3. From *The Bell Jar* by Sylvia Plath. Copyright 1971 by Harper & Row, Publishers, Inc. Reprinted by arrangement with Harper & Row, Publishers, Inc.

REFERENCES

Baker, R. (1982). *Growing up*. New York: Signet, New American Library.

Becker, D., & Margolin, F. (1967). How surviving parents handled their young children's adaptation to the crisis of loss. *American Journal of Orthopsychiatry, 37,* 753-757.

Bowlby, J. (1980). *Attachment and loss, Vol. 3, Loss*. New York: Basic Books.

Buchsbaum, B. (1978). Remembering a parent who has died: A developmental perspective. *The annual of psychoanalysis* (Vol. 15, pp. 99-112). New York: International Universities Press.

Buchsbaum, B., & Bethea, W. (in press). Choices considered and decisions made in the treatment of two maternally bereaved siblings. New York: Foundation of Thanatology.

Caine, L. (1974). *Widow*. New York: Wm. Morrow and Co.

Furman, E. (1974). A child's parent dies: *Studies in childhood bereavement*. New Haven, CT: Yale University Press.

Hummer, K. M., & Samuels, A. (1988). The influence of the recent death of a spouse on the parenting function of the surviving parent. In S. Altschul (Ed.) *Childhood bereavement and its aftermath* (pp. 37-64). Madison, CT: International Universities Press.

Kaffman, M., Elizur, E., & Gluckson, L. (1987). Bereavement reactions in children: Therapeutic implications. Israel Journal of Psychiatry and Related Sciences, *24*(12), 65-76.

Koocher, G. (1983). Grief and loss in childhood. In C. Walker and M. Roberts (Eds.), *Handbook of clinical child psychology* (pp. 1273- 1284). New York: Wiley.

Krementz, J. (1981). *How it feels when a parent dies*. New York: Knopf.

McCarthy, M. (1946). *Memories of a Catholic girlhood*. New York: Berkley Publishing Corp.

Plath, S. (1971). *The bell jar*. New York: Harper and Row.

Raphael, B. (1983). *The anatomy of bereavement*. New York: Basic Books.

Samuels, A. (1988). Parental death in childhood. In S. Altshul (Ed.) *Childhood bereavement and its aftermath* (pp. 19-36). Madison, CT: International Universities Press.

Simpson, E. (1987). *Orphans, real & imaginary*. New York: Weidenfeld and Nicholson.

Widowhood:
The Labor of Grief

Robert J. Dunn
Amelia Vernon

SUMMARY. This article briefly reviews the psychological literature regarding widowhood. The two major scientific models for understanding grief, the developmental model and the medical model,
are compared and contrasted.

This article suggests a view of grief as [birth] labor may be a
useful means of reconciling medical and developmental models of
grieving, particularly as pertains to widows.

Note: Amelia Vernon, one of the authors, lost her husband and two
children in an airplane crash several years ago. The article contains
excerpts from her *Passions of Grief.*

From the car, I watched them get ready to take off. My
husband, Bob, was checking the plane and looking serious —
dear as usual. Ang, our skinny, blond sixteen-year-old son,
was standing by the plane flexing his arm muscles in a strong-
man pose. Within a few minutes, they had left on a ski trip.
Later that day, they picked up our daughter, Laura, and two of
her college friends. That evening the plane crashed and they
were all killed. (Vernon, 1985, p. 1)

Robert J. Dunn, PhD from Iowa State University (1974), is Associate Professor of Psychology at Loras College, Dubuque, IA. Address correspondence to the
author at Department of Psychology, Loras College, Dubuque, IA 52001. Amelia
Vernon recently completed her Master's degree in Applied Psychology from
Loras College. She also holds a Bachelor of Science in Nursing from Johns
Hopkins University. Ms. Vernon is a free-lance writer. Address correspondence
to the author at 120 Hill Street, Dubuque, IA 52001.

131

In the United States, there are over 700,000 new widows each year (U.S. Bureau of the Census, 1983). One of every eight adult women is a widow. By its very nature it is a role for which women are ill prepared and enter with unclear expectations or goals (Hiltz, 1978). Greenblatt (1978) maintains that loss of spouse presents serious risks to the psychological and physical health of the survivor, especially for women. Widows, in general, need more emotional and physical help than they get and are particularly vulnerable to reduced financial status and social isolation (Lopata, 1979).

Factors thought to aid a widow's grieving include religious involvement (Ball, 1976-1977), good health (McGlosen & O'Bryant, 1988), an emotional support network (Bankoff, 1981), an opportunity to express one's feelings (Diamond, Lund, & Johnson, 1983). Some evidence suggests an important role for the widow's siblings as support figures (Diamond et al., 1983; Walker, MacBride, & Vachon, 1977). Strong ties to neighbors and neighborhood may also contribute positively to a widow's adjustment (Ferrarao & Barresi, 1982). When available, the bereaved adult's parents are the most effective source of support (Bankoff, 1983). In a recent study (Lehman, Ellard, & Wortman, 1986), survivors rated contact with a similar other and an opportunity to express feelings as most helpful in grieving. Giving advice and encouraging recovery were rated as most unhelpful.

DEVELOPMENTAL MODEL

The two major scientific paradigms for understanding grief are the developmental (growth) model and the medical model. The developmental model suggests that grief be seen as a dynamic, constructive activity with the potential for personal growth — an adjustment to loss, a process of healthy psychological separation.

Freud (1917/1953), an early proponent of the developmental model, describes mourning as a normal dynamic process that serves an important function; it is not a pathological condition, and, generally, does not require medical treatment. This "normal mourning" was distinguished from pathological forms of mourning where the normal process was distorted by mental illness.

Lindemann (1944),in his classic study of the Coconut Grove fire survivors, sees grief not as a medical or a psychiatric disorder but as a normal reaction to a distressing situation. Erikson (1968) views grief as associated with the developmental task of integrity versus despair. Maslow (1968) describes grief in terms of growth toward self-actualization.

Using a variety of animal and human studies, Bowlby (1980) perceives grief in the context of other losses, such as the separation of a mother from her baby. Grief is an attempt to recover a lost object which is not recoverable—a normal reaction to loss. The individual traverses stages of numbing, yearning and searching, disorganization and reorganization.

MEDICAL MODEL

> With newly discovered medicines, doctors could cure formerly incurable diseases and relieve formerly intractable pains. It was assumed that the doctors could handle the problem of grief in the same way. Thus the medical model of grief came into being. ("Is Grief," 1976, p. 134)

The medical model speaks of grief more as a pathological condition, often a specific type of clinical depression or a "normal" depression brought on by loss. Emphasis is often on differentiating the normal depression of mourning from pathological grief. The latter condition is identified by such symptoms as protracted grief, irrational despair, hopelessness, loss of identity, impaired self-esteem, self-blame, and loss of interest in the future (Wahl, 1970).

The 20th century has evidenced an increasing presence of physicians and health-care professionals in the assessment and treatment of grief. Abraham (1924) provides an early psychiatric viewpoint of mourning as closely related to depression. Even Lindemann (1944) uses medical terms in his description of grief—"symptomotology," "syndrome," and "pathognomonic." A recent review of the literature evidences continuous use of medical model concepts and language in articles pertaining to grief (Clayton, 1979; Vachon et al., 1980; Vachon et al., 1982).

Within the medical model of grief, an oft-used analogy is the comparison of grief to a physical trauma, particularly to a "wound." Engel (1964) places this analogy at the center of his model of grief.

> It [grief] involves suffering and an impairment of the capacity to function, which may last for days, weeks, and even months. We can identify a consistent etiologic factor, namely, real, threatened, or even fantasized object loss. It fulfills all the criteria of a discrete syndrome, with relatively predictable symptomatology and course. (p. 93)

A strong relationship or equivalence between grief and depression seems to be the underlying assumption of the medical model of grief.

CONFUSION BETWEEN DEVELOPMENTAL AND MEDICAL MODELS

> I knew that I was supposed to withdraw my attachment from my husband. And I knew that I was supposed to withdraw it in the right way or I would later suffer adverse consequences. But How? No one had ever told me how. (Vernon, 1985, p. 5)

The current situation suggests that while many helping professionals may prefer the developmental model of grief, the concepts and vocabulary of the medical model have become a part of the language of grief. This results in serious confusion for individuals who are grieving. The developmental model suggests that grieving should be entered into fully. The medical model tells one that grief is a condition to be monitored and treated and, to some degree, traversed as rapidly as possible. Even more confusion arises when helping professionals are not clear about which paradigm they endorse. Caroff and Dobroff (1975) cite the difficulty of sustaining a conceptual approach to grief that includes in it the notions of bereavement as illness and of bereavement as normal and natural.

Parkes, who has written extensively about grief, provides an example of the changing perspective of the research literature. While his early work (Parkes, 1964, 1972) emphasizes a medical or illness model, a more recent article (Parkes & Weiss, 1983) regards grief as the "normal" accompaniment of a major loss. A recent review of both professional and lay publications (Vernon, 1988) finds medical-model language and concepts used in over half (11 of 19) of the professional publications sampled and exactly the same number (11 of 19) of sampled large-circulation popular magazines. She concludes that the medical model's familiar and comforting language (i.e., "healing," "recovery") is probably one reason for its continuing usage. The grief literature remains hallmarked by the continuing tendency of authors to "mix and match" the illness and developmental models.

GRIEF AS LABOR: A UNIFYING METAPHOR

Following the death of my husband, I was struck with how like labor pains the pains of grief were. The pain would consume me for a minute or two and then it would be gone . . . until the next all-consuming pain. (Vernon, 1985, p. 8)

The labor analogy perhaps offers a way of reconciling medical and developmental models of grief. Labor implies both physical pain and normalcy. It is a natural, not a pathological event. Both labor preceding a birth and grieving after a death accomplish a separation. In labor, the time has come for the baby to be separated from the mother so that both may continue growing in a normal, healthy way. In grief following death, the time has come for the survivor to separate herself psychologically from the dead person so that she can continue growing in a normal, healthy way.

In both labor and grief the pain is not steady, it comes in short episodes or "waves" (Lindeman, 1944). It seems most effective to flow with the pain. The best way to achieve the separation is not to try to get to the goal, but to relax and be accepting of what nature sends. In labor, the unsolicited contractions of the uterus are nature's way of separating the baby from the mother. In grief, the unsolicited torrent of emotions are nature's way of psychologically separating the griever from the person she has lost.

If, in labor or in grief, the person seeks only to get to the separation as quickly as possible she is apt to miss the goal. Separation cannot be achieved without time and space to accomplish the work. The object of grief is not only to go through it, but to be *present* to it. It involves the entire person. The griever is asked to flow with the labor of grief and arrives at the goal when all emotions have been brought up and found expression.

My grief asked me to flow with her wherever she took me. Eventually, she washed me ashore on a peaceful beach. (Vernon, 1985, p. 7)

REFERENCES

Abraham, K. (1924). A short study of the development of the libido; viewed in the light of mental disorders. *Selected Papers on Psychoanalysis*. London: Hogarth.

Ball, J. (1976-1977). Widow's grief: The impact of age and mode of death. *Omega: Journal of Death and Dying, 7*, 307-333.

Bankoff, E. (1981). Effects of friendship support on the psychological well-being of widows. *Research in the Interweave of Social Roles, 2*, 109-139.

Bankoff, E. (1983). Aged parents and their widowed daughters: A support relationship. *Journal of Gerontology, 38*, 226-230.

Bowlby, J. (1980). *Attachment and loss. III. Loss: Sadness and depression*. New York: Basic Books.

Caroff, P., & Dobrof, R. (1975). The helping process with bereaved families. In B. Schoenberg et al. (Eds.), *Bereavement: Its psychological aspects*, New York: Columbia University Press.

Clayton, P. (1979). The sequelae and nonsequelae of conjugal bereavement. *American Journal of Psychiatry, 136*:(12), 1530-1534.

Diamond, M., Lund, D., & Johnson, R. (1983, November). *The role of social support in the first year of bereavement in an elderly sample*. Paper presented at 36th Annual Scientific Meeting of the Gerontological Society of America, San Francisco, CA.

Engel, G. L. (1964). Grief and grieving. *American Journal of Nursing, 64*, 93-98.

Ferraro, K., & Barrese, C. (1982). The impact of widowhood on the social relations of older persons. *Research on Aging, 4*, 227-247.

Freud, S. (1953). Mourning and melancholia. In J. Strachey (Ed. and Trans.), *The standard edition of the complete psychological works of Sigmund Freud*. (Vol. 14, pp. 237-258). London: Hogarth Press. (Original work published 1917.)

Greenblatt, M. (1978). The grieving spouse. *American Journal of Psychiatry, 135*:(1), 43-47.

Hiltz, S. (1978). Widowhood: A roleless role. *Marriage and Family Review, 1*(6), 1-10.

Is Grief an Illness? (1976, July 17). *Lancet*. p. 134.

Lehman, D., Ellard, J., Worthman, C. (1986). Social support for the bereaved: Recipients' and providers perspectives on what is helpful. *Journal of Consulting and Clinical Psychology*, *54*(4), 438-446.

Lindemann, E. (1944). Symptomatology and management of acute grief. *American Journal of Psychiatry*. *101*, 141-148.

Lopata, H. (1979). *Women as widows*. New York: Elsevier.

Maslow, A. H. (1968). *Toward a psychology of being*. New York: Van Nostrand Reinhold.

McGloshen, T., & O'Bryant, S. (1988). The psychological well-being of older recent widows. *Psychology of Women Quarterly*, *12*, 99-116.

Parkes, C. M. (1964). Grief as an illness. *New Society*. 7, 11.

Parkes, C. M. (1972). *Bereavement: Studies of grief in adult life*. New York: International Universities Press Inc.

Parkes, C. M., & Weiss, R. S. (1983). *Recovery from bereavement*. New York: Basic Books.

U.S. Bureau of the Census. (1983). *Statistical Abstract of the United States: 1984* (104th ed.) Washington, DC.

Vachon, M., Lyall, W., Rogers, J., Freedman-Letofsky, K., & Freedman, S. (1980). A controlled study of self-help intervention for widows. *American Journal of Psychiatry*, *137*:(11), 1380-1384.

Vachon, M., Rogers, J., Lyall, W., Lancee, W., Sheldon, A., & Freeman, S. (1982). Predictors and correlates of adaptation to conjugal bereavement. *American Journal of Psychiatry*. *139*:(8), 998-1002.

Vernon, A. (1985). *The passions of grief*. Manuscript submitted for publication.

Vernon, A. (1988). *Use of medical model terms in articles on grief*. Unpublished master's research project. Loras College, Dubuque, IA.

Wahl, C. (1970). The differential diagnosis of normal and neurotic grief following bereavement. *Psychosomatics*. *11* 104-106.

The Ties That Bind:
Loyalty and Widowhood

David B. Seaburn

SUMMARY. This paper will explore the role of loyalty in the process of grief. Loyalty will be discussed as a phenomenon of families and case material will be used to illustrate its relevance to widowhood. Some implications for clinical work with widows and widowers will be suggested.

The death of a spouse or partner is one of the most critical events in a person's life, requiring more adjustments than most other life events. The relationship between spouses is one of caring and support, love and loyalty. The process of grief, described elsewhere (Barrett, 1977, 1981; Glick, Weiss, & Parkes, 1974; Lindemann, 1944; Shuchter, 1986), takes months and even years to complete. How well one grieves can play a part in how well one is able to enter relationships in the future.

In this paper we will explore the role of loyalty in the process of a widow's grief. We will discuss the nature of loyalty bonds, how they may influence a person's capacity to grieve a partner's death, and what implications there may be for psychotherapy.

LOYALTY

Loyalty is one of the strongest threads in the fabric of human relationships. Loyalty commitment begins in the raising of children

David B. Seaburn, MS, is a Family Therapist who practices and teaches in the Departments of Psychiatry and Family Medicine at the University of Rochester School of Medicine. Address correspondence to the author at 77 Hillcrest Drive, Spencerport, NY 14559.

and is an important factor in maintaining family cohesion. Parents are the pillars of a child's existence. They nurture, guide, protect, and impart values to their children that foster attachment and loyalty. Even in cases of childhood deprivation, such as sexual or physical abuse, it is not unusual for children to remain loyal to their parents.

According to Boszormenyi-Nagy (1973) a child balances his or her ledger of loyalty by internalizing the family's values, living up to family expectations, and eventually transmitting those values and expectations to the next generation of offspring. By doing so, the child passes on a family "legacy" (Boszormenyi-Nagy, 1976; Boszormenyi-Nagy & Ulrich, 1981) based on rootedness and continuity.

The child's map for human experience and development is drawn within the family. The child learns how to form attachments, express affect, make decisions, assume responsibility, deal with authority, cope with loss, and much more. The child's map is drawn with conscious and unconscious loyalty to the family's tradition with regard to how its members will live their lives.

The degree of trust generated by family loyalty can determine how well the maturing individual will be able to form new attachments, relationships, and commitments. If a person is too tied to his or her parents, the development of new relationships may be seen as a betrayal of old ones. By the same token, if a person feels little family loyalty, new relationships may be difficult to establish because of a basic lack of trust. Individuation, to a certain degree, depends on how well one balances old and new loyalty commitments (Boszormenyi-Nagy & Spark, 1973).

BALANCING LOYALTIES

Over the course of a lifetime a person develops both vertical and horizontal loyalties (Boszormenyi-Nagi & Spark, 1973; Van Deusden & Van Den Eerenbeemt, 1987). A person has vertical loyalty to previous and future generations. This includes parents, grandparents, and one's offspring. Horizontal loyalties are established with friends, peers, and partners.

Vertical and horizontal loyalties can come into conflict. This is particularly true at developmental transition points in the individual's and family's life. Leaving home, marriage, the birth of children, and the death of loved ones are times in a person's life when loyalties may shift. At these entry points and exit points the individual can feel pulled in what may seem to be different directions. For a majority of people who develop committed relationships or marry, loyalty to one's own family and its traditions are continually being balanced with a commitment to a new relationship and its future. The birth of children calls for yet another rebalancing of one's loyalty commitments. Will there be room enough for a child in the marital relationship? Will the families of origin give their sanction and blessing to this new member? How will commitment to both families of origin and the marriage influence or be influenced by the commitment to the child? Balancing and respecting these shifting loyalties throughout the life cycle will have an effect on the health and stability of both the individual and his or her relationships.

LOYALTY AND LOSS

Of particular interest here is the impact of vertical and horizontal loyalties on a person when his or her spouse dies. How does loyalty to a deceased partner and one's offspring influence the grief process? How does loyalty to one's family of origin and their traditions around spousal loss play a role in grieving? The following case illustrations will be used to explore these and other questions related to loyalty and loss.

Odd Man In

Clara Boone had been married to her husband, Bob, for nearly 30 years when he was diagnosed with inoperable stomach cancer. Over the ensuing months, Bob and Clara, along with their two sons and three daughters who ranged in aged from 16 to 29, worked to hold the family together despite their anticipation of loss. Bob, a warm, genial man, whose children respected him deeply, found it hard to deal with his own or his family's feelings. Clara, the family caretaker, was often the recipient of the anger, sadness, and fear that her sons and daughters felt. In family therapy they worked successfully to enable Bob and his children to talk more directly to each other and to share difficult but important feelings. The family grew closer as Bob's death neared.

The 10-month illness ended with Bob dying at home. During the following 18 months, Clara's children provided steady support as they navigated the many anniversaries and other family changes that occurred. Clara's youngest son graduated from high school, two daughters moved out of state, and Clara became a grandmother for the third time. She also met another man.

Joe was a local repair man who had been to Clara's house to fix an appliance. He was rough hewn, at times abrupt, but also gentle. Joe was seeing two other women when Clara met him. She vowed she would not get involved. But they struck up a friendship that evolved into romance, much to the chagrin of Clara's children. To a person, all of Clara's children disliked Joe. He was "nothing like Dad," who was generous and understanding. Joe had been rude to two of Clara's daughters and did little to endear himself to the others. Clara insisted that he met an important need in her life, but she did not intend to make a serious commitment to a man who was involved with two other women. She wished her children were more accepting of him.

During a family consultation with the Boones, it became apparent that their strong feelings about Joe were only thinly veiling unresolved grief over Bob. Clara was caught between their loyalty and love for Bob and her children and her own needs as a woman that were being met by Joe. She did not want to replace Bob in her children's eyes or in her own heart. Her choice of a partner was an interesting compromise. Joe had very few of Bob's qualities and so could hardly be seen as replacing Bob as the head of the family. In fact, Joe's qualities only enhanced the children's respect for their own father. Clara also acknowledged that Joe's entanglements with several women may have been part of what attracted her to him. She felt there was little danger of any premature commitment on her part. In fact, Clara's feelings for Joe waned when he expressed his intention to end his other relationships.

The strength of a widow's or widower's loyalty to a spouse resurfaces when she or he contemplates a new relationship. Whether a new relationship is developed soon after a death or years later, the original commitment of loyalty will reawaken feelings of grief. That loyalty is not only to the spouse (vertical loyalty) but also to the children (horizontal loyalty) who are the fullest, living expression of what the partnership has meant.

It is important for the new person who has entered the family picture not to become a scapegoat. The widow or widower and family members must readdress their attachment to the deceased spouse and parent. They must find ways to maintain a connection while also creating room for others to enter the family.

The Ties That Bind

Frank and Nancy were married for 5 years. It was a second marriage for both. At the time of the wedding Frank understood the seriousness of Nancy's kidney disease, which already limited her daily functioning. During the course of their marriage, Frank was a devoted partner who took care of Nancy at home on a daily basis,

When Nancy died Frank felt intense remorse that would not abate. He continued his daily routine of staying at home even though there was no one to care for. He developed few new relationships and withdrew to the safety and familiarity of his house and his memories. Three years passed. Frank's new primary care physician became concerned about Frank's depression and suggested he see a therapist with whom the physician often collaborated. Frank reluctantly agreed.

The therapist learned of Frank's feelings of guilt because he wanted to move on with his life but did not want to abandon the memory of his wife. At first the therapist thought that Nancy's dependency on Frank was the primary factor contributing to his inability to resolve his grief and continue his life. Frank indicated that he and his wife depended a lot on each other but that Nancy had talked openly with Frank about the importance of Frank developing new relationships and new interests after she died. Frank did not feel Nancy was holding him back.

The therapist did learn, though, that Frank's family had much experience with the lengthy illnesses and deaths of spouses. Frank's stepfather died 3 years earlier of cancer. Frank's mother had taken care of him for more than a year. Frank's brother-in-law had also died of a long debilitating illness. When asked how his mother and sister dealt with their losses Frank reported that neither had done well. He felt his mother had not completed her grief. In fact, her health had seriously deteriorated over the past 2 years. As for Frank's sister, she had been a widow for 17 years. She told Frank he would "never get over it."

Several members of Frank's family had married partners who died of lengthy illnesses. Grief over these losses was not only unresolved but was not expected to be resolved. These widows stopped living as a way of honoring the memory of their deceased partners. This legacy of unresolved grief was inherited by Frank. It provided the model for how he would grieve his wife's death despite her understanding injunction that he go on living. After 3 years of grieving, the problem for Frank was not his loyalty to his wife (vertical loyalty) as much as his loyalty to his family of origin (horizontal loyalty). There was no clear permission for him to grieve differently. To be a loyal family member he needed to grieve continuously and without end.

Frank eventually met another woman. He was extremely hesitant to move forward with this friendship until his mother encouraged him to go ahead. By giving her blessing to Frank's new relationship, Frank's mother also gave him permission to resolve his grief without being disloyal to his family.

CLINICAL CONSIDERATIONS

Our discussion of loyalty and loss emphasizes a multigenerational, family perspective on widowhood and grief. This perspective can be helpful when working with an individual widow or widower or a family. Some clinical considerations follow:

1. **Construct a family genogram** with your client. This will aid in assessing the nature of past losses and how the family has dealt with them. Questions to pursue include:

    - Who in your family has experienced the death of a spouse or partner?
    - How have they coped with the loss?
    - What have they suggested to you about dealing with your grief?

2. **Discuss the vertical and horizontal loyalty pulls** that your client may be experiencing.

   * How would your spouse expect you to deal with his or her death?
   * How do your children and other family members expect you to deal with this loss? What do they want from you at this time? What do you want from them?

3. **Normalize the need to balance loyalty** to one's partner, loyalty to one's family and children, and loyalty to one's self.

4. **Whenever possible include other family members** in therapy as a resource for helping the client through the grief process. The support of family members can permit the patient to complete his or her grief without feeling disloyal to the loved one or to the family. The involvement of family members in the widow's or widower's grief can also provide an opportunity for family members to address their own issues related to loss.

Widows and widowers do not experience loss in isolation. The death of a partner reverberates throughout the family and across generations. The use of loyalty as a concept for understanding these connections can prove fruitful in helping clients resolve their grief.

REFERENCES

Barrett, C. (1977). Women in widowhood. *Journal of Women in Culture and Society*, 2, 856-868.

Barrett, C. (1981). Intimacy in widowhood. *Psychology of Women Quarterly*, 5, 473-487.

Boszormenyi-Nagi, I. (1976). Behavior change through family change. In A. Burton (Ed.), *What makes behavior change possible*? (pp. 103-113). New York: Brunner/Mazel.

Boszormenyi-Nagi, I., & Sparv, G. (1973). *Invisible loyalties: Reciprocity in intergenerational family therapy.* New York: Harper and Row.

Boszormenyi-Nagi, I. & Ulrich, D.N. (1981) Contextual family therapy. In A. S. Gurman, and D. Kniskern, (Eds.) *Handbook of family therapy* (pp. 159-186). New York: Brunner/Mazel.

Glick, I., Weiss, R., & Parkes, C. (1974). *The first year of bereavement.* New York: John Wiley.

Lindemann, E. (1944). Sympotomatology and management of acute grief. *American Journal of Psychiatry, 101,* 141-148.

Shuchter, S.R. (1986) *Dimensions of grief: Adjusting to the death of a spouse.* San Francisco: Josey-Bass.

Van Heusden, A., & Van Den Eerenbeemt, E. (1987). *Balance in motion: Ivan Boszormenyi-Nagi and his vision of individual and family therapy.* New York: Brunner/Mazel.

Widowhood as a Time
for Growth and Development

Jeanette Hainer

SUMMARY. Widowhood brings about role changes for the individual and shifts in the family and social systems. This paper illustrates how the crisis of widowhood provided the opportunity for a 55-year-old woman to resolve earlier developmental issues, her former dependence on her husband, her role in caring for aging parents, her relationship with her adult children, and her evolving maturity as an independently functioning woman.

She called me because she knew I worked with older people. She wanted to talk about her parents. Sitting in front of me was a woman in her middle 50s, attractive, well groomed, and for all initial appearances a well-functioning adult. Her strained voice and her shrugging shoulders accompanied by the outward and inward turning gesture of her palms communicated feelings of frustration and helplessness.

Mrs. Salter was an only child of parents who had been dependent and ill equipped all their lives for the job of parenting. The father was an unambitious man who took little responsibility for himself. He had always been a gambler in cards, and while he never went to the extreme of putting the family in debt he never allowed savings to accumulate. As a result, now, in their years of retirement, they had to manage on very little income. He was in poor health, a heavy smoker, and suffered from emphysema. He rarely left the house but had friends in for cards daily.

Jeanette Hainer, ACSW, is on the staff of the 92nd Street YM-YWHA in New York City as Associate Director of the Group Service Department, in charge of Senior Services and is in private practice. Address correspondence to the author at 160 West 96 St. #4N, New York, NY 10025.

147

Mrs. Salter's mother was a diabetic and had failing eyesight. She spent her time socializing with friends at a nearby beach club but complained about lack of satisfaction in her life. She, too, was not well and had difficulty being responsible for her eating habits and her doctors' appointments.

Mrs. Salter's presenting problem was her concern for her aging parents — about their having enough money for their daily living, the maintenance of their home, and their increasing ill health. She was additionally concerned about their inability to handle their financial affairs responsibly and was feeling overwhelmed by the burden of this dependent dyad.

Why now? The question almost always asked — the precipitant, if you will, that motivates clients to pick up the phone at the moment they do. Roberta Salter said that up until his death almost 5 years ago, her husband, who had been an accountant, had handled all the details around her parents. Roberta Salter was a widow.

While we know that widowhood plays a prominent role in our society, it is not usual or expected that the widowed person will have aging parents as dependents (or, for that matter, as sources of comfort), although, as we see an increasing aging population, these expectations may change.

Statistics tell us that the average age of widowhood is 56 and brings with it a major life change requiring more adjustment than almost any other life event (Porcino, 1983). Far too often married women have lived as if their marriages would last forever without realistically planning for a time when they would be on their own. While it is always advisable for women to be continually developing themselves through education and interesting work, they should also be acquiring social and business skills and an ability to spend time alone — even within a marriage. Given the statistical data that the average woman can expect up to 10 years of widowhood (Porcino, 1983), I believe that the use of fantasy can serve in tapping into a person's coping capacity. Imagining what these years will be like can be helpful in developing plans and strategies to minimize the impact of this period of crisis.

We know that the condition of widowhood is accompanied by many complex transitions (Hainer, 1988). At first there are several stages of grief and mourning (Kübler-Ross, 1969; Silverman,

1981). The successful completion of this initial task yields to confronting the strangeness, isolation, and loneliness of widowhood. Adaptation to widowhood takes place in the last stage of the process with the redefinition of one's role, an acceptance of one's changed status, and a new sense of one's self. At each of the stages the stress of the transition can be eased by appropriate interventions: for example, support services; individual counseling; and social, self-help, and therapeutic groups (Hainer, 1988). How had Mrs. Salter's stress around her parents affected her adjustment to widowhood?

Erikson (1980) speaks of developmental crises which are induced by the special tasks necessary at each new developmental phase in the psychosocial maturation. Lindemann (1944) sees the pain of grief as a normal reaction to stress caused by loss. In contrast to which, stress tends to carry with it a negative connotation with pathogenic potential; crises are conceived to have a growth-promoting potential. Crisis can be a catalyst that disturbs old habits, evokes new responses, and becomes a major factor in bringing about new development (Rapoport, 1962; Volkhart, 1951) and new coping mechanisms, strengthening the individual's adaptive capacity and self-esteem. These developmental opportunities allow for the reworking of early incomplete psychosocial developmental tasks.

The treatment of the presenting problem around her aging parents gave Mrs. Salter the opportunity to accomplish some of these tasks.

Mrs. Salter had married at a young age. Having been a parentified child who did not fare well in that role, the man she married was a "gift" to her parents. He managed their finances and assisted them in buying a small house near the beach. Mrs. Salter's parents felt good about the relationship they had with their son-in-law and for the first time Mrs. Salter had someone in her life who could take charge of matters in an adult, responsible way. The Salters had two children, now grown and living across the country, three thousand miles away.

The family system worked well for Mrs. Salter and her family of origin: Mr. Salter as head of the household, Mrs. Salter as wife and homemaker and friend to her mother. Mrs. Salter's mother would enjoy her daughter's friends and the "girls" would hang out together often.

Mr. Salter's death was sudden and a shock that threw the family into disequilibrium. He had been a good wage earner and provided for his wife but not so affluently that she would be totally free from financial concerns. The loss not only left Mrs. Salter a widow — it left both her and her parents in a sense "parentless" since that was the role Mr. Salter assumed in that family. To add to the crisis of his sudden death and the stress of her parents' dependency, Mrs. Salter discovered that her husband had been having an affair for many years.

Mrs. Salter related that she had been in treatment earlier and had worked through some of her feelings of grief and anger and that she had received medication for her depressed mood. It was with this information in mind that I formulated the parameters of our work: focusing concretely on the problems she was having around her parents — their health, their living arrangements, and their financial situation.

When I saw Mrs. Salter for the first time it was almost 5 years after her husband's death. She had recently moved and had just ended an affair with a married man. It appeared that her affair may have been an attempt to recreate the original relationship she had in her marriage by triangulating into this new family system. While, temporarily, it brought her some balance, it did not include her parents. This interlude may have given Mrs. Salter some of the distance necessary to accommodate to her new role. Her taking a small apartment in the city and ending the affair was an attempt to achieve some independence and differentiation. This move also meant she had to give up her car and was living further away from her parents. Visiting them now necessitated taking the railroad and a taxi unless her mother picked her up at the train station.

Since the loss of their son-in-law, Mrs. Salter's parents' health declined, making them increasingly more dependent on their daughter. Feeling resentful at being placed in the position of having to take up her husband's role in relation to her parents, Mrs. Salter was overwhelmed by her feelings of anger and resistance to assuming that role and the resulting feelings of guilt these feelings incurred. Mrs. Salter saw no other choices.

At the same time, her parents' behavior frustrated whatever attempts Mrs. Salter made to be responsive to them. Although they had requested that some of the financial arrangements their son-in-law had made be put back in their control, they would neglect the necessary obligations this entailed. They would receive dunning notices, be without fuel for their house, and have no organized record-keeping procedure. Mrs. Salter's mother would complain about being lonely, and yet when Mrs. Salter would make the trip to her parents' home her mother would not be there. Her father, often engaged in a card game, would not speak with her when she arrived. A series of phone calls would ensue until Mrs. Salter located her mother and she would wait for her to come home or try to meet her wherever she was at. Mrs. Salter was feeling like an outsider in the family where she very much wanted to belong.

The move to an apartment in the city had increased Mrs. Salter's living expenses. To meet her needs she had taken a job to supplement the income she was receiving from what her husband had left her. She worked for a woman whom she experienced as demanding and ambiguous in her communication. With little respect for Mrs. Salter's time she would ask her to take care of something when it was time to leave, with the expectation that Mrs. Salter would do so. She would express no appreciation for the effort nor provide any monetary acknowledgment for what was a fairly low-paying wage.

While Mrs. Salter had a fairly large network of friends with whom she socialized, she had no real confidante with whom she shared some of her deeper feelings of anger, confusion, and frustration. Nor did her children know of the situation and difficulties she was experiencing around her parents. In an attempt to not repeat her parents' pattern of dependency, Mrs. Salter was reluctant to "complain" to her children and have them feel burdened by her problems. She felt they were building lives for themselves and believed she was a good mother by not interfering in their lives and not intruding upon them with her problems. She would speak to them regularly and send gifts on appropriate occasions. The children's image of their early widowed mother was quite different from what Mrs. Salter was actually experiencing.

We started our work together by my asking Mrs. Salter what she wanted in relation to her parents. How involved did she want to be? What was she willing to be responsible for? What did she not want to have to deal with? Mrs. Salter was committed to ensuring that her parents had the best possible quality of life. She in no way wanted to abandon them. Beneath her anger and frustration was a little girl who very much wanted their love, approval and recognition, and the feeling that she was a good daughter.

The initial supportive and educative work was to have Mrs. Salter see that caring for her parents did not mean that she had to do it directly. (Indeed, although unconsciously, she had already made those arrangements once when she married.)

The responsibility of making arrangements for her parents was different from carrying out each task herself. Thus, she was able to contact a local social service agency and refer her parents to a social worker who was able to arrange for entitlements for which they were eligible. Her parents, once known to the agency, were able to receive additional support from them and the agency became another resource and support for Mrs. Salter as well.

The issue of her parents' home remained paramount to Mrs. Salter. The house that her parents lived in had been neglected over the years. Her father was unable to make repairs and there was no money to hire someone to do the work. The house was realistically a burden. Mrs. Salter's mother, whose driving was becoming more limited because of her failing vision, was becoming isolated. The elderly parents spoke of selling the house and taking an apartment closer to the center of their small town, using the proceeds from the sale of the house to yield them additional income for living expenses. It was wise to sell before there was greater deterioration and a deep decrease in value. However, giving up their home was a difficult thing to do. Consideration was given to how this would impact upon their health and how they would take the loss. Yet another consideration was whether or not they should remain where they were or move to Florida.

Their ambivalence displayed itself over and over again. They would contact realtors and arrange for the house to be shown. Mrs. Salter would arrange to be there and at the last minute her father would say, "No! We're not selling." At this time Mrs. Salter, whose concern for her father's fragile health left her unclear as to the right course of action for them, disengaged from any of their plans to sell. She felt that by deferring to her parents she was fostering their autonomy around this issue and thought that might serve them well.

Mrs. Salter responded well to my encouraging her to set some boundaries and limits. She would no longer chase after her mother when her mother was not home. Nor would she wait for her beyond a reasonable amount of time. Mrs. Salter began to integrate her visits to her parents with visits to her friends. Visiting with a friend in the suburbs, they would drive to her parents' home for a visit. When Mrs. Salter's mother knew her daughter was coming with a friend she was invariably home. This reconstituted the original family system of being one of the girls when Mrs. Salter would bring her friends home from school. For Mrs. Salter it provided yet another support that enabled her to care for her parents while also caring for herself.

Mrs. Salter was also able to accept the fact that she could involve her children. She was able to see that she and her husband were not the dependent parents to her children that Mrs. Salter's parents had been to her. She did not need to protect them. Telling them of her difficulties, asking their advice and opinion, was not burdening them but including them in the family system in a respectful way. As a result of their concern for both their mother and their grandparents, the children made more frequent contact and were an additional source of support to Mrs. Salter.

Mrs. Salter began developing a more appropriate role in relation to her parents and began making more definitive interventions. What was truly interesting to observe was that throughout this process Mrs. Salter was always focused on what would be best for her parents. She was helped to see that this could be accomplished without total subordination of her own needs and that, indeed, when she was able to make clear and distinct interventions a new sense of competence emerged for her, and her parents felt good about what she had to give them.

With this emerging sense of competence Mrs. Salter left her job and found one that was part-time with better pay and flexible hours, enabling her to enjoy her friends and to tend to her parents with less stress and tension.

In once again evaluating her parents' living arrangements, an additional major consideration was the cold weather and her father's health. Mrs. Salter took a trip to Florida and investigated living accommodations and arrangements available that would fit the parameters of her parents' needs: affordable rent, accessibility to the beach and shopping, socialization, availability of social service resources. Informed and confident in what she had seen, she introduced this alternative to her parents. On a subsequent trip she took her mother down to see the accommodations and areas available. Her parents sold their house and successfully relocated in a community with peers.

Sometime after her parents moved to Florida Mrs. Salter relocated there as well. Many of her friends had retired there and she enjoyed the continuation of her increasing separation and individuation without having to have the physical distance between her parents and herself. She remained there for about a year and then moved to California to be closer to her children and to enjoy the new grandchildren who were coming into the family.

Mrs. Salter's role had evolved into that of an adult child to aging parents and a parent to adult children.

I saw Mrs. Salter eight times over a period of 8 months. Her style was to take what we would deal with in a session and go home and work on it, coming back when she got stuck or was prepared to move ahead. Over the next 18 months she called me three times. The first was to tell me of her own move to Florida; the second was to tell me of her move to California. The third call, a message on my answering machine, was to let me know she was getting married and was hopeful that it was going to be good.

While our focus was always on her situation around her parents, Mrs. Salter was able to continue to work through her anger around her husband's death and affair by recognizing what her marriage to him had saved her from having to face and, equally, how it prevented her from her own growth and development. Slowly, she was able to undertake the tasks necessary to experience a sense of competence and heightened self-esteem.

REFERENCES

Erikson, E. (1980). *Identity and the life cycle*. New York: W.W. Norton.

Hainer, J. (1988). Groups for widowed and lonely older persons. In *Group therapy in the mental health treatment of the elderly*. Madison, CT: International Universities Press.

Kübler-Ross, E. (1969). *On death and aging*. New York: Macmillan.

Lindemann, E. (1944). The symptomatology and management of acute grief. *American Journal of Psychiatry, 101*, 141-149.

Porcino, J. (1983). *Growing older, getting better*. Reading, MA: Addison-Wesley.

Rapoport, L. (1962). The state of crisis: Some theoretical considerations. *The Social Service Review, 36*(2). Reprinted in H.J. Parad (ed.)., *Crisis intervention: Selected readings*, (pp. 22-31). New York: Family Service Assoc. of America.

Silverman, P.R. (1981). *Helping women cope with grief*. Beverly Hills: Sage.

Volkhart, E. (Ed.). (1951). *Social behavior and personality contributions of W.I. Thomas to theory and social research*, (pp. 12-14). New York: Social Service Research Council.

Whom God Has Joined

Bruce J. Schell

SUMMARY. This paper briefly examines the modification of identity that occurs in the long-term marriage. It is concerned with aspects of the bereavement process following the literal or symbolic death of one's spouse. Two case studies of adjustment to the loss of a spouse are presented.

To be widowed is to have lost from life one's spouse. I intend to look briefly at what is created in the long-term marriage, to look at the bereavement process, and then to use two case studies as illustration. I shall use the term marriage to refer to a relationship which has involved, at a minimum, living together for an extended period of time with a sense of commitment to one's partner, being recognized as a couple by their community, and having a passionate element. This relationship may or may not have been sanctioned by religious or legal ceremony.

The traditional Christian wedding vows emphasize that a joining of the pair is created in the wedding ceremony. Indeed the traditional Protestant service contains the phrase "whom God has joined let no man tear asunder." The symbolic joining that is an aspect of the wedding ceremony points to a process where, over the years of the relationship, part of one's identity comes to include the other. This identity shift is not unique to the long-term marriage, rather it is a normal aspect of the psychologically important long-term relationship. An element of it may be seen in psychotherapy when the patient unconsciously takes on aspects of the therapist's dress or

Bruce J. Schell, PhD, is a clinical psychologist. He is on the faculty of the Department of Family Medicine at the University of South Carolina. Address correspondence to the author at Department of Family Medicine, Five Richland Medical Park, Columbia, SC 29203.

157

manner. This transference phenomenon is the surface manifestation of the internalization of the therapist. In the long-term relationship the "I" that develops includes within its boundaries important aspects of the partner as well as an identification with being part of a couple. Over the years the lives become so interwoven that death or divorce cuts across the fabric of one's life's meaning and leaves, for a time, a major gap in one's sense of "I."

In beginning to consider the issues faced by the surviving spouse following the loss of a partner two important variables need to be considered. They are the nature of the death itself and the number of the years the couple has been together. A sudden unexpected death produces more shocked disbelief and difficulty in coming to grips with the death than does an expected death following protracted illness. The effect of loss in a new couple is different than it is for a couple whose relationship has lasted for many years. The difference may not necessarily be in intensity of reaction but perhaps more in the nature of the loss to the sense of self. I am suggesting that over the passage of time there is a shift from identifying one's partner as love object to including one's partner as an aspect of one's own identity. This appears true whether this is a "good" relationship or a "bad" one.

The gross manifestation of this identity shift can be seen in the functional aspects of a couple's relationship. In the stereotypic couple, the man is responsible for the yard and automobile while the woman is responsible for the house. We still see, in the older widow and widower, women who have never written a check or driven a car and men who have never fixed a meal or washed clothes. At one level this can be seen as a deficit in skill acquisition along conventional sexist lines; at another level it points to the shift in identity wherein aspects of the singular self wither or never form in favor of a sense of self that includes important aspects of the spouse. The trauma associated with the loss of one's spouse and accompanying experience of loss of self (Parkes, 1972) is such that thoughts of suicide are not uncommon. The widowed are at greatest risk during their first year of bereavement when they commit suicide four or five times more frequently than their married counterparts (Resnick, 1980).

Whether the couple (or the survivor) would describe himself or herself as happily married or close is not germane to the shift from a singular sense of self to a joint sense of self; rather what is relevant is the absence of factors interfering with the process of identity shift. The major interfering factors are those personality wounds that prevent emotional bonding, psychopathy or autism for example, and where the spousal relationship is always, at most, secondary to other emotional relationships.

In addition to a normal modification of identity the longer term relationship is also where we grapple again with major unresolved issues of our childhoods. The upsurge of these unresolved issues, in relationship to our partner, imbues him or her with awesome meaning that resides mainly in potential and cannot be fully realized. Those who persist in the marital relationship must bind that meaning in such a way that the relationship is not destroyed by unrealizable unmet childhood needs and so that the energy of the need is not free to be attached to another. The loss of our partner releases this bound emotional energy but does so in the presence of all the meaning associated with the loss. Thus, while a tremendous amount of psychic energy is freed and therefore the possibilities for change are great, the tendency will be to harness it with the historical meaning we have attached to loss and to ourselves as the kind of people who sustain losses.

As beings who inhabit literal and symbolic reality we face the possibility of experiencing the death of all that our partner symbolizes to us as well as his or her literal death. With literal death there is generally also a symbolic death of the partner and the loss is grieved without the necessity of differentiating the deaths. However, the symbolic death of a partner is frequently not accompanied by his or her literal death. The most common arena where a spouse may symbolically die is in those events culminating in divorce. I would include, as a special type of widow,[1] the woman who has been left against her desire. Clinically she goes through much of the same process as the widow whose spouse has died. The major difference is that she goes through this without benefit of the normal community support following the death of a spouse, without rituals of leave taking, and frequently without an internal awareness that

---

1. My focus on the widow, in this paragraph, reflects my clinical practice.

supports the extended grieving that must take place. A consequence may be to deny and thereby submerge and prolong the grief. For example, one woman whose divorce was abruptly initiated by her husband exclaimed, "I wish he had actually died—it would be much easier." In addition to having fewer feelings of rejection to cope with, his literal death would have provided a socially supported context in which to mourn her loss.

Normal aspects of the larger context of the bereavement process are the rallying around of families, the funeral scene itself, the burial, the signing of legal forms, the sorting out of possessions, and the reading of wills. All of these features help to move along the grief process and provide a culturally sanctioned context for the grief.

In the main these are absent in the divorce and so the mourning of the symbolic death is not well supported culturally. There is the absence of all the legal and cultural events that signify a death, and one is only faced with the legal details signifying struggle or rejection. This is likely an important factor in the great number of legal divorces that are not accompanied by a corresponding emotional divorce, which involves the death of the symbolic meaning of the spouse. There is no cultural support for the important sorting out of life details. To have lost one's spouse through his or her decision to leave, as in literal death, brings first shocked disbelief followed by a host of feelings. Friends tend to give brief support for the grief and longer support for the expected anger—anger that may be submerged in the initial grief. The tendency is then to quickly push for resuming one's life, including dating. That a death—albeit a symbolic one—has occurred, is not recognized even by the one who was left. An important difficulty is making conscious the loss to oneself and then communicating this to one's friends.

It is unusual for a patient to voluntarily enter therapy during the initial grief of bereavement. We are more likely to see them during an intermediate stage marked by intense emotional states, as they are struggling with the meaning of the loss, and searching to reduce the pain of grieving (Lamb, 1988). The exception to this are those individuals who enter psychotherapy during a painful divorce.

An important consideration in looking at the mourning process is the capacity of the bereaved to tolerate the pain associated with the

loss. Because of psychological vulnerabilities preceding the relationship or concurrent stressors that deplete psychic resources, the
individual may be unable to tolerate reviewing more than minimal
aspects of the loss. Similarly, when the "I" of the relationship
functioned to buttress major aspects of the bereaved's psychological
world, the grief work must procede slowly.

Maddison's work (Raphael, 1983) with widows suggests that
when there is an adequate social network that supports the widow in
reviewing positive and negative features of the person and relationship and supports her in expressing the concommitant affect, the
adjustment is likely to be satisfactory. His work reveals a less satisfactory outcome when the widow's support system fails to support
her affect, interferes with the review process, and attempts to pre-
maturely orient her to the future.

As psychotherapists, we do not see, professionally, those who
successfully traverse the stages of grief. We see those individuals in
whom some aspect of the bereavement process has gone awry. The
following case studies illustrate some ways by which the grief process may be extended and the consequences of that. In both cases
the relationship to the lost partner was seen as to a "soul mate"
(Leonard, 1986).

April, a 39-year-old and her husband, George, 48, first presented for marital therapy after a marriage of 13 months. They
were residing in different homes at the time of the first session. Both had been previously married, with his marriage of
16 years ending in a protracted and painful divorce approximately 3 years prior to this marriage. Her marriage of 12 years
had ended when her husband suffered a sudden massive coro-
nary about 3 years before this marriage. She had a 10 year old
daughter, with whom she was very close. The daughter was
the one who discovered that her father was dead and received
professional help for this which seemingly had been of little
avail. Following their marriage George moved into April's
home, where she had lived in her first marriage. He left when
he no longer could stand "living with a ghost" or with her
daughter's hostility. April had been unwilling to remodel the
home in any fashion or to have him bring any of his furniture

to the house. She explained that she just felt that was wrong and became increasingly anxious when the subject was pursued. She described her daughter's devastation following her father's death and how she had set her own grief aside in caring for her. Her descriptions to me of that marriage and of her dead husband were uniformly idyllic. This was also the tenor of what she had told her daughter of her father and their marriage. When pressed, there was tentative acknowledgment of "occasional problems," which was initially followed by another positive description of their life.

George had been the first man she dated following her husband's death and they had married within 3 months of meeting each other. It was apparent that much of her grieving for the lost relationship had never occurred. The course of therapy was marked by George's continued withdrawal and unwillingness to deal with anything "negative" and her deepening grief for her lost husband. She also began to articulate how much she wanted the marriage to "work out." Our exploration of the "marriage that works out" revealed that she was hoping to regain the marriage lost when her husband died. With marked ambivalence she agreed that she had to face that loss and what it would mean about her current life. The ensuing months were marked by her grieving for what had been. As her life changed therapy appointments became more sporadic. An important step in dealing with her grief was resuming work, which had ended with her initial marriage. The next major piece of her grief work ensued with her decision to sell their home. The activity of preparing and then selling her home flooded her with grief for her lost relationship, with a major upsurge of memories and dreams of him. Now the dreams and memories also included less flattering features of him and their marriage. The decision to divorce George brought grief for the lost hopes, more memories of her dead husband, and little seeming grieving for George.

The major factor in her arrested grief was her decision to invest herself in her daughter's recovery from the trauma of finding her dead father, at the sake of her own grief work. What began as providing solace to her daughter became a joint focus on remembering and speaking solely of the positive memories. The inability to remember and grieve the whole relationship distorted her grieving for the man to mourning the loss of a "golden age." The marriage to George brought to the fore the degree to which she and her daughter lived their lives unconsciously awaiting the return to their "golden age."

Mary, a 36-year-old woman, entered individual therapy primarily focusing on her depressed mood and the increasing, seemingly inexplicable, cruelty of her lover of 15 years. Over the previous 3 years, he had radically changed, embracing the values of a markedly self-centered adolescent. She was an only child who grew up with a profound sense of estrangement from her distant alcoholic father. Her overly present mother's greatest need was to mold Mary into her image. Larry has been the major love relationship of her life. He has been described as "the center of her life," "her mentor," and "the person who will be there and that she can trust under any circumstances." He was the one who filled a void untouched since the failed parental relationship. As his unexplained absences and verbal attacks increased, he insisted that her reactions were evidence of how deeply she was emotionally disturbed. He refused to participate in psychotherapy as it was "her problem that she couldn't be happy." The months preceding separation were marked by her increasing confusion and despair as the fundamental reality about herself and their life clashed with the reality of his behavior. As her struggle between realities continued and her self-blame for his behavior decreased she increasingly found him repugnant and yet still essential to her. Shortly after meeting one of his girlfriends she left their home and established her own apartment. Leaving their home did not mean destruction of his central role in her psyche but it did allow time to view it without constant turmoil.

The reconciling of her two realities began with the splitting of Larry into lost-loved aspect of Larry and the current not-to-be-trusted Larry. This dual context for her feelings freed anger and began the grieving for the lost, still-loved, Larry. She began to see that the context for her continued love was in their past—in the good years they had lived and not in the man or relationship today. At that point, with friends impatiently pushing for her to move on with her life, she was beginning to mourn for the death of her lover while the man yet lived. This grappling with the difference between what is (not-to-be-trusted Larry) and what was (loved Larry) is best facilitated through the use of symbols to differentiate them. As she was mourning the loss of loved Larry the symbol we evolved was his ritual burial.

This was done in steps: first selecting a photograph of him from the good years, discussing with a close friend the good and bad memories from that time, and then saying good-bye to the photo which was placed in a box. Accompanied by a friend, she returned to a special place in the history of their relationship where she buried the box. This produced an increase in sadness, an upsurge of memories, and a marked decrease in vulnerability to current Larry. As she continued her mourning the occasional contact with him was now less disruptive of her sense of reality.

Mary's effort to differentiate what is real today from what was real in her yesterdays is common to all whose spouse has been lost. The relative absence of cultural support for handling our symbolic deaths and the difficulty in getting validation for the loss tends to prolong the mourning and make it more covert than in the literal death of a spouse.

It may be that the culture's relative unwillingness to validate and support mourning the symbolic death of a spouse is symptomatic of our individual resistance to face the many deaths that are inherent in a rapidly changing culture. That is, accelerating social and technological change requires of us the facing of the death-rebirth of the fixed form of the self not once but many times in order to support the growth of the essential self. In addition to accelerating change, we are also culturally bereft of rituals that support transitions of the self.

REFERENCES

Lamb, D. (1988). Loss and grief: Psychotherapy strategies and interventions. *Psychotherapy: Theory Research and Practice, 25,* 561-569.

Leonard, L. (1986). *On the way to the wedding.* Boston: Shambhala Publications.

Parkes, C. (1972). *Bereavement: Studies of grief in adult life.* New York: International Universities Press.

Raphael, B. (1983). *The anatomy of bereavement.* New York: Basic Books.

Resnick, H. (1980). Suicide. In H. Kaplan, A. Freedman, and B. Sadock (Eds.), *Comprehensive textbook of psychiatry* (3rd ed., pp. 2085-2098). Baltimore: Williams and Wilkins.

My Granddaughters Cope
with the Death of Their Father

Neil Lamper

SUMMARY. A narrative description of a family trauma with emphasis on the natural way three children dealt with the death of their father. Beginning with the scene of the accident in California and moving to the grandparents' farm in Michigan the author makes a case for the value of openness instead of denial around such an event.

"Do you know what happened to my Daddy?" Summer Lee is five and in constant motion.

"You tell me."

"He drove off the cliff and got dead." She does a somersault and scampers the length of the back of the couch like a squirrel.

"Got dead," echoes Cassia Rose. She takes two fingers from her mouth to talk and do her own rollover and tumble as she is two-and-a-half and wants to be like Summer.

Lia gurgles. She is 7 months old. Pat and I have come here from Michigan, summoned by a nighttime call. Grief, confusion and anger are already in motion; our daughter Kim has been a joy to us for 30 years. She also tumbled and scampered like a squirrel when she was little and though she is older and wiser this pain is unexpected, sudden.

Summer Lee asks me the same question three more times in the next few hours. Cassia adds her refrain and this is how they begin to handle the death of their father.

This family of five lives and works at Esalen. Kim is our eldest

Neil Lamper, PhD, is a psychotherapist specializing in group retreats worldwide. Professor of Counseling for 25 years, he now focuses his work at his Michigan farm. Address correspondence to the author at 1546 Spruce Dr., Kalamazoo, MI 49008.

daughter and the three little girls go to the Gazebo School at Esalen. Bob is their father and a carpenter. Often he drives the shaggy Big Sur coast of California and the one night he was a passenger the driver of the van missed the sharp curve at the south end of the Bixby bridge. Both bodies were brought up the cliff in the morning and now what's left is the ceremony and the rest of life.

"May we play with the shells, Mommy?" asks Summer.

"We wanna play shells," adds Cassia. They sit cross legged like little girls at jacks and make piles of the small bits of gray and white shells gathered from the Pacific shore.

Our voices are low and we talk and there is even laughter. Friends and visitors touch this circumstance, each in their own way. Someone begins a volleyball game outside. As the prophet put it: Let the dead bury the dead.

Sunday, Kim and I drive the same curved coast to Monterey. Her signature is needed for the cremation. I fill with love even more for this daughter of mine as she talks her heart out and I hear her first steps to accommodate this event. She does not go gentle into that good night: There is rage against this dying of the light. At the bridge I look far down to where the van still rests on its roof. It is on the beach, and already someone lives in it and has a red tent attached.

By Monday the bone fragments are in a small, brown plastic box.

"May we see, Mommy?" asks Cassia.

"They look like our shells," says a subdued Summer. The mother and three girls make a game on the floor. The goal is to separate bone from shell.

"Is this a shell?" Summer looks at a piece.

"This is Daddy," Cassia holds a fragment. Lia crawls close and her random movements scatter and mix the pile.

On Wednesday, the ceremony at Esalen is also like a mosaic of mixed materials. With no instructions or plans other than "on the lawn around ten," a circle of 60 people in costume forms around a mound of flowers. In the center is the small box of bones. Up from the lawn curious seminarians pass on their way to the lodge. Duty staff come out to the terrace and this entire panorama of color edging the ocean does honor to this family they love. The morning sun stretches down the western slope of the mountains; someone composes a tune on a recorder and two others tap a muffled background on drums. One by one, as they choose, some speak: in anger, in praise, in memoriam, and in grief. A man mentions Bob's need to live on the edge; he is angry at his manner of going over the real edge. A scripture is recited from childhood memory, a song begun and broken. Through tears Kim shares her gratitude for family, both the primal family of her beginning and this extended Esalen family. Summer and Cassia take flowers from the hands of people and run to add them to the mounded festoon. It is clear through the misty eyes of many that these little girls have many fathers and mothers. It is also clear that this circle of love and life is unbroken.

Suddenly there is the motley music of 20 voices. The children from the Gazebo School surge down the path and spill onto the lawn. Each has a helium balloon on a long string and one each is given to Summer and Cassia. Little legs circle the clump of flowers; yells and calls create a carnival fervor and these children are not intimidated by ashes. Their churning life keeps death in its box.

Now the whole group goes through the vegetable garden, down across the canyon, and up the trail to Gazebo. They cluster at the old tuna boat mounted on skids. This boat, now a classroom, is the project that brought Bob, the carpenter-boatbuilder, to this place. His early family fractured, this was his only home and his ashes will stay here.

The musicians dangle their legs from the highest roof edge. Kim, her daughters, and a few friends stand on the main deck. Children and balloons garnish the slopeside. Flute, recorder, and drums merge with the sigh of leaves and the steady beat of the sea. Kids and adults dip into the brown box and scatter ashes; some tie the larger bone bits to the balloons and Kim cries out, "Let 'em go." The balloons leap up through the trees into the sky and head out over the ocean. Someone says, "There goes Bob, on another adventure." This is the end of the beginning.

* * *

The Midwest is gentle, solid, and corny. This 140-acre farm is used for some of the same seminars, workshops, and groups as at Esalen. It is the same and it is different. The pace is slow and the space wraps around woods, fields, and swamps. Everything that's here is for eyes to see and ears to hear. Kim is in California with Lia and her ebbing memories; Summer and Cassia are here at the farm to tie up the tags of this trauma. There is no seminar on death, no workshop on dying. These little girls do the best they can among the movements of strangers seeking their own susurrus. They make use of everything here.

"Do you know my Daddy?" Cassia asks the man from Toronto.

"No."

"My Daddy died."

"Yes, I heard; I'm sorry."

"I won't see him again." Cassia remounts her hotwheels and pedals off down the long barn hallway. The cooks in the kitchen resume their work put on hold during this conversation. It is clear to those who watch and listen that this 3-year-old is a teacher. Every visitor here during these 5 weeks is engaged with this central issue. Some are met at the door with the statement, "My Daddy died," or Summer announces, "My Daddy got killed." The month is more magic than mourning.

"May we make something, Grandpa?" Summer holds a board, a hammer, and a nail.

"You may do whatever you want with that pile of wood in the corner; that's my junk pile."

Summer and Cassia spend as much time in the shop as I do. Their major project is two pieces of wood crossed, held together by a huge nail in the middle. Cassia also takes heavy tractor tools and fixes her plastic hotwheels in pantomine. Summer looks at her work with satisfaction. "We're carpenters, Grandpa, just like my Daddy."

Tuesday it rains. The group gathers in the big meeting room for an art session. The stereo spins the concise music of the flute, and in silence we explore some nuance of our psyche with crayons on large sheets of paper.

"Lookit my flowers." Summer works hard and fast and covers a dozen sheets with a multicolored riot of long-stemmed flowers. She hangs them on the walls and finally I see that they are a harvest of helium balloons.

The important thing is that death is not denied. Whatever these little girls are thinking, doing, or feeling is woven into the fabric of dancing, music, working, meditation, and searching.

The man from Kentucky is here to reduce stress. Summer is his teacher. She is creative and active and makes everything fun. She also sits on his lap for a long, warm, and quiet snuggle. The couple from Canada are students of relationships; Cassia shows them how as she bonds in some way with everyone here.

The visitor from Philadelphia is often morose and doesn't know what to do with himself. He folds his arms and broods, staring out the window. Near lunchtime, Cassia and Summer invite him to a tea party. Wearing high heels, they set up a table and chairs in the corner of the dining room. They put a cloth on the table and one on his lap. He is served a small pan of sand and a cup of mud and when Pat announces lunch he smiles and says he's sorry, but he has a previous engagement. He looks across the cloth at the two little girls who sip their mud and of course expect him to stay. It is now too difficult to be morose and he smiles. He is the same age and has the hair style of the father of the little girls. Their eyes sparkle.

The girls create an extended family here; no one is left out. Whoever is here, no matter the mood, Summer and Cassia sidle up, climb up, look up, and all are aunts and uncles. Early one morning Cassia comes walking into the kitchen carrying all her clothes from one entire dresser drawer. Wearing only her shoes, she clambers up into a lap. They select her wardrobe. Summer dresses in a long gown and head kerchief and invites someone for a walk. They seek contact; they make family. Their approach is as natural as flowing water.

Then comes a special evening dinner. The table is large, a solid slab of heavy wood. The centerpiece of farm flowers and dried grasses is circled by candles and kerosene lamps. Eyes glow and soft voices reach across the table. Cassia has been saying a blessing. She does this by asking everyone to join hands while she closes her eyes and sings, "This land is your land." It is the end of August and she is now three. Tonight she varies it.

"Did you love my Daddy?" she asks the person on her right.

"Yes, I did." It does not matter that many did not know Bob. These little girls have created such a presence through their image that it is natural to say yes.

"Did you love my Daddy?" Cassia's small blonde head turns to each person at the table. Her eyes look straight and intent at each one and time seems to stand still. She is in full command of this entire scene. A dozen misty adults are mesmerized, caught up in high drama as they circle the table with Cassia. She turns last to Summer.

"Did you love our Daddy?"

"Yes."

There is a hush; the world is still. Cassia looks one last time around the silent table. Suddenly she claps her hands and says, "Yeah," and runs off to her hotwheels. Behind her the set dissolves as the devastated supporting cast exhales and begins to breathe. Each of us is too limp to move. The lamps flicker and we are left, each by ourselves, to deal with this drama made ours by the casting of one little girl. Such unsophisticated improvization has a power all its own. The candor of this child is simple and clean.

Deaths are not good-byes. Once someone has life the body absent does not kill memory. Life is for life; life is always, not some cheap joke making the rounds for three-score years and ten. Bob was here for almost half of his allotment and then moved on. Unexpected moments continue to underline his existence. The memories of the little girls are inscribed with this fact.

Months pass and Summer and Cassia crawl onto the lap of the young man Kim is dating. They pull his beard, they giggle, they tease. They are so available. We are all in the Midwest again and tonight I am making a late bedcheck. I bend down to study Cassia's little face and am surprised by eyes wide open at midnight.

"Are you dreaming?"

"Uh huh."

"About what?"

"My Daddy."

And the one that still fills me with awe: Summer and I walk out of the barn early on a warm morning, only weeks after the accident. She looks around and then stands still. "It's all so beautiful," she says softly. This is grace, given, amazing grace.

Now it is Thanksgiving and Kim is in Hawaii to rest and search out her own life. Valerie and Stacey, two of her sisters, have the little girls in Los Angeles. They are young and know how to be aunties and also have fun. In a corner store a man sells helium balloons from a tiny kiosk. Cassia jumps up and down and insists she must have a balloon. With the balloon barely up she steps to the curb and lets it go.

"This is for you, Daddy."

And this is the way my granddaughters cope with the death of their father.

Therapists Raised by Widowed Fathers

Merle R. Jordan

SUMMARY. There is a profound impact on the work and love relationships of therapists who have gone through the experience of losing their mothers in childhood and of being raised in some new family configuration by the widowed father. Such a child often becomes a "little therapist" in the family of origin as a reaction formation. The concepts of repetition compulsion and projective identification are applied to such therapists' unconscious selection of mate and to their therapeutic style and client relationships. Two cases illustrate some implications of such early maternal death and of the resultant child rearing by the widowed father.

The myth of the macho male dealing readily with the death of his wife is rapidly disintegrating. Recent literature on the widower clearly indicates that generally the widower has a much more difficult time in dealing with the death of the spouse than a widow has. As Campbell and Silverman (1987) point out in their study of the widower,

> It is assumed that widowers have it easier than widows, that men don't grieve as long or as much, that men just want a housekeeper, or that men just want sex, and that men prefer to talk to women about their most intimate feelings. But in fact, men have as hard a time with bereavement as women do, and often for as long or longer. At the same time, they are often

Merle R. Jordan, ThD, is Associate Professor of Pastoral Psychology at Boston University. He is a Fellow and Approved Supervisor in the American Association for Marriage and Family Therapy. He is also a Diplomate in the American Association of Pastoral Counselors. Address correspondence to the author at Boston University, 745 Commonwealth Avenue, Boston, MA 02215.

Portions of this article were written with the collaboration of Ann Marmesh.

175

willing to learn how to run a household themselves; they often not only don't want sex, they are incapable of it; and they often find it difficult to talk to another woman in intimate terms after losing their wives. (p. 3)

Burgess (1988) points out in her research on widowers that "men suffer more problems of loneliness and social isolation than do women during all periods of grief" (p. 153). She also points out that men often have fewer confidants with whom to bare their souls than women do, and the "frequency of interaction with friends and family usually declines more rapidly for the widower than it does for the widow" (p. 153). Also men often lack the necessary social skills to enable them to make the desirable social contacts. "The first few months after my wife's death were almost unbearable – the loneliness, the emptiness," is a typical statement made by men who have lost a wife (p. 155).

The literature indicates that widowers who have experienced a high-grief death in which there was a sudden and totally unexpected death of the wife usually have a more difficult time in coping with their loss than a widower who goes through a low-grief death in which there was anticipatory grief because of a lingering terminal illness and some opportunity to prepare for the future. Some authorities believe that such anticipatory grief does not diminish the grief experience, but rather that the emotions are more intense when the death is unexpected. In any event, the research suggests that becoming a widower is a devastating experience for most men. Campbell and Silverman (1987) suggest some startling implications for the nearly one-quarter of a million new widowers every year in the United States. They project that a widower's chances of being killed in a car accident have increased 300 per cent, the chances of committing suicide have increased 400 per cent, the chances of dying from heart disease have increased 600 per cent, and the chances of dying from a stroke have increased 1000 per cent (p. 1).

The evidence challenges the prevailing idea that "women grieve and men replace" when they lose a spouse. There are also indications that most widowers do not ask for professional help, and therefore the children of widowers generally handle their bereavement and adaptations without the benefit of professional help also.

In this context of the widower being overwhelmed by his grief, it is important to investigate the impact of the total grief experience upon children who are raised by widowed fathers. I propose to explore one dimension of this systemic bereavement experience by looking at therapists who have been raised by widowed fathers.

Little attention has been paid to the professional and personal implications for therapists who lost their mothers when they were children and were then raised in a home with the widowed father. Experience in doing both therapy and supervision with therapists who suffered maternal death in infancy or childhood and who stayed with the widowed father in some reorganized family system indicates that there are profound personal and professional consequences from that significant loss and from the reconstructed family of origin. While it is not realistic to lump all such therapists into one category as a result of such childhood bereavement and reconstituted family, nevertheless it is valid to highlight certain themes and common experiences from the lives of some of these therapists.

It is important to remember that these therapists have had two significant things happen to them in tandem when they were children: the death of their mother and the often overlooked or undervalued grief crisis that their father goes through as a widower and surviving parent. Some of these therapists have come to realize in adulthood that they had not appreciated the magnitude of what their child self had to cope with in dealing with their own sadness in addition to coping with the resulting consequences of their father's reactions to becoming a widower. The child of a widowed father is often thrust into a situation where the very stressed father is not able to be of much help to the child in going through the child's loss and readjustment, but in fact the father may well need the child to become the one who in a variety of ways has to adapt, adjust, and possibly even take care of the father. Often children who have grown up in these circumstances have to sacrifice the child part of their life and become the caregiving "therapist child" to others.

As children, these persons learned that they had to deny and repress many of their own needs and feelings and be attentive to the needs and feelings of others in their environment. They literally were programmed into the roles and functions of listener, comforter, caregiver, healer, mediator, substitute wife and mother, counselor, and so on. Their survival strategy, which was not consciously planned, was to bury their own anguish and grief, their own need to be listened to and comforted, their own need to be parented, and their own need to be authentic for the sake of taking care of others in the family and thus try to gain some sense of safety and security for themselves in the process. The solution of sacrificing the child self for a parentified and therapeutic self was in many instances an important strategy of survival, only it left unresolved the fundamental needs and feelings of the inner child of these persons. The solution of loving too much as a strategy for childhood survival often becomes the adult dilemma and problem. The "reaction formation" dimension of being a parentified child usually catches up with one. Therapists whose inner child has not been healed from its wounds may find two major areas where they are potentially vulnerable to serious problems and even tragic mistakes.

The first area is in the unconscious selection of mate which usually is based upon the unresolved conflicts in object relations from early childhood. If the therapist is operating as a parentified child and is out of touch with some significant aspects of his/her childhood experience, then one is liable to marry someone with whom the parentified child role is continued but with the secret yearning and desire that the spouse will at last become the ideal parent who will take care of the inner, starved child of the therapist. What usually happens in these instances is that there is a replication in the marital relationship of the unresolved intrapsychic conflicts from the family of origin. The therapist may marry someone who in some ways may play out the role of the absent, deceased mother and/or the stressed-out, detached and perhaps needy father. In such situations, the spouse does not turn out to be the ideal mother who replaces the deceased mother, nor does the spouse become transformed into the ideal father who takes appropriate care of the child instead of the roles being reversed. So when the spouse does not mature in the way desired in order to end up parenting the therapist, the therapist's inner child is left in the same predicament as in childhood with having the most intimate people betray one because one is rejected or abandoned by the spouse or else the mate is so needy and dependent that he or she wants to be taken care of by the therapist. Thus it is not uncommon that the marriages of such therapists end up duplicating the childhood trauma and the destructive patterns of the family of origin. No matter how hard the therapist loves, gives and tries to help the spouse and to improve the relationship, the therapist's marriage may end up on the brink of divorce or in serious jeopardy with the therapist profoundly unfulfilled.

The second area in which such therapists are particularly vulnerable is in their vocational choice, role, and function as a therapist. Oftentimes these people, who suffered the deep wounds of the mother's death and the father's continuing struggle with the loss of his wife, became overly responsible care-givers or "little therapists" in their family of origin. They then tend unconsciously to move naturally into professional therapeutic roles as adults and to continue living out in their professional world and with their clients the same patterns and types of relationships that they were accustomed to in their childhood environment. A common parallel is the adult child of an alcoholic parent (ACOA). Many ACOAs were overly responsible children who took on significant caregiving roles and functions in their families of origin. Often in adulthood they move into the professional world of caregivers, including working in alcohol treatment programs and as therapists. So too the bereaved child raised by the widowed father may become a "therapist who loves too much" and transfers the parentified child role into the professional therapeutic role. Thus these therapists can have a determinative history which literally programs them into (a) their choice of profession as therapist being based upon their therapeutic and healing role which was assigned to them in their family of origin and (b) a restructuring in their professional work of some of the same patterns of listening, caring, comforting, rescuing and healing that were present in their childhood family relationships. Thus such therapists may on occasion be vulnerable to burn-out because once again their inner child's needs and feelings are not fulfilled by their professional work because they are so continually in the role of doing the loving, giving and helping. These therapists may also be particularly vulnerable to certain clients whose needy, dependent, and demanding child selves pull on the therapist to feel the emptiness and grief which the therapist has not been able to acknowledge within himself or herself. Supervision and therapy with therapists who "love too much" and their clients who "need and demand too much" can disclose the unresolved conflicts and dilemmas in these therapists.

There are also two other concerns that are relevant in the discussion of the lives of such therapists. The first is the concept of *repetition compulsion*. In this instance it means that the therapist who was a bereaved child and who has not come to grips with the affective experience of his or her own wounded child will unconsciously set up and participate in professional and personal situations which occasionally will duplicate the trauma and unresolved conflicts from childhood. It is possible, for example, for such a therapist to unconsciously seek to bring the dead mother to life in the raising of a client or an intimate other from her depression and deadness into dynamic life. Or the therapist may seek to be the listening, comforting, nonconfronting counselor to the client or to the beloved who reminds one of the widowed father. The script for such therapists in their professional and personal lives is like an attraction to a fatal flame in which the unresolved intrapsychic conflicts and pain from early childhood are repeated in the relationships with clients and with significant intimate others. Thus therapists whose traumatic childhood has not been significantly healed live with the same role and affective experience with certain clients and with some intimate others without an awareness that the problems of today have been sought out as if by a deep inner emotional magnet that attracts one to relationships and circumstances similar to the unresolved dilemmas of childhood.

The second important concept is the idea of *projective identification*. Often such a wounded therapist has blocked out and repressed much of the intense grief, rage, pain and anxiety of childhood. So this therapist is extremely vulnerable to connecting with intimate persons in one's personal life or with certain clients in one's professional life who have similar pain, anguish, grief and trauma as the hidden wounded inner child of the therapist. However, what the therapist attempts to do in his or her personal and professional life is to unconsciously project into the other person those repressed and disowned painful parts of one's experience and then seek to heal the beloved or the client through one's therapeutic or parenting efforts in the unconscious hope of receiving "bootleg therapy" for the inner child of the therapist. In other words, the therapist seeks to do for the client or for the loved one what the therapist wishes that the idealized parent had done for him or her as a child. In this way, the therapist's loving too much keeps him or her out of the awareness of the painful struggles of childhood and continues the role of parentified child in trying to help certain clients or significant others in one's life.

ILLUSTRATIVE CASES

First of all, let us look at two therapists with different genders, different times of loss of the mother, and different styles of the widowed father at coping with the loss.

The first example comes from doing supervision with a female therapist in her mid 30's whose case material again and again was connected with issues from the experience of losing her mother as a 10-year-old child and then trying to take care of her widowed father in the ensuing years. This therapist's life situation offers an example of a multi-layered grief process. Her mother died after 15 years of marriage. This was the second major loss for the father, who had also lost his mother when he was age three when she was in the process of giving birth to his youngest brother. Thus from age 10 on this therapist became a living symbol to her father of these two lost women in his life because her facial and secondary sex characteristics were a striking blend of her mother's and his mother's characteristics. Thus she became a target for her father's rage at times since she was a walking, talking reminder of the women he could not be with because death had stolen them from him. The situation was inherently, or at least potentially, incestuous due to the father's blurring of boundaries with the loss of his wife. While the father did not invade the daughter's sexual boundaries on a physical level, he did invade her emotional and psychic space because she could experience how deeply he wanted her to replace one or both of these women in his life. Thus in some sense she became a pseudo-wife/mother to her father until he died at the age of 56. The therapist was then 23. Interestingly enough, her father died three months before her wedding, and she had been engaged four months prior to his death. It was as if he could not bear a third loss of a significant woman in his life by seeing his daughter marry.

Since this therapist had taken on the loving, giving, helping role in relationship to her father, which Carmen Renee Berry speaks of so exquisitely in her book *When Helping You is Hurting Me: Escaping the Messiah Trap*, she continued the same pattern of "loving too much" in her own marital choice and marital interaction. She chose a man who appeared to her to be like her father minus his rage, only the underside of her husband was also filled with separation anxiety and rage due to the fact that his father had died when he was only 11 years of age (the exact year that the therapist's mother had died), and he had lived with a mother who was filled also with her own unresolved grief. So the therapist and her husband were in a marital relationship in which the unresolved dilemmas of childhood were re-enacted. In some ways they were unconsciously small children seeking connection to the lost same-sex parent. Over time it became evident that she had to be financially and emotionally the strong one in the family because even though he had much promise he was unable to keep a steady job. Also ultimately there was the dynamic of an affair in the relationship so that the marriage experienced its own form of death in a divorce.

At the same time the therapist struggled with doing too much for her clients and feeling overly responsible for their success in therapy and in life. She had some difficulties in dealing with clients' resistance and defenses because they thwarted her power and ability to bring about transformation and change. To care for people in their freedom to be in whatever spot they were and to allow herself to be in a helpless and powerless place sometimes was very uncomfortable and anxiety-producing to this therapist. As she was able to let go of trying to take care of some of her clients as she had taken care of her father, as well as allowing herself to feel helpless and sad in the face of strong resistance from stuck clients as she had felt powerless and sad during her mother's long terminal illness, was a major transformation for her in her clinical practice. The supervision also encouraged her to go back into her own personal therapy in order to find more freedom from the bondage of the past due to the death of her mother and her parentified child care-giving to her father.

The second case concerns a male therapist in his mid 50's who sought therapy as a result of being overwhelmed by a client with a primitive personality disorder. The therapist had literally become exhausted by his efforts to rescue his client, having been available to her literally 24 hours a day. He had lost a sense of the need for boundaries in the therapeutic process with her as he tried to fill her emptiness instead of helping her to gain ego mastery over it. This therapist had not been aware of the projective identification that had gone on in this therapeutic relationship in which his repressed primitive feelings of losing his mother were projected onto the disturbed client. This therapist had lost his mother at 5 weeks of age as a result of her contracting a serious illness in the hospital following the childbirth. The infant was thus separated from his mother for these first few weeks in the hospital and then had to deal with the infant trauma of being separated from her permanently by her death. His father had been deeply grief stricken by the loss of his beloved wife, but he had also felt caught in the dilemma of what to do about raising a new baby son and a 2-year-old daughter. So the father brought in a neighbor who was a practical nurse to take care of the children, and within four months the father married the nurse who then became the stepmother to the children. However, this therapist was aware of overhearing his stepmother say on a couple of occasions, "I'm not sure whether I married the man or the baby." In other words, the father had apparently remarried in order to have someone to take care of the children even though it was clear, including to the stepmother, that the father's love attachments were always to his first wife. The boy was raised in an environment of a conspiracy of silence in which there was no conversation about his mother and her death except for a 30-second announcement when he was six in which his stepmother told him that she was afraid that she would lose his love because she was not his biological mother. She told him that she considered herself to be his real mother even though his biological mother had died when he was a baby. There was such a fear of losing a second mother and of the consequences of betraying the stepmother as well as upsetting his father that there was not a single question raised to the stepmother nor to the father through this man's youth and young adulthood. In fact, when the father died when the young man was 20, there had never been one word of discussion between them about the biological mother.

In the process of therapy this man came in contact with the lost little boy inside of himself and he wrote about his experience in the following way.

Once upon the time there was a lost little boy who had to keep the fact that he was lost a secret. He couldn't tell his father, his stepmother, his sister, his grandparents, aunts, uncles or cousins. He couldn't even tell his friends. In a way he didn't even let himself know that he was lost, though he was always searching for something. He had been lost since he was just an infant, and his mother had gone away and never come back. In losing his mother, he had also lost himself and to some extent he had lost his father. His true identity had been in limbo. He needed to be with someone who would let him name the truth that he was lost. He wasn't even allowed to name the fact that he was the son of his natural mother and his father. But he had to pretend that he wasn't lost, and no one really guessed the truth about the lost little boy. In fact, many people thought that he was very much grounded in the reality of life. But he did not really know the topography of his own inner terrain. He did not truly have a map of his own inner reality. He wandered and searched, without daring to let others or even himself know that he was lost. He was afraid of some kind of negative impact if he let on that he was lost, so he pretended to be in the know. He pretended to be among those who really knew their way around. He picked up the cues as to how one tries to be okay in this world, and he mastered the art of pretending to cope and of knowing the map of reality for his life. No one was the wiser. And that was a sad fact, because then no one could help him name his plight. No one could join him in his realm of lostness and just be with him. He had to be lost all by himself, and all the time pretending that he was okay and those close to him were okay too.

In his unconscious selection of mate, he chose someone who was like the deceased mother in that she was an exciting but rejecting object. She was also somewhat like the stepmother and the father in participating in a conspiracy of silence not to talk about deep emotional factors in their marriage. While the therapist had an idealistic hope that his wife would both be a replacement for his lost mother and be an ideal woman who would love him and communicate with him in more mature ways than the stepmother and father did, his marital choice and the resulting patterns of interaction that were structured replicated for him the same isolated, sad and helpless roles that he had experienced as a child. Again through the process of repetition compulsion his basic object relations and emotional patterns were duplicated in the marital relationship.

Likewise in his therapeutic relationships this man tended to be a therapist who loved too much and who tried to keep his clients from experiencing separation anxiety and the unbearable pain and grief of early loss. Thus he tended to unconsciously be involved in projective identification, especially with his more seriously disturbed clients, whereby his unresolved primitive experience of losing his mother and the resulting consequences in the reconstituted family of origin were projected upon the clients. He tried to help fill the vacuum of their pains, hurts and losses rather than to help their adult ego seek to bear the unbearable and to master those losses. Thus he was readily hooked in to a countertransference disaster with a person who demanded that he be the ideal mother who would be always present, always giving, and have eternal love for her. He also came to the realization of how his collusion with his father never to talk about his mother and her death was occasionally replayed in a conspiracy of silence with certain clients, who usually reminded him of his father. He would not take initiative to explore certain secrets of their life and their patterns of interaction. It was necessary for this therapist to go back into his own history to relive the terrors of his childhood so that he could master intrapsychically his own inner hell both in dealing with the death of his mother and the lack of openness and closeness to his father. Then he began to be free not to try to pacify and ameliorate the emptiness and painful vacuum in the lives of his clients or his intimate other by being a therapist or partner who loved too much and sought relief through fusion.

CONCLUSION

While individual therapists who have lost their mother in childhood and been raised by their widowed father in some new family configuration may have various experiences which impact them both personally and professionally, it is clear that there are some key themes that need to be considered. Whether a therapist is doing supervision or personal therapy with such a therapist, one should be very sensitive to the profound impact of the loss of the mother in childhood and of the adjustments and adaptations made to the widowed father and to the reconstituted family of origin. The supervisor of such a therapist particularly needs to keep in mind the possibility of projective identification with a client who is undergoing deep experiences of pain, grief, anger and separation anxiety. The supervisor needs to be aware that the unresolved issues of the parentified child in the supervisee may create serious countertransference problems in the therapeutic process. The supervisor also needs to be conscious of any ways in which the supervisee may be unconsciously reconstructing in the therapeutic relationship the repetition compulsion of the unresolved intrapsychic issues from childhood. Likewise the therapist of such a person needs to keep in mind the various ways in which the therapist who was a bereaved child may be engaged in self-defeating and self-sabotaging strategies of living. Particularly one needs to be aware of the unconscious selection of mate and the often unfulfilling marriage relationships in which therapists may replicate the problematic object relationships of their childhood.

While much more research is indicated in this area to investigate numerous factors such as the gender and age of the person at the time of the loss, the nature of the reconstituted family with the widowed father, the father's ways of coping with his grief and widowhood, the patterns of communication in the family, the support of the extended network, etc., it is important for therapists of therapists and supervisors of therapists to be sensitively aware of the profound dual impact upon a therapist who suffered the loss of the mother in infancy or childhood along with seeking to cope with the reconstituted family with the widowed father.

REFERENCES

Altschul, S. (Ed.). (1988). *Childhood bereavement and its aftermath*. Madison, CT: International Universities Press.

Berry, C.R. (1988). *When helping you is hurting me: Escaping the messiah trap*. San Francisco: Harper & Row.

Brockman, E.S. (1987). *Widower*. New York: Bantam Books.

Burgess, J.K. (1988). Widowers. In C. Chilman, E. Nunnally, & F. Cox (Eds.). *Variant family forms*. Newbury Park, CA: Sage Publications.

Campbell, S., & Silverman, P. (1987). *Widower*. New York: Prentice Hall.

Treating the Bereaved Spouse: A Focus on the Loss Process, the Self and the Other

Simon Shimshon Rubin

SUMMARY. This paper reviews aspects of the bereavement response to loss and sketches a time frame for viewing psychotherapeutic intervention. When a person suffers a loss, not only the real other, but the intrapsychic representations of the other-in-connection-with-the-self has to be mourned. Therapy can assist the bereaved return to what they have always had — a relationship to themselves that enabled attachment to and interaction with highly significant others. Two cases of intervention with bereaved spouses are presented. Taken together, they show the power of intervention to make significant inroads in the response to loss, the relationship to self and other, and to rework basic early issues in the bereaved's personality and intrapsychic life.

Treating the bereaved spouse involves working with one's client's pain, fear, anxiety, loneliness, self-deception and unhappiness. These all touch our own. The client who has come to us has already been overwhelmed by the task of responding to loss. We are invited to help the mourning proceed along its melancholy course within the limits of not being overwhelmed ourselves as well. Our knowledge, our experience, our skills, our humanity, and our fi-

Simon Shimshon Rubin received his PhD degree from Boston University in 1977. Dr. Rubin is Chairman of the Clinical Psychology Program at the University of Haifa and Director of the Child, Adolescent, and Family Clinic in that city. He maintains an active interest in issues of professional training in both Israel and the U.S., as well as in the areas of research and intervention with the bereaved. Address correspondence to the author at Department of Psychology, University of Haifa, Haifa, Israel 31999.

niteness are what we take into our meetings with the bereaved. We join the grieving client in a quest to understand and to effect change. Yet paradoxically, our interventions are both desired and feared. For inevitably, therapy will bring with it still more process-ing of the loss, and another level of realization of what must be given up. We become in effect, messengers of a reality that says life can have something to offer. It is true that life may be forever shad-owed by the loss of the spouse — but life can still have something to offer.

In this article, I wish to highlight a few of the basics of adaptive and maladaptive response to loss, to sketch a time frame for view-ing our interventions and our goals, and to consider a number of affective and cognitive processes the therapy can provide to assist the bereaved return to what they have always had — a relationship to the self that enabled attachment to and interaction with highly sig-nificant others. When a person suffers the loss of another, he or she has to mourn the deceased as that person affected his or her external *and* inner worlds. Not only the real other, but the intrapsychic rep-resentations of the other-in-connection-with-the-self has to be mourned (Rubin, 1984b; 1985). The basis of the relationship to the self (even in its most intimate communion with another in a dyadic relationship) is a structural feature of personality that must serve to contain the bereaved if the adaptation to the loss of the other is to be assimilated.

BACKGROUND

The ultimate goal of the bereavement process is to allow the be-reaved to perceive, assimilate, and integrate the reality of loss into the life structure. Freud (1917/1957), in his classic article, "Mourn-ing and Melancholia," organized his understanding of the bereave-ment process as centered on the task of relinquishing the attachment to the deceased. During the mourning process, the bereaved is highly and almost singlemindedly focused on the loss of the valued other. Psychologically, the bereaved uses this period of intensive preoccupation and emotional upheaval to part from the deceased. In the months and years following loss, the tasks and commitments of life gradually exert their influence on the bereaved (Rubin, 1984b;

in press). The survivor is forced to deal with the mundane but dynamic details that characterize the living and is thus drawn back into the mainstream of the life cycle.

Current thinking on bereavement is well represented in the work of Bowlby (1980) and Parkes (1972). They have presented a paradigm wherein the bereaved responds to loss via a progression through the stages of shock/numbness, searching, disorganization, and reorganization. As with most psychological stage theories, one is generally talking about a relative preponderance of certain elements which coexist with other features highlighted in additional stages. The searching stage, for example, contains within it elements of shock, disorganization, and reorganization. The highlight of the response at this point in time, however, involves being responsive to cues and associations linked to the physical presence of the deceased. These continue alongside a major reorganization of internal and external reality that takes into account the absence of the deceased. Similarly, years later, where searching phenomena predominate, they can be assumed to mark features related to a fixation characteristic of the relatively early adaptation to loss.

Chronologically, the process of responding to loss traverses three rough phases. The initial stage can be considered the acute grief phase and can last from 1 to 3 months. Numbness, hollowness, strong somatic responses, anger, confusion, and helplessness are among the characteristics of this period (Lindemann, 1944; Shuchter, 1986). This is a most dramatic and confusing state for many bereaved people due to the newness, strangeness, and incomprehensibility of much of how they respond physically and emotionally. The bereaved are often not prepared for what they experience here. This acute phase is followed by a chronic and somewhat less florid phase of protracted mourning where depression and anxiety characterize the response to the empty life confronting the bereaved. At this point, the bereaved attend concretely and emotionally to the tasks of living—while they undergo mourning. In this mourning period, the major characteristics are the central focus on the deceased, the relationship to him or her, and life without the partner. The somatic and psychological responses continue, but with less intensity. The phase of mourning for a spouse can last for several years (Parkes & Weiss, 1983).

The third stage is one that I term the epilogue to bereavement (Rubin, 1984b). For those individuals whose mourning progresses to this third stage, the memories of the deceased and the relationship to him or her are integrated into a life picture. The surviving spouse is open to remembering the deceased, but is not significantly reworking or processing the relationship to the deceased. The deceased is not forgotten, but a steady-state relationship to the couples of memories, associations, and feelings vis-à-vis the deceased have crystallized in a non-compulsive, non-anxiety-provoking manner. In interviewing a client at this stage of response to the loss, the sense of perspective, of a significant but not the only significant relationship, emerges from discussion.

Clinical and research literature have identified maladaptive response to bereavement as difficulties in entering, traversing, and/or exiting the grief and mourning process. The majority of problems encountered are those with entering into and exiting the bereavement response. Absence of grief, too hurried coping, denial of emotional response to loss, and a sealed-off response to the loss represent one extreme. Chronic involvement with grief and bereavement, continued thinking about the deceased, and preoccupation with the loss represent the opposite pole of continued overinvolvement with loss. Many clinicians and researchers believe that the latter is both more common and more difficult to treat than the former (Bowlby, 1980; Mawson, Marks, Ramm, & Stern, 1981; Osterweis, Solomon, & Green, 1984).

In the initial period following loss, the newly bereaved are often unprepared to deal with the sheer force and nature of the emotions that follow loss. It is not uncommon for latent as well as verbalized concerns about one's sanity to surface in initial weeks following loss. In general, people vary widely in their response to loss so that the clinician can expect a broad range of responses to the experience. While much knowledge about the process of bereavement is available via self help groups, the media, and common interactions in the community, knowledge about the process of loss is apt to be defended against until an individual faces the crisis of loss personally. The naiveté of the recently bereaved responds to information about the process and course of loss.

At later points in time, therapists can work to help people achieve structural changes in their relationship to themselves and to the deceased. In my research and clinical experience, the significance of the incomplete bereavement response as a barrier to post-loss adjustment is striking (Rubin, 1981; 1984a; in press). Many bereaved individuals do not complete their mourning to a point where the term epilogue to bereavement would apply the them. While some of the effects of loss and some of the involvement with the relationship to the deceased are typically permanent—overinvolvement with the loss and the lost are characteristic of an incompleted response to loss. Psychotherapeutic intervention in these cases can benefit from an understanding of the significance of the relationship to the deceased for the bereaved.

To illustrate some of the points made here, two cases of intervention with bereaved spouses are presented here. The first case briefly considers a woman who was unable to move from her sense of numbness and shock into an adaptive grief process following her husband's recent death. The second case follows in detail a man 8 years after the loss whose mourning did not progress adaptively to a stage consistent with the features characteristic of the epilogue to loss. Both cases show the power of intervention to make significant inroads on the response to loss, the relationship to self and other, and to rework basic early issues in the bereaved's personality and internal life.

A CASE OF AVOIDED MOURNING
IN A RECENTLY BEREAVED WIFE

Donna W. referred her 14-year-old son for evaluation and treatment to a child guidance clinic 2 months after her husband, Mike's, death. In the initial intake meeting, the necessity of intervention for the bereaved family and the bereaved mother were recognized. Dr. B., a postdoctoral fellow, provided a set of family sessions followed by a period of psychotherapy with the mother alone. In the initial sessions, Donna presented as a cold and narcissistically preoccupied woman who was emotionally unavailable to her children. As therapy progressed, it became clear that this behavior was reactive to the loss process rather than rooted in personality difficulties as had been initially hypothesized.

History: Donna described an ambivalent and strained relationship to her husband prior to his illness. Their marriage had undergone a dramatic but encapsulated shift when Mike was diagnosed as having cancer. Prior to his illness, Mike had been a nonintrospective counterdependent man whose time was spent alternating between working in the construction trades and visiting with his gambling buddies. With the realization of the severity of his illness, he became a "new person." Mike terminated his relationships with his male cronies and began to depend heavily on his wife for emotional support. As the cancer rapidly spread, he became fully homebound and made demands on his wife for 24-hour care and availability. She provided these completely and "wholeheartedly." Her own relationship to him which had incorporated sizable aspects of rage and attraction shifted to a caretaking stance. In the final half-year of his illness, the children were sent off to school and spent the remainder of each day at the paternal grandparents home, returning only at night to sleep in the house. Donna was totally preoccupied with caring for her husband and with the closeness of their relationship. Following Mike's death, Donna could tolerate little of her children's behavioral or emotional reactions.

Meeting Donna in her current emotional state, Dr. B encouraged her to share the circumstances of her husband's illness and death. She related information in an intellectually bland fashion, but she also conveyed an undercurrent of seething anger not far below the surface. Dr. B. provided support and a nonthreatening atmosphere in which to gradually allow Donna to experience her emotions. Donna's rage at being left with the children by a man who had neglected to provide either emotional or financial support was one of the family issues directly tied to the grieving process. The attentive and sympathetic listening allowed her to relax the protective wall that had frozen her rage and person in a manner so dysfunctional for her and her family. After a number of sessions, Donna was able to emotionally confront the course of her husband's physical deterioration. Donna cried as she spoke of the difficulties and fears she had experienced in those last months. No longer walled off, the ambivalence she had always felt reemerged and mingled with the experiences of Mike's illness. Poignantly, Donna described how she and Mike had, for a time, been together as they had not been for most of the marriage. Yet, she realized that the problems of their previous years together had not been resolved.

As treatment progressed, Donna's sadness deepened and a range of issues appeared. There were angry attacks upon Mike, an evaluation of what the marriage had been like, and an apportionment of responsibility and blame. In addition to issues of their relationship, Dr. B. helped Donna link her mourning to significant themes of her life's relationships.

Donna began to see that in her relationship to her parents, the interplay of dependence and independence had been a central theme. When marrying, she had chosen a man with whom she had replayed aspects of her family drama. An additional link of early history to present response to loss was rooted in Donna's parents' history. Donna had been born the child of two holocaust survivors whose life experiences had shaped them and affected their daughter in important ways. Donna's mother and uncle had been imprisoned in a concentration camp during their early adolescence. By adapting to the harsh realities of life in the camp, and by denying all internal feelings, Donna's mother had been able to save both herself and her younger brother. The role that Donna had assumed with her husband during his illness was modeled on her mother who responded to the other's need with intense caregiving but with an absence of emotion. In contrast, Donna's father had survived the war as a partisan. He had not been exposed to the helplessness of the concentration-camp regimen where retreating into oneself was a valuable defensive maneuver. He represented for Donna the freedom to experience emotions and to function simultaneously. The latter parts of the short-term treatment saw Donna recover and build upon her identificatory attachments to her father that served to connect herself with her internal emotional states. These links played a role in helping Mrs. Donna W. experience and undergo open mourning. Simultaneously, Donna's increased tolerance for her children's responses to their dislocation, father's illness and death produced positive changes in the behavior and emotional status of the children.

Comment: This case sketch described a woman having difficulty making the transition from the grief to mourning stages of the response to loss. The significance of the case emerges following the initiation of the treatment process. The therapist's assessment of Donna's problems as rooted in personality difficulties changed as it became clear that aspects of her response were related to relationship difficulties with spouse and parents. The extent to which ambivalence in relationships with the bereaved is associated with increased difficulties in mourning is well known. Less often stressed is the potential for diagnostic error in assessing clients at the early stages of the loss response. In this case, the 5 months of psychotherapeutic intervention emphasized support, a history of the loss, a review of the relationship to Mike, and the links to Donna's patterns of relationships and identifications with her parents.

In considering the effectiveness of the psychotherapeutic intervention so early in the loss response, we are somewhat limited. The evidence suggests that the bereavement response in this case resumed an adaptive course. Yet many of the questions regarding outcome to bereavement require the passage of several years in order to determine the adequacy of the adaptation for the bereaved. The next case will allow us to consider adaptive and maladaptive response from the vantage of years following spouse loss.

A CASE OF UNFINISHED MOURNING IN A LONELY WIDOWER

Joseph G. was a 40-year-old accountant who sought psychotherapy because of an inability to maintain a relationship with a woman for purposes of marriage. In the year prior to entering treatment, Joseph had become serially involved in relationships with two women that had progressed well on a casual basis. When he began to consider marriage, however, he became uneasy and each time terminated the relationship.

Joseph was a tall, well-dressed erect man who sat stiffly during the initial interviews. He spoke in a obsessive, pedantic tone and had minimal awareness of his internal emotional state or of his feelings. Anamnesis yielded the following information. Joseph's wife had died in a boating accident 8 years earlier in which he himself had been seriously injured. Four children ranging in age from 9 to 17 lived with him in a small town and were "well adjusted." According to Joseph, the children were interested in having a mother figure in the home. He indicated that it was important for him to remarry and father additional children while he still had the energy and virility to do so.

In his family of origin, Joseph was born late in the marriage and was one of three children. Both of Joseph's parents were deceased. His father had died one year before treatment and his mother had died when he was 16 years of age following a long and debilitating bout with breast cancer. According to Joseph, he had not been unduly upset by his mothers' death either at the time or later. Joseph had met his wife Molly when he was 22 and his wife 16. After a year and a half of dating, Molly became pregnant and at Joseph's urging agreed not to have an abortion but to marry him instead. Description of the family life hinted at an undercurrent of conflict between husband and wife whose course was interrupted by the tragic accident.

An exploration of Joseph's general interpersonal relationships indicated that his relationship with his children were his warmest and were not a source of conflict. Interpersonal difficulties were apparent in his relationships to colleagues and co-workers although he did not appear sensitive to his role in the difficulties. Increasingly isolated from sources of interpersonal support, Joseph tended to respond with cynicism stemming from a kind of hurt pride.

Comment: I was intrigued by Joseph, found him overcontrolled and angry, with disturbing schizoid-like qualities that favored liking people in the abstract over meeting real people in the flesh. My interest in the general issue of long-term response to bereavement, however, provided an initial curiosity and empathy for him which sufficed to carry me through the early phase of relationship building. In the initial interviews, I was struck by the mix between Joseph's significant losses (including the recent of father) and of his rigid personality structure that was ego syntonic for the client and not likely to respond to a focal intervention.

Three areas were outlined to Joseph as central to the proposed psychological contract. My formulation accepted the client's description of his difficulty in bringing a relationship to the point of marriage. In addition, his interpersonal difficulties seemed to be linked to the problem of finding a spouse — that is, that his interpersonal difficulties were operant in both areas. One aspect of our work would focus on these issues. A second area of therapeutic work would address the further working through of aspects of the relationship to and loss of his wife, Molly. Potential links between the grief over his spouse and the loss of his mother years before would be explored as well. The third area of our work would involve expanding Joseph's affective repertoire to help him recognize and experience a broader range of feelings than were available to him at present. Joseph accepted the treatment contract as presented to him. He did not understand what his mother or his general feelings had to do with any of this, but he was willing to give treatment a try.

Treatment spanned 18 months and followed the course of a psychodynamically oriented psychotherapy. At its conclusion, each of the three areas outlined in the treatment contract has proved to be of importance in effecting significant change in Joseph's life patterns. The focus of the therapeutic work occurred within an evolving therapeutic relationship which sufficiently supported Joseph so as to enable him to explore areas of difficulty, to achieve insight, and to practice patterns of interaction. In this, the treatment of this individual did not markedly differ from that of any traditional psychotherapy. There were, however, several nodal points in the therapy which I wish to highlight. I shall do this as we follow the course of the treatment.

Within the first 4 months of treatment, Joseph had described his abandonment by his friends and the difficulties he had with his daughters' seeking greater autonomy. The predominant issue, however, remained the extent of his longing for his wife. In response to questions, he spoke about his feelings when passing the place of the boating accident, and such things as the mementos of his wife, his pictures of her, and his gravesite visits. There were pictures of his wife in his bedroom and a large box of her clothes that he was saving to dress his children in. Shortly thereafter, he would begin to court a young woman who reminded him of his wife. In response to her rebuffs, he would desist for a number of months before returning to this in earnest.

Comment: Joseph's presenting complaints had suggested difficulty in achieving intimacy with a potential life partner in a man who had suffered significant losses in midadolescence, adulthood, and within the past year. Although theoretically available for a new relationship, he was unable to actualize his interest. The possibility of an inability to complete the bulk of his mourning and progress to the postmourning or epilogue-to-loss stage following bereavement was confirmed in this phase of treatment. Elements of searching (Bowlby, 1980; Parkes, 1987) were manifest in his retention of numerous articles of his wife's wardrobe and in his search for a second version of her. These indicated that, despite significant progress in the reorganization of his life post-loss, the mourning process had not adequately addressed his clinging to tangible and intangible reminders of his wife. It was not the presence of these features, but rather their degree, that signalled the difficulties.

As we spoke about his late adolescence and early adulthood, the link between mother and wife became clearer. Joseph had suffered the loss of his mother to a lingering illness in his middle adolescent years. To protect himself from the flurry of emotions, he had intensified his intellectual interests and set about denying his feelings of sadness, anxiety, and anger. In his initial relationship with his future wife, he had chosen a woman who looked up to him by virtue of his relative age and wisdom. Seeking to recapture the closeness that he had been missing, he quickly set about encouraging the construction of a family to serve as a framework to supply his needs for closeness and caring.

Prior to the death of his wife, however, there were hints of a process of estrangement and unease which had begun to take the form of separate vacations and less time spent together. In contrast, the retrospective reconstruction of Joseph's memory of his years with Molly emphasized a concrete description of his relative dominance, marital tension, and disappointment. Joseph ignored all that in his thinking of what those years had been like. Asked as to the quality of the relationship, Joseph had nothing but superlatives for Molly and for their years together. In ignoring the details in favor of a distorted but soothing construction, he managed to repeat the pattern of relating to his intellectualized analysis as if it were reality. This maintained his social ineptitude and insensitivity to other people. Although ostensibly in interaction with others, Joseph was really dealing with himself and how he saw the world, and his view was both idiosyncratic and defensive.

Comment: Perhaps the most seductive and potentially harmful aspect of the relationship to the memory construct of the deceased — and where these differ most strongly from the relationship to people who are living and in contact with us — is the fact that living people provide feedback and reality testing whereas the deceased do not. The gap between Joseph's descriptions and his construction of reality in his relationship with Molly made me question what it felt like during their years of marriage together. That same gap continued to present Joseph with many difficulties in how he lived his life at present. In contrast to the frustrating reality in which he found himself, Joseph was able to soothe himself and seek comfort and support in the idealized reveries involving his deceased wife. Dead wives do not complain or criticize, are always available in fantasy, and when the memories are organized selectively (or heavily edited) who among the living could compete?

A turning point for this therapy occurred approximately 6 months into the treatment. Joseph had become very attracted to a young woman whose age, body size, and mannerisms reminded him strongly of how Molly had been during their courtship. Responding to his internal signals, he had heavily pursued the woman on the basis of his desire for her. Strongly motivated by his own needs, he was unable to attend or respond to this young woman's needs. Spurred on by his choice of a replacement and continuation of the ideal Molly, he was also unable to consider the limits of the resemblance. Not surprisingly, Joseph was not succeeding as a suitor and was not terribly interested in looking at what about his behavior might be contributing to this development. Clarification and drawing parallels between his general difficulties with individuals and his difficulty with this woman were tolerated as unwelcome intrusions by the client. My seeking to have him observe his behavior and how it was dominated by his needs were of no avail. The avenue that provoked the least resistance consisted of asking Joseph to again describe relevant features of Molly and how this new woman resembled and differed from her.

The idealized picture of Molly that Joseph presented coincided with his failures with the new woman. Once again this focused the difficulty on the client's choice of living with his distorted but foolproof inner reality as a welcome haven from dealing with the complexity of people and relationships in the real world. With the treatment relationship well developed, I chose to intervene here at the juncture of Joseph's general tendency to stay with a distorted but soothing picture of reality (irrespective of interpersonal cues from those around him); his idealized picture of Molly; and his unwillingness to surrender his interest in a living attachment to a dead woman — who could not be revived by his willingness to see in another the opportunity to continue on with the former.

Listening to the resemblance of the new woman to the young Molly, I asked Joseph to describe again how Molly would have been if she had lived, and what things would be like for them now. He gave a placard-like sketch of a family with many children, with a wife at home to care for them and her husband, and with a fairy-tale quality to it. "You know something Joseph?" I said. "It seems to me that if Molly had not died in the boat accident, there was a good possibility she would have divorced you." In shock, he replied: "What — what did you say?"

I repeated my words and elaborated by weaving together the elements of the worsening marital relationship in the last years that Joseph had previously dismissed. Using these details in the context of his reawakened attachment to Molly/Molly the II proved catalytic. It effected a clear shift in the course of Joseph and his therapy. In the next session, Joseph came in quite subdued and spoke of the power of the previous meeting. He had gone to his wife's grave and had been flooded with pictures of the complexity of their interaction and of the frustration and distance he had experienced but ignored both at the time and for years thereafter.

From this point on, the impact of the change process facilitated by psychotherapy progressed. Almost immediately, Joseph stopped phoning and writing Molly the II. Over the next months, Joseph's anger and depression began to surface. We did some work linking his feelings to the loss of his mother and how this had emerged in his current feelings of anger at the world and at the therapist. We spoke of his identification with his children as motherless and what that served for him. He became more demanding. The dominant theme in this period was his fear of loneliness, his depression, and his seeking solace at his wife's gravesite. The loneliness of the transition phase was useful. It served as a bridge to the linking of his mother to his wife. Still, his anxiety continued and his depression increased. There also emerged Joseph's wish for greater closeness to his deceased father and to his therapist. These were apparent but difficult for him to accept. Alongside his exploration of how his wife had at times served to serve him emerged the readiness to tolerate change. Alongside this shift were increasing demand on the therapist. The strength of his wish to remarry heightened in response to my forthcoming summer break.

Comment: With the beginning rupture in his self-object relationship to the memory representations of his wife, depression, loneliness and mourning reappeared for the first time in years. I spoke to the self-object features of his wife being dead and how that allowed for a greater closeness than the reality of human interaction would tolerate. Although he had lost his wife many years before, now he was losing the defensive but reassuring closeness to her inner representation. Anger, frustration, and neediness began to mount. This phase also allowed for the exploration of his sense of aloneness. At this juncture in treatment, Joseph was able to more directly confront his feelings about the loss of his mother as he began to understand his identification with and overdetermined closeness to his children as motherless.

Faced with the upcoming separation from me, he focused again on his interest in remarriage. We worked on his longing for a woman, and how he was reminiscent of Western posters proclaiming "Wanted, Dead or Alive – A WOMAN." Again, the confrontation and stimulated mourning were helpful to Joseph. For in response to this session he reported a dream in which his wife and family had left him for a day. It was the first separation dream that he could recollect. He saw this as a positive development speaking to his progress. The content of the previous session and my upcoming vacation combined to allow him greater interaction with his loneliness.

The final stage of therapy began with the resumption of therapy after the particularly prolonged summer break. The break foreshadowed my future sabbatical that would start in 4 months time. The time limit on the current phase of treatment was clear. In this time frame, the break and resumption of relationship, the forth coming termination (or a minimum cessation of treatment for 3/4ths of a year) framed the final phases of treatment. The culmination of the changes facilitated by treatment found expression in Joseph's increased ability to mourn the loss of his wife, to tolerate being alone, and to feel open to the feelings that emerged. Themes of father-son, and mentor-junior relationships emerged as one the of major content areas of the treatment in this phase.

Comment: The treatment had progressed from the prominent focus on the loss of his wife in reality, to his willingness to mourn her intrapsychically. In addition, a level of work on his relationship to his mother and their significance vis-à-vis his relationship to his wife was achieved. Also, the third loss, that of his father, began to emerge as the transference and reality aspects of the client-therapist relationship and its limits became clear. If Joseph couldn't have a wife, had lost his mother too soon, and couldn't be as one with his children – the relationship to the father figure was all the more important. Yet here too, he would have to say good-bye. The recency of that loss had in all probability influenced his entry in to therapy in the first place. Joseph's current capacity to tolerate his feelings, to be alone but in thought, allowed him to begin to integrate his therapeutic experience and make use of the process for the present and the future.

In the last stage of treatment, Joseph began to talk about the closetful of his wife's clothes that were taking up too much space in the house. He wondered whether he should do something about them. Soon, he sold the double bed of his marriage and bought a single bed to enable the addition of a desk in his bedroom. He realized that to give his teenage daughter her mother's clothes was something she neither wanted nor could use. He reported how each of his children had begun to differentiate and assert their own needs. For example, the eldest was pursuing age-appropriate relationships with friends and limiting her extensive caretaking for the younger siblings. Joseph had moved from the stage of mourning to that of the epilogue to loss.

The final contract of termination neared. Joseph considered the option of terminating or continuing treatment and opted to work toward termination. We agreed that a period of sessions focusing on termination was appropriate in order for him to review the meaning of the separations: the separations from Molly, from Molly the II, from his mother, from his father, and from me. He used his time well.

CONCLUSION

In spouse loss, the bereaved has a formidable task. He or she must function while grieving, relinquishing aspects of the attachment and gradually redirecting attention to the outside world. Bereavement sets in motion the need to painfully become preoccupied with impact of the relationship to the deceased. Because of the power of the loss experience, because of the retrospective focus on the relationship, and because of the intrapsychic rather than the interpersonal nature of the process, a number of distortions do result. Among the most potent of these is the distorted and seductive pull of a relationship where the memories of the relationship, determined by the bereaved and by the unconscious, can conspire to create a psychological reality which beard minimal relationship to the reality of life lived previously.

The cases presented above reflect therapeutic work with individuals whose bereavement responses had not proceeded well. In the former, the therapeutic task had involved assisting the client to enter into her loss process. In the latter, the therapeutic task had focused on assisting the client to relinquish his continuing heightened attachment to his deceased wife. The delicate interplay of the relationship of the bereaved to the deceased, to the self, and to significant others all played a part in the examples presented. The links drawn between these features allow the bereaved spouse to proceed with the bereavement process.

Much of what we do in dynamic psychotherapy related to helping clients reassess their relationships. Working with the bereaved spouse requires many of the skills that are in our general psychotherapeutic repertoire. To be willing to lead/follow into the pain of rearranging the complex, powerful, and yet fragile connection that the bereaved have with the deceased triggers strong emotions in all involved. The relationship that develops in psychotherapy can serve to support the bereaved who is experiencing the pain of loss.

Supporting the bereaved as well as supporting the bereaved *confront the loss* are significant elements in psychotherapeutic work with those who have experienced loss.

REFERENCES

Bowlby, J. (1980). *Loss: Sadness and depression*. London: Hogarth Press.

Freud, S. (1957). Mourning and melancholia. In J. Strachey (Ed. and Trans.), *The standard edition of the complete psychological works of Sigmund Freud* (Vol. 14, pp. 243-278). London: Hogarth Press. (Original work published 1917)

Lindemann, E. (1944). Sumpomatology and management of acute grief. *American Journal of Psychiatry, 101*, 141-148.

Mawson, D., Marks, I.M. Ramm, L., & Stern, R.S. (1981). Guided mourning for morbid grief: A controlled study. *British Journal of Psychiatry, 138*, 185-193.

Osterwies, M., Solomon, F., & Green, M. (Eds.). (1984). *Bereavement: Reactions, consequences and care*. Washington, DC: Institute of Medicine.

Parkes, C.M. (1972). *Bereavement: Studies of grief in adult life*. London: Tavistock Publications.

Parkes, C.M., & Weis, R.S. (1983). *Recovery from bereavement*. New York: Basic Books.

Rubin, S. (1981). A two-track model of bereavement: Theory and research. *American Journal of Orthopsychiatry, 51*, 101-109.

Rubin, S. (1984a). Maternal attachment and child death: On adjustment, relationship and resolution. *Omega, 15*(4), 347-352.

Rubin, S. (1984b). Mourning distinct from melancholia. *British Journal of Medical Psychology, 57*, 339-345.

Rubin, S. (1985). The resolution of bereavement: A clinical focus on the relationship to the deceased, *Psychotherapy: Theory, Research, Training, and Practice, 22*(2), 231-235.

Rubin, S. (1986). Child death and the family: Parents and children confronting loss, *International Journal of Family Therapy*, 377-388.

Rubin, S. (in press). Death of the future?: An outcome study of bereaved parents in Israel. *Omega*.

Schuchter, S.R. (1986). *Dimensions of grief: Adjusting to the death of a spouse*, San Francisco: Jossey-Bass.

The Construing Widow:
Dislocation and Adaptation
in Bereavement

Linda L. Viney

SUMMARY. This account of the dislocation and adaptation of the construing of a bereaved widow begins with a description of the major assumptions of personal construct theory and of the therapy that is based on that theory. These assumptions include constructive alternativism, the range of convenience of construct systems, and the centrality and superordinancy of constructs, as well as the tightening and loosening of construing during therapy. Then I use a constructivist model of bereavement to cast light on the reported experiences of a recently widowed woman and her therapy. This account concludes with some comments on the roles of clients and therapists who take this view of bereavement.

This is an account of a personal-construct therapist's work with a bereaved client. Since some readers will not be familiar with personal-construct theory, a brief description of it and the psychotherapy based on it are first provided. I then go on to show how it can be applied with people who are experiencing the dislocation and adaptation of mourning. This account is followed by a discussion of the experiences of an elderly client, Betty G. She was referred to our team of general-hospital-based personal-construct psychologists because of her emotional distress and the lack of family to support her

---

Linda L. Viney, PhD, FAPS, is affiliated with the Department of Psychology, at The University of Wollongong, P.O. Box 1144, Wollongong, N.S.W. 2500, Australia.

at the time of her husband, John's, death after a series of heart attacks.

This account shows how a focus of the construing of people who are dealing with an irrefutable, world shattering event such as death can help to promote better leave-taking. Hopefully, it will be helpful in clarifying the normal and appropriate psychological processes which underlie the distress of bereavement for all of us who must eventually experience these events. This account should also be helpful to therapists who work with the bereaved. You will have your own beliefs about death and bereavement. I want to ask you to set those aside for a time, while you try to experience the simultaneous dislocation and adaptation of construing that takes place during bereavement. To set aside one set of beliefs in order to try out another is the essence of personal-construct therapy.

PERSONAL CONSTRUCT THEORY

A History

Personal construct theory was originally proposed by George Kelly (1955) in two large and rich volumes. As a practicing psychologist he was satisfied with neither the behavioral nor the psychoanalytic approaches which were available to him in the '30s. and began to develop some of his own ideas. However, the more clinical work he became involved in, the more Freud's notions made sense to him. He liked Freud's ways of making explicit the distress of inarticulate clients. After some time, however, he became suspicious of the success of his psychoanalytic interpretations when they were offered to clients (Kelly, 1969). The results of experiments like this eventually convinced Kelly that people live their lives on the basis of a system of interpretations. These interpretations or constructs are used both to make sense of the past and present and to anticipate the future. Also, the construct system of each individual changes during his or her lifetime. Consider, then, the huge number of different construct systems which can occur for all human beings over historical time! Kelly inferred from this consideration that "reality" provides no basis for judging the validity of any of these constructs. In other words, "all of our present interpretations of the universe are subject to revision or replacement" (Kelly, 1955). This philosophical assumption of constructive alternativism has many implications for personal-construct therapists. The most important of these is that the value of a person's construct system lies, not in how accurately it mirrors "reality," but in how well it explains past and predicts future life events.

The Theory

The basic assumption of personal-construct theory is that people are always trying to interpret what has happened and to anticipate what is going to happen to them (Bannister & Fransella, 1986). We make these interpretations and predictions through our systems of personal constructs. Each person has a unique construct system. A construct is really a way of viewing the world. Constructs allow us to differentiate between objects and events, and even people and concepts. They are two-sided, like a coin, for example, "fancy-plain," "generous-mean." By applying our systems of constructs, we make sense of what is going on. We develop meanings from our experiences.

When we construe objects and events, people and concepts, we find that some of our constructs are more useful than others. The range of experiences to which a construct may be usefully applied is called its range of convenience. Core constructs are those by which people maintain their sense of identity and existence. These constructs lead us to behave as if certain of our attitudes and beliefs were reflections of some real and lasting core, the inner self. Core constructs become those which are used most frequently to construe oneself and others very close to oneself. Betty G. will show how difficult it is for people to change these core constructs. There is less difficulty with those which are of less central importance, or, in other words, are more peripheral. For example, "I like apples" is a peripheral construct which can easily be changed, when they become tasteless and soft, to "I don't like end-of-season apples."

Another set of constructs which it is hard for us to change are those which are high in our hierarchical system of constructs. These constructs have many patterns of influence, so that, if they are changed, many other constructs must also be changed. These constructs high in the hierarchy are called superordinate constructs. Those which have fewer paths of influence in the construct system are known as subordinate constructs. An example showing the relationship between particular subordinate and superordinate constructs may be useful here. The process by which the higher level construct is arrived at is called "laddering" (Bannister & Fransella, 1986). It starts with the lower level construct. For example, a woman was helped to describe one of her constructs by asking her to thing of a way in which some of the shoes in a shop window were alike and others were different. She replied with the construct I mentioned earlier: "plain-fancy." This was a subordinate construct for her. To help her to ladder she was asked the question, "Why is this important?" The higher level construct she then produced was "sensible-silly." With further laddering, through the asking the "why?" question, she eventually could go no further than the superordinate construct "useful-useless." To be personally useful and to have friends that she could value for this quality was central to her construct system.

Our construing and evaluation interpretations and anticipations are constantly being revised, as are our construct systems. We are always making adaptive revisions so that our interpretations and anticipations remain based on experienced events. When faced with the likely death of a loved person, people experience major changes in their lives. They may therefore require major changes in their construct systems (Epting & Neimeyer, 1983). Such changes are unlikely to occur without emotional distress. Anxiety, for example, is said by personal-construct theorists to occur when a new experience is beyond the range of convenience of people's construct systems, that is, when they can't make sense of what is happening to them. Negative feelings, in general, occur when peoples' construct systems do not permit effective interpretations and anticipations so that they experience invalidation. Positive feelings, such as hope, contentment, and joy, result from confirmation of their construct systems, that is, they come from validation. When a couple have conflicting expectations about who will put the garbage out, ("It's your turn!'' ''No, it's your turn!''), they both experience invalidation of their constructs. When the same couple take the time to understand one another's constructs about the garbage, they experience validation.

PERSONAL-CONSTRUCT THERAPY

Reconstruction

Reconstruction is central to personal construct psychotherapy. Kelly (1955) has provided a highly detailed account of this in his second volume. Other accounts include a recently published book of therapeutic practice (Epting, 1984) and earlier case reports of mine (Viney, 1981; 1987). These accounts focus on the reconstruing by the client. Such reconstruing is achieved chiefly through the loosening of constructs for the purpose of freer exploration, and the tightening of constructs for better predictive power. The aim of such psychotherapy is for the client to become more aware of the options available to him or her (Fransella 1985). It is achieved by a sharing of constructs between client and therapist (Landfield, 1971). The psychotherapy relationship can be viewed as a laboratory in which the therapist works with the client as a co-researcher to test and secure validation for some of the client's constructs (Kelly, 1955).

Clients in personal construct therapy have a range of therapeutic movements available to them. Loosening and tightening are the most important of these (Viney, Benjamin, & Preston, in press-c). I describe them here in some detail, as well as the way in which the client can change the content of constructs, modify them, and move out of traps formed by those constructs. Therapeutic movements in which the client takes the initiative, as well as the therapist, are also considered. All of these therapeutic movements are also possible for the common constructs and forms of construing of formulae in constructional family therapy (Viney, Benjamin, & Preston, in press-a).

Loosening and Tightening

Loosening and tightening of the client's construing is necessary when constructs have become inflexible in the predictions they make. For example, a client who, complaining about her husband not helping her in the house, used construing which was too tight when she said: "If I ask him to help, he never will." When her therapist opened up other interpretations of the situation for her, she was eventually able to show the loosening which had taken place: "If I ask him to help before he starts to watch TV, he may help." Tightening of construing, on the other hand, is necessary when the construct system provides only a vague, confused view of the world. Another client showed this problem: "I don't know what all this fuss about my health is about. It's all beyond me. I'll let the doctors decide what to do with me." His understanding of his physical condition was minimal, and insufficient to allow him to plan a life style suited to it which also met his psychological needs. His construing was tightened by helping him to set physical and psychological goals for himself and to monitor their achievement.

Modifying old constructs is another form of therapeutic movement. This example is from another client who was dealing with illness and disability: "I've lost a leg from diabetics; and that is just too much for me to cope with." Her construing of her disability as "overwhelming" was, in time, modified to "very difficult, a challenge." Such movements include, too, clients moving out of traps laid by their own constructs. An example follows from a socially isolated man: "I'm a Scot; and Scots are unforgiving." The implications of this pair of constructs were that he had to maintain grudge-bearing relationships with his family and work colleagues. When he was able to modify the second of the pair, he was freed to establish and maintain relationships which were more satisfying both to himself and to those around him.

Initiatives by Therapists and Clients

Some therapeutic movements occur after initiatives taken by the therapist. For example, the therapist can emphasize the alternative perspectives available to the client, for example, "You can choose to see your relationship with your daughter as finished or as something the two of you could work on together." The therapist can also encourage the client to search for validation of his or her constructs outside the therapeutic relationship: "You say that your wife doesn't understand you; but had you thought that if you put your view of things to her, the way you did to me, that she might be able to?" In order to help the client understand his or her construct system better the therapist can also initiate the use of techniques employed by other types of psychotherapists, such as analysis of the client's dreams.

The client also takes initiatives leading to therapeutic movements. He or she can check out some constructs with the therapist, especially when no validation for them is available from elsewhere. For example, "No one seems to agree with me, but I'm sure that if I work harder I'll get a promotion. What do you think?" This forms an invitation to the therapist to explore his or her possibly different construing of the situation. The client can also use the therapy as an opportunity to become aware of some as-yet-unarticulated nonverbal constructs. A client who had, for example, only a nonspecific, unspoken comprehension of the link between her migraines and the tensions she was experiencing at work, was able to use her therapist to put this link into words for her. The client can also secure help from the therapist in reorganizing his or her construct system. A recently widowed client had moved to live with her daughter after her husband's recent death. Her core constructs were based on her ability to work in a team, as she had with her husband. Her daughter's already established routing permitted the client little teamwork. She therefore used her therapist to help her reduce the importance of these constructs and put others, concerning the pleasures she could give herself, in their place.

PERSONAL-CONSTRUCT THEORY
AND THE BEREAVED:
BETTY G'S LOSS

I shall now turn to an account of the psychological processes of bereavement which introduces some special personal construct concepts designed to deal with mourning: dislocation, and adaptation in its two forms of assimilation and accommodation. These concepts are described below. These psychological processes are illustrated by the case of Betty G.

Betty's History

She worked with a different personal construct therapist for a month before her husband, John's, death and for another 3 months afterwards. During this time it became apparent that Betty had grown up with a younger sister in comfortable financial circumstances, and with parents who provided the girls with a powerful model of conjugal care. Betty, although she did well in school, left at 14 years of age to take a secretarial course. Her parents did not want her to work but she was eager to do so, "so I could meet people." It was through her secretarial job that she met John G. When John's family refused to accept her because she was not a Roman Catholic, she wanted, for a few months, to withdraw from the relationship for his sake. She finally consented and settled down in their new home to wait for a family to arrive. The garden bloomed and her ability with a needle became well known, but the awaited family did not eventuate. Betty, while feeling guilty about this, became very involved with her sister's children. During John's rise in his profession, she had developed into an excellent hostess and had many friends; but she had been enjoying the opportunity to spend more time with him which his retirement provided.

Before his death Betty worked hard to prepare herself for the loss of John, but felt guilty as she did so.

> I keep saying to myself: "You're going to have to learn to live a life without him, my girl." I know I ought to start thinking of this, taking up with my friends again. Many of them are widows. I'll have no trouble fitting in. But I feel so awful about it! It seems so disloyal to John! I just want to stay as close to him for as long as possible.

She was aware of the importance of the psychological tasks that waited for her but, sensibly, she wanted to make the most of her remaining time with John. When he died her initial reactions were very mixed.

> I feel so confused. I tried to be ready for this. But you can't live your entire life with a man and then be whole the moment he is gone. I feel angry, guilty and most of all almost overwhelmingly sad. And yet I have such good memories of John. I have so many feelings, it is almost too much for me. I wish I could turn them all off for a while.

A Constructivist Account of Bereavement

Theories about bereavement have tended to assume that it occurs in a series of separate, identifiable stages (Bowlby, 1980; Freud, 1967; Kubler-Ross, 1969; Raphael, 1983). Certain bereavement processes, such as denial, are therefore assumed to occur initially. Betty's mixed set of reactions would, however, be expected by a personal-construct therapist. The personal construct approach to bereavement sees it as resulting in dislocation and adaptation of the construct system which can occur simultaneously for the bereaved person (Viney, 1985; Woodfield & Viney, 1985). Dislocation represents the failure of the bereaved person to anticipate new experiences in her world. Adaptation can take place in two ways. When it occurs through assimilation, the construct system of the bereaved person does not change but his or her perceptions of some events do. Where adaptations occur through accommodation, parts of his or her construct system change to account for some events.

Dislocation of the personal construct system of the widow is apparent in the shock and numbness, anger, guilt, sadness, despair and anxiety shown. The last of these emotions will serve as an example. Anxiety can be experienced as "waves of discomfort" lasting 20 minutes to an hour. They may be nonspecific and vague. Or they may be specific fears, such as being concerned about how to behave in the new role of widow. As has been noted, anxiety occurs when the events which are experienced are beyond the range of convenience of her construct system. The bereaved person who is anxious recognizes that constructs are failing her now or in the future. Events seem to call for new constructs, which the bereaved person does not have. She becomes anxious if the most important constructs do not allow acceptance of the implications of the death of the loved one, that is, incorporation of them without involving significant dislocation of her construct system. If the implications of the death involve the dislocation of core rather than peripheral constructs, the anxiety of the widow will be more pervasive.

Assimilation is one way in which the widow adapts using her construct system (Viney, 1985). She tries to change or assimilate the confronting event by denying its existence or by insisting that other people agree with her interpretations of such events. Some of the psychological manifestations of this assimilative processes are denial, hostility and idealization. Accommodation, the other adaptational process, involves a change in the bereaved's constructs. It is manifested in defenses against distress, depression, and aggression. It involves the active elaboration of the personal-construct system. The widow who is distressed senses a need to reorganize her construct system. This is done slowly because the system is an essential chart for her personal adventures, and such reorganization must take into account the relationships between superordinate and subordinate constructs. The widow will usually manage to live with the anxiety and keep opening herself to moderate amounts of confusion in order to be able to revise the construct system continuously.

From the vantage point of this personal-construct approach, each bereaved person can be seen as involved as an active participant in his or her bereavement reaction. The bereavement reaction is a conscious experience, accessible to evaluation, introspection, and, if necessary, psychotherapy. By applying personal-construct theory the bereavement reaction can be anticipated, understood and helped. The adaptability of the personal-construct system of each bereaved person determines the efficacy of his or her adjustment to bereavement. For example, the widow who has defined her identity and the meaning of her life inflexibly in terms of her marriage and husband may become a prisoner of her own construct system. The widow whose prior beliefs about herself and her marriage have encompassed a broader perspective has a better chance of discovering those choices which lead to her freedom.

Betty's Dislocation and Adaptation

Betty's initial reactions to John's death included several signs of dislocation of her construct system. For example, the guilt which she had described earlier became much stronger.

> I don't know if I did the right thing about the funeral arrangements. When I've had to do things like that before, John's been here to help me. I'm afraid that coffin was too fancy, with those great curly handles! John wouldn't have liked that! He would have thought that I was being too ostentatious! Maybe I spent too much! Oh dear!

Further discussion of Betty's guilt feelings soon revealed that it was not so much John's view of her that she was worried about but her own. It was her own core and superordinate constructs which she was in danger of violating (Hoadland, 1983). Constructs such as "as John's wife, I do things well" were being invalidated for her. Further exploration of her constructs with her therapist helped her to understand why she felt this guilt and at the same time to resolve it.

Denial was another sign of the dislocation of her construct system. Like may widows (Rapheal, 1980), she found ways of distorting the fact of John's death. Sometimes this distortion was to the extent of seeing him physically in places he had often occupied in their home. These "manifestations" frightened her; but she was reassured to hear from her therapist that they are not unusual for people who have lost a loved person. They faded after the first month of bereavement. More persistent was her clinging to constructs that still assumed her major role in life to being John's wife. That construct of hers noted earlier, "as John's wife, I do things well," was one example of this. Although changes in the constructs lower in her hierarchical system were quicker, this kind of protection of her core constructs was expected to continue some time after she and her therapist agreed to end her therapy.

Some of the assimilation in Betty's construct system after her bereavement was apparent in her hostility. This was rarely directed at her therapist but often at others.

> I find myself looking at other women of my age whose men are still with them, and thinking: Why are they so lucky? Why have they still got their husbands? They didn't put into their marriages what I put into ours. Honestly, I could smack their faces. They look so smug! They don't deserve them!

Betty was trying here to secure validation for some of her constructs which had been invalidated by her bereavement. In this case, an important construct of hers was identified, in part, as "if I work hard, I deserve to be happy." She gradually came to accept that, although it might have been a useful, predictive construct when she was a child in school, as a mature woman it might prove to be too tight. As she loosened this construing in therapy, she also began to use up some of her energy generated by her hostility in playing tennis with her neighbors.

Another element of her initial bereavement reaction which indicated that as she adapted, she was assimilating, was her idealization of John. This, too, is a very common element (Parkes, 1972).

> He was the best husband a woman could have. He was always kind and considerate. He often brought me flowers, not just for birthdays but to surprise me. He never raised his voice to me. And I never needed to raise my voice to him.

Now John's view of their relationship had been somewhat different. He valued it greatly; but before he died, he had also admitted to his therapist that they had argued. This idealization by Betty may have been in part a result of the guilt she was experiencing. After a marriage which had not been successful, a bereaved partner can sometimes maintain this idealization for years. Since the marriage of Betty and John had been a successful and rewarding one, Betty did replace this idealized picture of her husband but not until a month after his death. The psychotherapeutic work on her guilt probably also helped with this adaptational process.

Signs of accommodation in her bereavement processes were apparent, that is, she began to change the content of some of her constructs. At first this was a very painful process.

> I'm so tense and jumpy. I can't seem to concentrate. I can't read a book, not even a newspaper. Even when I'm getting myself a meal, which I don't really want, I'll stop in the middle and forget what I was doing.

This anxiety was evidence that John's death had brought about other experiences for her which were beyond the range of convenience of her construct system. The apparently simple statement of "I'm a widow now" caused her to sob with an intensity she had not shown when talking of other events. Exploration of this was helpful to her. She learned that it was a construct with many implications, from making sure the roof gutters of her house don't block with leaves when it rains to maybe being someday available for a relationship with another man. It was 2 months after his death before she could start to deal with some of these implications. When she was able eventually to include the construct in her system, her anxiety would fall considerably; but it would be many months before her construct system would change to accommodate this new care construct of widowhood.

Accommodation was further apparent in the feelings of depression Betty expressed.

> There are times when I feel so empty and lost . . . It's as if there is nothing left for me . . . Now that John is gone . . . I feel so lonely. It's as if a part of me has gone, forever.

She, like many other bereaved people, was tightening some of her constructs too much in the face of her loss (Niemeyer, 1983). This had an immediate advantage for her in that it restricted the number of unpleasant events stemming from John's death with which she had to deal. These feelings of depression were, however, very distressing to her. This tightening would have, however, also limited her ability to adapt to her new situation in the long term. She was therefore encouraged to explore and to accept her feelings of sadness and loneliness. She was also encouraged to try loosening her constructs, both in working with the psychotherapist and in talking with her friends. This is one way in which the support of friends is very important during bereavement, that is, validating new and appropriate constructs. Her friends also helped her, of course, to deal with some of her loneliness.

THE CONTRIBUTIONS OF CLIENTS AND THERAPISTS TO BEREAVEMENT THERAPY

This personal-construct therapy account of the major psychological reactions to bereavement has been presented in four sections. In the first section I introduced personal-construct theory, providing descriptions of constructs and of how people's construct systems adapt or fail to adapt to change. Superordinancy of constructs, core constructs, and the concept of validation were all discussed. In the second section I provided a description of personal-construct therapy, and of the therapeutic movements which occur for clients in such therapy. In the third section I applied personal-construct therapy to aid in the understanding of the psychology of a widow. A range of emotional reactions of bereaved people to their loss was explored, with some of Betty's reactions as examples. They included guilt, denial, hostility, idealization, anxiety, and depression. The personal-construct-therapy account of the dislocation and adaptation underlying her distressed reactions were accompanied by descriptions of therapeutic techniques drawn from personal-construct theory for the relief and working through of her distress.

What occurs in personal-construct therapy between any client and therapist depends on the construct systems of the client, as well as that of the therapist. Clients are likely to differ in their construing, for example, according to the point in their life span they have reached (Viney, 1987). Betty, being towards the end of her span, had a wider range of constructs available to her than a younger client would have had. For this reason, her therapy may have been shorter and her therapist less directive than with other clients. Whether this is so generally is not known as yet. Had she been older, she might have been more likely to work through her bereavement by reminiscence (Viney, Benjamin, & Preston, in press b). For personal-construct therapists, the unique value of each individual client construct system requires that the form each psychotherapeutic intervention takes — its timing and the roles played by each participant — must be negotiated anew with each client as they learn to work together. Some comments about the role of the personal-construct therapist, however, may be made.

How similar is this role to other types of therapist roles? Is, for example, reflection used? Yes, to help in identifying the client's constructs. Is interpretation employed? Yes, to help expand and develop his or her construct system. Is there a period at the beginning of psychotherapy, when the client is taught some of the concepts of personal-construct theory? Usually, no. The therapist introduces the theory to the clients as they explore the construct system of the client. In order to encourage this exploration, an active therapist is likely to be the most effective, but only during some phases of the therapy. Active interventions are made only after some phases of the therapy. Active interventions are made only after some understanding of client's construct systems is achieved through empathic listening. This understanding by the therapist is only possible if he or she has such an extensive and permeable construct system that it can encompass those of many other people, including that of the client. This understanding is best expressed by a therapist with good verbal ability. Indeed much of the client's eventual understanding of and choice within his or her construct system depend on the therapist's ability to verbalize what for the client are vague constructs yet to be articulated. In these ways, the choices available within the client's mind are clarified so that a fuller range of his or her actual choices also become available.

REFERENCES

Bannister, D., & Fransella, F. (1986). *Inquiring man*. Beckenham: Croom Helm.

Bowlby, J. (1980). Loss, sadness and depression. *Attachment and loss* (Vol.3). New York: Basic Books.

Epting, F.R. (1984). *Personal construct counseling and psychotherapy*. New York: Wiley.

Epting, F., & Neimeyer, R.A. (Eds.). (1983). *Personal meanings of death*. New York: Hemisphere.

Fransella, F. (1985). Individual psychotherapy. In E. Button (Ed.), *Personal construct theory and mental health*. Bechenham: Croom Helm.

Freud, S. (1967). Mourning and melancholia. In *Collected papers* (Vol. 4). New York: Basic Books.

Hinton, J. (1967). *Dying*. Harmondsworth: Penguin.

Hoagland, H.C. (1985). Bereavement and personal constructs: Old theories and new concepts. In F. Epting and R.A. Neimeyer (Eds.), *Personal construct meanings of death*. New York: Hemisphere.

Karst, T.O., & Trexler, L.D. (1970). Initial study using fixed role and rational emotive therapy in treating public speaking anxiety. *Journal of Consulting and Clinical Psychology*, *34*, 360.

Kelly, G.A. (1955). *The psychology of personal constructs* New York: Norton. (Vols. 1 and 2).

Kelly, G.A. (1969). The autobiography of a theory. In B. Maher (Ed.), *Clinical psychology and personality*. New York: John Wiley.

Kubler-Ross, E. (1969). *On death and dying*. New York: Macmillan.

Landfield, A.W. (1971). *Personal construct systems in psychotherapy*. Chicago: Rand McNally.

Neimeyer, R.A. (1984). Toward a personal construct conceptualization of depression and suicide. In F. Epting and R.A. Neimeyer (Eds.), *Personal meanings of death*. London: Hemisphere.

Parkes, C.M. (1972). *Bereavement: Studies of grief in adult life*. London: Tavistock Institute of Human Relations.

Raphael, B. (1980). A psychiatric model for bereavement counseling. In M. Schoenborg (Ed.), *Bereavement counseling: A multi-disciplinary approach*. Westport: Greenwood.

Raphael, B. (1983). *The anatomy of bereavement*. New York: Basic Books.

Viney, L.L. (1981) Experimenting with experience: A psychotherapeutic case study. *Psychotherapy*, *18*, 271-278.

Viney, L.L. (1985). The bereavement process: A new approach. *Bereavement Care*, *4*, 27-32.

Viney, L.L. (1987). Psychotherapy in a case of physical illness: "I have a choice." In R.A. and G.J. Neimeyer (Eds.), *A casebook in personal construct therapy*. New York: Springer.

Viney, L.L. (1987). A sociophenomenological approach to life span development complementing Erikson's sociodynamic approach. *Human Development*, *30*, 125-136.

Viney, L.L., Benjamin, Y.N., & Preston, C. (in press-a). Constructivist family therapy with the elderly. *Journal of Family Psychology*.

Viney, L.L., Benjamin, Y.N., & Preston, C. (in press-b). Mourning and reminiscence. Parallel psychotherapeutic processes for the elderly. *International Journal of Aging and Human Development*.

Viney, L.L., Benjamin, Y.N., & Preston, C. (in press-c). Personal construct therapy for the elderly. *International Journal of Cognitive Therapy*.

Woodfield, R.L., & Viney, L.L. (1985). A personal construct approach to bereavement. *Omega*, *16*, 1-13.

Object Loss
and Pathological Consequence:
A Study in the Psychological Treatment
of Loss and Self-Injury

Louis Birner

SUMMARY. The loss of a parent or mate can produce profound emotional disharmonies for the immediate survivors, especially when the loss is part of a continuum of traumatic events. The level of pathological interaction with a lost object on the part of the survivor can be both intensified and redefined over the passage of time. A basically healthy survivor can repair and restructure the life patterns after a loss. Successful mourning of a parent or mate in a good relationship often leads to renewed strength and hope. In a very negative and pathological relationship, there is no true mourning when a spouse or parent dies. In the shadow of a melancholic night, evil and tragic consequences often follow such a loss. The dead object then becomes empowered with the ever present force of a negative introject, damning and stifling the life force of the survivor.

Treating such a survivor in psychoanalytic practice requires a knowledge of the human condition, especially as it relates to tragedy and the loss of significant persons. One must work to free the patient from an object who could not provide growth and emotional support in life and who, in death, entraps the living by serving as a self-destructive directive and influence. Psychoanalytic treatment must demand that the dead are to be buried along with their injurious directives so that the living may survive.

Louis Birner, PhD, is a member of the National Psychological Association for Psychoanalysis and The New York Center for Psychoanalytic Training. Presently he is in the private practice of psychoanalysis and group therapy specializing in the isolated and creative patient. Address correspondence to the author at 823 Park Ave., New York, NY 10021.

223

Mary was seen in psychotherapy for 5 years during her first treatment experience. She presented the problems of anorexia, paranoid ideation, and masochistic submission. However, the initial and major complaint was one of intense anxiety. At age 19 her life history was a patchwork of tragedy, injury, and survivorship. By a quirk of biological fate, she was born the lightest skinned member of a black family and was resented for her "light color" by her family members, especially her mother, sister, and brother. Shortly after her brother was born, her father left the family for another woman. The mother later became sick with tuberculosis and had to be hospitalized. At the age of five, Mary was placed in a foster home where she was the victim of cruelty and discrimination. She, her older sister, and younger brother suffered the object loss of both parents at an early age, along with the cultural shock of a loveless foster home.

For 5 years, along with her sister and brother, Mary stayed in the foster home and endured abuse and racial discrimination. The only positive emotional consequence of her foster-home experience was that she discovered that she was intellectually gifted and was one of the best students in her school. She was resented for being black by the whites in the school and resented by the blacks for being "too light."

At age 10, Mary was reunited with her mother who had recovered from her tuberculosis. The mother was a highly sadistic and exploitative woman who showed her daughter very little love or affection. In the first part of her life, Mary was separated from her mother and father and discriminated against by both whites and blacks. She was then returned to her mother to be abused again. Her first decade centered on abandonment, loss, and reunion with her mother.

Where Mary found the psychological strength to survive her first 10 years is uncertain. Her survival and ability to function is a testament to her courage and will to live. What she could not get emotionally from her mother, her absent father, or siblings in terms of love and caring, she found in the world of art and in the literary treasures of her local library. Sound and sight were a part of her creative world; she dipped deeply into this well of discovery and would listen to opera records and visit museums. She studied art in high school and, after graduating from high school, established herself in a productive career in the commercial art field.

When she was reunited with her mother, Mary also started living out the role of a Cinderella. The mother was both a man-hater and sadistic, and would berate men and beat her for any reason, especially when she suspected her daughter of committing the crime of masturbation. The mother would often fly into psychotic rages and whip Mary with an ironing cord, shouting insults and accusations. Because Mary could sew and make clothes and made money through babysitting and other chores, her mother would frequently exploit her talents and labor and borrow her money, repaying her only with promises.

Mary had boyfriends through adolescence but did not maintain a relationship for any period of time. Although she enjoyed sexual contact and intercourse, her attitude toward the opposite sex was one of distrust and ambivalence. It was at the time of her high-school graduation that her father reunited with her mother. Her father was alcoholic, depressed, and suffering from a heart condition. Although the mother hated the father, she took him back into the home. When drunk, the father would make sexual passes at Mary. When she was 19, a friend told her about psychotherapy and referred her for treatment.

It was noted during the first session that Mary was an extremely thin and graceful young woman. She spoke well and demonstrated that she was intellectually bright. She volunteered that the reason she wanted to come into treatment was because she felt nervous. When asked to explain what she meant by that, she indicated that if she was on the bus or in the street, unless she felt and looked perfectly dressed and neat, she knew "people would look at me." She experienced nightmares but was never suicidal. Her reality sense seemed somewhat impaired. At age 19, she had no involvement with drugs. She was seen on a once-a-week basis with the therapeutic goal of "getting rid of my nervousness."

Mary's sessions provided for her the much-needed verbal release of expressing her conflicts, fears, and angers. However, it was indeed horrific for me to hear of some of her family scenes with her sadistic mother and/or alcoholic, lecherous father. After being in treatment for a short time, Mary was encouraged to leave her parents home and find a place to live by herself. She did soon move out of her parents home and established a single life-style. This gave her a chance to grow emotionally inasmuch as it removed her from so much constant abuse and devaluation. The focus of treatment was to assist her in maturing in the areas of enjoying herself and giving up her fear and paranoid expectancy. She was also anorexic; her inappropriate weight was a reflection of her not being able to find the vital supplies of love and caring. Most of her life there were no consistent loving figures who provided positive emotional and narcissistic supplies for her. She had had little emotional feeding and reassurance. What was, of course, not stated by Mary was her underlying residue of conflict from her childhood depression. Although her creativity and curiosity enriched her, it did not remove the scars of her childhood and abandonment depression. The anorexia as such was not dealt with as a treatment issue, but as she became better Mary did put on some weight. She became more comfortable with food and with nurturing herself.

The goal of treatment was for Mary to claim her self and to work through some of her depression. She did make progress in these areas. The one area that was not resolved when she left treatment at the age of 24 was her gross ambivalence toward men. Men were emotionally killed off by her if they were not "perfect." Although she had a strong and healthy sex drive, she could not work through her basic distrust of men. Her father left her in early childhood and returned home to later abuse her sexually when she was an adolescent. His behavior toward her was indeed a trauma and a narcissistic humiliation. An additional trauma was to be found in her seeing him drunk and stuporous. The father at one time was a hard-working electrician. In cups, he was a pathetic, unemployed alcoholic waiting to die.

When Mary terminated treatment, life was going in positive directions and, indeed, she had accomplished much in the time she spent in therapy. She was doing very well vocationally, had a number of friends, and was enjoying her life. She also maintained a passionate interest in art and music.

*   *   *

Some 20 years later, Mary left a drunken message on my answering tape that I should call her back because she wanted to see how I was doing. The smell of tragedy seemed to emanate from her alcoholic words. When I returned her call, she stated in an inebriated tone that all was well and that she wanted to find out how her former shrink was doing. Her denial covered up some severe problems. I called Mary again the next day. Fortunately she was sober, and an appointment was made for a consultation.

The 20 years that had elapsed since she last saw me were a tale of loss and sadness, much like the first 5 years of her life. Mary had met and married a young man who left her after their child was born, never to see her or his son again. Her mother and father had died after she left treatment, her brother was in prison, and for good reasons she had disowned her sister. All she had presently were her 16-year-old son and her other interests which were now work and drinking. Somehow Mary sensed that she was in deep trouble and realized that she needed help once more.

If there is some truth to the idea that enough straws can break a camel's back, fate insulted Mary sufficiently to break her emotional back. It was one final insult that put her in a mental hospital, after which she started drinking and became an alcoholic. For 10 years, Mary had a love-hate relationship with her boss who also supervised her work. Jane, who was her boss and supervisor, was an impassioned, perfectionistic sadist who looked to demean Mary at every turn. Mary fought back and they related to each other by becoming very devoted enemies. Jane was a refugee from Hitler's Germany. In many ways she was the daily evil reincarnation of Mary's mother. When Jane died suddenly, Mary went into a state of disbelief, a denial of reality, and an extreme paranoid reaction. Something was the matter, she felt, and she went to her medical doctor who wisely had her institutionalized for a 2-week period of time. After she left the institution, she was medicated and returned to work. With Jane's death, a newly empowered introject was incorporated into her superego to insult her psyche. Mary now had an additional enemy: alcohol. No doubt every drink she consumed was also sanctioned by tragic examples of her deceased father.

Because her mother, father, sister, and brother related to her in an exploitative way, Mary raised her son, John, by indulging him and giving him everything he demanded. Her own masochism motivated her to reward her son's unrealistic narcissistic expectations. In effect, she used her son to continue her life pattern of being exploited. At 16, her son was an extremely bright and able student who had no older males with whom to identify other than an uncle who spent time in prison on various criminal charges, including drugs and assault. The neighborhood in which they lived was also rife with drugs and crime.

When Mary returned to therapy again after 20 years, she seemed pleased to see me once more. Time had changed her. She had put on some more weight, but was still thin. Her face showed lines of sorrow, and the tone of her voice was uncertain. As in her very first session, she was still very anxious and paranoid. Her life had lost much of its meaning. She had suffered bouts of drinking, followed by periods of drying out and attending A.A. There was a certain depressed and beaten quality to Mary. As she reviewed her life, she thought that being alive was almost too much for her. She did admit to having suicidal fantasies and feelings. Her initial transference was one of sorrow and despair, emptiness and uncertainty.

As for my own countertransference reactions, I experienced a feeling of sorrow. In truth, this once bright and beautiful woman was now an emotionally broken wreck. My successful patient of 20 years past was no more. The work of her first therapeutic experience seemed almost lost. Most of the accomplishments of her life appeared to be undone as she sat in the consultation room entrapped in a veil of depressed hopelessness. The immediate therapeutic challenge was to stabilize her life, to contain her self-destructiveness, and to assist her in becoming once more a sober person. Since she appeared to be in crisis, she was referred for medication and seen in psychotherapy on a twice-weekly basis. She was also told to stop drinking totally.

It was striking to observe how regressed Mary had become during the initial stages of therapy. She had designed for herself a cruel life of work and drink. When she became dry, she did not know what to do with her time when she was not working. Her free time was for self-torture. I suggested that she find an enjoyable interest to fill her idle hours. She followed this suggestion and began playing the piano once more. Since her son had discovered girls and was involved with being a 16-year-old, he was not now a major part of her life. Music began to become a vital part of her existence, and then fate stepped in in a curious way. Her neighbors were so impressed with her playing and practicing that they asked her to give music lessons to their children. Mary now had a new part-time profession! Quite a pleasant switch from being a chronically depressed evening alcoholic.

In a few months Mary was taken off her medication and was once more very involved with her interests in art and music. She was slowly beginning to recover. As her recovery started, Mary's son began acting out by being defiant and demanding. His need to extract money from her for any excuse increased. John also started to become threatening and abusive. Mary was cautioned not to indulge her son, but not to provoke him either. He was a physically huge and aggressive adolescent. It seemed now that something was amiss. New tragedies were about to become a part of Mary's life.

After 6 months in treatment, Mary missed a session and called me to tell me she was in the hospital and would have to come to her session the following week. When she was asked what had happened, she stated that her son demanded money from her and she said no. The "no" provoked him to take a pot of hot chili off the stove and hit her with it on the side of her face and head, burning her skin and almost blinding her. "What should I do? What should I do?" she cried on the phone. Realizing that she could not now return home to a potential assault or murder, I said, "Have him immediately arrested. You cannot stay in the same home with your son any longer." When John was arrested, she learned that he was free-basing crack with a friend of his on and off for the past 6 months. He was probably living under a chemically induced psychosis.

Once more Mary had to deal with a negative and hurtful object whom she had once truly loved and cared for. Therapy took on a different focus for her in terms of her own emotional and physical survival. She had to reclaim her role as a mother and also as a self-loving person. Through much effort, she arranged for the court to place her son in a group home and be given psychotherapy. Mary herself had to realize that she was limited in terms of offering discipline, guidance, and direction to her son. His therapist, the court, and the group home were now his maturational agents of new realities. Of course, with these new and terrible problems she brought to treatment a sense of guilt and self-accusation. Mary was freqently confronted with the legal and emotional reality that nothing justified her son's assaultive behavior and that nothing justified his taking crack. Still, there remained the problems of mastering her depression and of restoring and assembling a life out of the debris of recent tragic events. What follows is a theoretical discussion on these issues and treatment approaches to dealing with the deep psychic hurt of the tragic events of her son's betrayal and physical assault.

TREATMENT APPROACHES TO DEALING WITH THE VICTIMS OF TRAGIC EVENTS

No therapist enjoys dealing with a patient's tragedy. Indeed, Searles (1979) notes that depressive and suicidal feelings in a very disturbed patient can induce suicidal feelings in the analyst. The therapist who has emotionally mastered similar types of tragic events in his or her own life can more fully understand the patient's reaction to monstrous blows of fate. The most vital psychological construct for the therapist is that tragedy is a life event that has to be mastered by the ego. Whatever the situation, the analyst has to work to move the patient from reactions of self-hate, depression, and melancholia to some sense of psychic peace and resolution.

Any true therapist in practice today must have a deep sense of the many tragedies of our time and a personal approach to dealing with such events, along with an understanding of these horrors. We live in the age of nuclear weapons; poverty and homelessness; AIDS; cancers; holocausts; sexual, racial, and religious hatred and discrimination; drug wars and the everyday crimes of murder, rape, and mugging. The psychic landscape has grown dark in the 20th century. A number of psychoanalytic writers have noted that we live today in a nonhuman and toxic world. Therefore, a responsible therapist realizes that he or she works in a time in history that is framed in tragedy and insanity. The personal tragedies of the patient are often a part of the historical events of our time.

Mary was the child of racial bigotry, poverty, and a sadistic and cruel institution for the homeless. She was also the product of her family's hatred of her. When she returned to treatment, she was broken and alcoholic, depressed, in despair, and in the throes of a schizophrenic depression. Nothing in her life was working for her. She was reliving and suffering loss and grief. She had the schizophrenic vision of a cold, empty world full of dead and hateful objects. Mary was caught in pathological reaction to object loss, self-hate, and a grief that she could neither mourn nor resolve.

It was Abraham (1911/1927, pp. 137-156) who first made the observation that healthy people mourning a loss can recover. Mourning is a normal and natural way of handling loss and grief. Melancholy and prolonged depression, however, are grief gone wild. A depression mixed with psychotic postures and drugs is a statement that there are shocking events in process that the ego cannot integrate and bring into psychic balance. My patient, like many of us, had felt overwhelmed by the events and moods of her life and, like some of us, had lost her ability to cope adequately. She was, in effect, done in by the pressures of her past and the realities of her present. Her ego could not integrate the final blow of the loss of her hateful boss whom she needed to psychologically maintain her emotional stability. The boss-lady probably regulated her daily amounts of projected anger and self-hate and served as mother substitute. Without her boss in her life Mary drowned in a sea of self-hate. She hated herself instead of hating her boss.

When Mary returned to therapy, there was an implicit demand on her part that her therapist should help her. She wanted to be healed. She also wanted to die! In the very first moments of the therapeutic encounter, there has to be some type of conviction *expressed* to the patient that the therapist feels able to take on the huge task of treatment and to work with the patient to lighten the burden of psychic pain and make things better. Especially in the schizophrenic depression or panic, patients have to feel that there is someone out there who is deeply concerned for their welfare. The feeling and conviction that the therapist can be helpful is not necessarily a verbal statement; it is a conscious and unconscious communication. It is an essential communication. Staying alive and getting better is to be valued, and it is the main therapeutic communication for people in despair.

A patient's profound grief, shock, and depersonalized responses along with a weakened hold on reality make specific emotional demands on the therapist. No classical psychoanalytic treatment can be employed if the patient is significantly regressed to the psychotic level. Hence, the temporary use of medication and a need to design and reinforce a therapeutic environment for the patient is indicated as a treatment procedure.

While it was clear that Mary had great hostility and anger toward the boss/mother figure, she reacted to this hostility by behaving like her father and becoming an alcoholic. Further, she vented her anger toward her mother by attacking herself and giving up her high level of functioning. She was no longer the bright, hard-working, good daughter/employee. Mary was working on murdering her psyche, attacking her self; and she was caught in a ritual of narcissistic humiliation and devaluation. The ritual was an encapsulation and repetition of her being unloved as a young child who was later abandoned and hurt by her parents. She eventually became a wreck who had to be institutionalized. What caused her to fall into her psychotic-like grief with an alcoholic defense was probably the reality that the death of her boss was another narcissistic wound, a statement that the dead could never love her again. When the boss was alive, there was a slender hope that the boss might change. With her death, there was no longer such hope for Mary. She was psychologically tied once again to another loveless mother and another cruel superego. In effect, she had integrated a new messenger of self-hate into her psyche; she incorporated an introject equally as vicious as her mother.

The literature provides concepts and approaches to treating a patient in despair. There are such treatment suggestions as the creation of support groups. No concept is valid and no treatment procedure is valid unless the patient emotionally perceives that the sorrow and the pain he or she is living with can be heard by the therapist. Talking about and sharing one's despair in the treatment situation gives the patient a chance to hear and review his or her grief and to study the language of despair. With a patient such as Mary, it is important for the therapist to be in touch with his or her own personal tragedies and attempts at the mastery of tragic sorrowful life events. Patients in despair elicit powerful countertransferences. In some of her sessions when her ego was falling apart and Mary was engulfed in anxiety, dread, and fear, I reminded myself that at times in my own life my own ego had almost fallen apart and somehow I made it back into reality. The past sorrow and despairs of my own life now became an emotional ally. Those events that once almost destroyed my own ego now in memory became an ego support and an ally to the treatment situation. The unexpressed countertransference to Mary was: "If I became somewhat free of my own despair, you too can be free of your despair."

In effect, in the mastering of grief and despair, the patient and the therapist serve each other as a form of mutual transitional objects. The patient validates the therapist's role and work by using the skills of the therapist and by not self-destructing. Growth is substituted for despair. To do the therapeutic work, the therapist must leave his or her neuroses and sorrows behind. In giving up personal grief, he or she makes a very powerful emotional statement of health. The therapist is to be seen as that vital transitional object that converts feelings of despair into words and then into hope. The patient is seen as that vital object that confirms the existence of the therapist. The patient is also a type of transitional object that moves the therapist in the direction of being what he or she should be. After all, therapy is another word for help. When the therapeutic relationship works, both parties thrive as they mutually help each other grow and mature (Searles, 1979, pp. 503-576).

Somehow Mary found her emotional strength again and was able to give up the negative influence of her former boss and all negative influences that she had symbolized. Some very interesting changes were noted as Mary worked her way out of her depression. She started to give up her virulent selfhate. Her creative and artistic interests were beginning to flourish and she would shift from discussing the hated objects of her past to talking about great operatic figures or great writers. (She was well versed in both literature and music.)

She made and renewed emotional investments in some good and friendly people from her present and past, such as her lawyer, doctor, accountant, and girlfriends. Pets were also added to her home life. It is noteworthy that an object of hate which produced an emotional breakdown was now being replaced by objects of love and caring. Mary was on the mend and was, so to speak, designing her own therapeutic environment and enjoying her life. Perhaps her son could not relate to her newfound mental health, because as his mother started to flourish John became involved with drugs. Mary first noted this when she discovered that money was missing from her purse.

The evil of the use of crack and its tragic influence has been well documented. Every day, large numbers of people commit crimes of violence and die under its influence. My patient had recovered her mental health, only to be assaulted by her son when he was under the influence of this drug. He took a pot of hot chili and assaulted her by hitting her in the face with it when she refused him money. She suffered a second-degree burn on her face and was almost blinded in one eye. Sometimes one's worst nightmare is replayed in reality. The burden of this crisis also creates the burden of making significant decisions. Realizing the gravity and criminality of the home situation, I told my patient to have her son arrested and to use the power of the court to deal with him. Murder or mayhem was probably avoided when he was arrested.

The patient brought into treatment feelings of guilt and negative grandiosity. Like the dead boss lady, the son had now become a negative introject. Mary would attack herself rather than face the rage and disappointment she felt toward her son. A series of battles now commenced in her life. Mary had to fight with the court system to get her son a good group-home placement and psychiatric help. She had to learn how to not indulge him and how to limit her relationship with him so that he could fully comprehend his responsibilities for his criminal actions.

When Mary was working with the court and various agencies, she was told she could not afford to be depressed and that she had to "take care of business." The court tends to be a bit slow in helping first-offenders and officials are not always overeager to help the disadvantaged. In effect, she was providing the interest and caring for her son that was absent when she herself was institutionalized as a child. The son did well in his group home, job, and high school. He is now preparing to go to college. Somehow he learned that his mother would no longer be there to indulge him and that if he committed another crime he would have a criminal record. Interestingly enough, he scored in the 98th percentile on his SATs.

When Mary would bring into the treatment her sorrow and despair about her son, she was confronted with the reality of her role as a mother and what she should *demand* from both the court and the social agencies. The crisis was used as a maturational experience. Mary acted on her behalf and on her son's behalf and developed the faculty of assertiveness. She was not indulged or pampered into a sense of helplessness. She, too, had to learn to accept the reality of her son's behavior and her own limitations. If her son wanted to become a crack-head, there was nothing she could do. If he wanted to grow, he had (through her efforts) a good institutional environment with a therapist to help him.

By a paradox of fate, she became the caring mother she herself was yearning to find in her own mother and boss-lady. Mary's mother died drowning in a sea of hate. Her father died in a sea of alcohol and incestuous lust. At this point, Mary and her son are separated; both are doing well and both are growing human beings. She has, through her efforts, reversed some of the tragedies this cruel world and her evil parents had in store for her.

Mary's music and art enrich her life. Alcoholism is a horror that is long past. Her life today has stability and rewards. Given the degree of tragedy and bigotry, psychosis and despair that she has endured and mastered, this patient is today an inspiration to her therapist. As is so often the case, a courageous patient emotionally enriches the therapist and justifies this form of professional work.

SOME THEORETICAL CONSIDERATIONS

The early writers who formulated the psychoanalytic theory and treatment of depression provided an intellectual understanding of the problems associated with object loss. The depressive process and pathological actions and reactions can also be viewed as the secret language of the ego in response to pain and insult. Later writers such as Jacobson (1975), Bowlby (1961, 1963), and Mahler (1966) clearly enrich our present-day understanding of the psychic mechanism of depression and depressive affects.

Jacobson makes the important observation that the depressive mood in certain cases can alter one's ability to test reality. Pathological depression clearly limits a true and full use of psychic energy. Indeed, for the pathologically depressed person too much energy is bound up in trying to handle early (or later) traumatic experience. *There is not enough of a sense of reality and self-love to understand and master the earlier traumas*. Hence, the earlier (or later) pathological traumas can be repeated and, alas, compounded through blind repetition. Conflicts that insult one's sense of worth can expand the distance between one's self-representation and one's ego ideal. The ego establishing friendly understanding of the self is lost. Hateful self-judgment can invade the psyche along with unconscious repetitions of unsolved sorrows. Bowlby (1961, 1963) has made the observation that prolonged mourning limits the child's ability to trust and to attach itself to a significant adult or parent. Mahler (1966) had noted that a depressed child has trouble individuating and becoming his or her own person. Indeed, depression is a force that works against maturation.

Depression and pathological responses are due to narcissistic insult and the sense that the self can no longer be esteemed. The chronically depressed person becomes, according to Fenichel (1945), a "love addict" who looks for a degree of love that he or she can never seem to find. Freud (1917/1957) and others have noted that depressives can react to the loss of a loved object by first identifying with it and then attacking their own ego as a way of expressing their own rage toward the dead object. Unresolved depressive conflicts tend to stop the maturational life processes and lead one into despair, apathy, and impulsive actions. In his psychosocial conception of the life cycle, Erikson (1968) noted that inhibition, trauma, and fixation totally confuse the flow and the promise of the developmental phases of the life cycle and lead the adult person to experience confusion, stagnation, and despair.

Many of our very disturbed and depressed patients speak the sad language of despair. Despair is definitely a form of language and a way of feeling and a way of looking at life. From my own perspective, chronic despair and intractable overwhelming depression are a false language and a moral lie. The depressed can be viewed as people who were forced to become emotional liars. While it is true that in reality they lost beloved objects and/or endured the cruel insults of fate, they have to be helped to learn that they must give up their pathological introjects and objects, and their depression as well. In terms of an approach to dealing with depression and tragic events, one must see them as events to be mastered. One must be intellectually and emotionally aware that one's ego is not to be crushed. Emotional health is always the ideal. The dead are always to be remembered in loving and self-loving ways.

In crisis one needs the support of people who have mastered their tragedies. Any patient who can emotionally grow and give up the negative effects and secondary gains of depression is an ego support to the therapist. Statements and acts of the patient's emotional courage are to be studied and used as future reference points. Churchill saved his nation in one of the most tragic and depressing moments of World War II, telling his people such things as "We must endure, we must persevere, we must struggle on," and "We shall fight them on the beaches. We shall fight them on the fields. *We shall never surrender.*"

In surrendering to pathology and to our hated psychic introjects, we lose hope and the precious right to claim the joys of life and to test the promise of our reality. The basic implication of life must be some form of gratification in experiencing the human condition. Surviving great loss and trauma gives one a chance to reclaim and rebuild one's life. Even the most resistant and pathetic patient on some level wants to be better. The therapist seeks to find that vital level. Gaylin (1968) states: "It is part of the wonder of man that even the state of hopelessness can be used to generate hope" (p. 391).

If anyone had a right to be depressed and irreconcilably sad, it was Freud during his last years in Vienna. His cancer had not improved; he lived under constant threat of the Nazis; the literal life or welfare of his family was most uncertain; and the nightmare reality of a concentration camp was quite possible. Whatever the possibility, Freud kept working and writing and never surrendered his human dignity. Schur (1972), in his marvelous book, relates the following:

> When things were at their worst and seemed hopeless, Anna asked Freud: "Wouldn't it be better if we all killed ourselves?" To which Freud replied with his characteristic irony and indignation: "Why? Because they would like us to?" Such was his fortitude and defiance . . . He wrote to his son Ernst on May 12, a few days after his eighty-second birthday: "Two prospects keep me going in these grim times: to rejoin you all and—to die in freedom." (p. 499)

And Freud did rejoin his family in England and maintained his dignity and continued his creative work. He achieved his final goal of dying in freedom. All of us must work to live and die in freedom from our hateful introjects, traumas, and childhood and adult depressions.

AFTERTHOUGHT

When I was in analytic school a "control analyst" who loved to show his vast erudition outlined to his classes that the true "analyst" should only work with "analytic patients." By his definition, the very depressed and the grossly disturbed would not have fit his pure standards. Therefore, they were not good candidates for treatment. Here was a man who considered himself a "true Freudian." In reality, such people are not even real human beings. In the true tradition of psychotherapy and psychoanalysis, a therapist must reach out and make contact with those who have suffered from depression, trauma, melancholia, and psychosis. "Pure analytic patients," if they do exist, are probably bores.

REFERENCES

Abraham, K. (1927). Notes on the psychoanalytic investigation and treatment of manic depressive insanity and allied conditions. *Selected papers on psychoanalysis*. London: Hogarth Press. (Original work published 1911)

Bowlby, J. (1961). Process of mourning. *International Journal of Psychoanalysis, 43*, 317-340.

Bowlby, J. (1963). Pathological mourning and childhood mourning. *Journal of the American Psychoanalytic Association, 11*, 500-511.

Erikson, E.H. (1968). *Identity, youth and crisis*. New York: W.W. Norton.

Fenichel, O. (1945). *The psychoanalytic theory of neurosis*. New York: W.W. Norton.

Freud, S. (1957). Mourning and melancholia. In J. Strachey (Ed. and Trans.), *The standard edition of the complete psychological works of Sigmund Freud* (Vol. 14, pp. 243-278). London: Hogarth Press. (Original work published 1917)

Gaylin, W. (1968). *The meaning of despair*. New York: Science House.

Jacobson, E. (1971). *Depression*. New York: International Universities Press.

Mahler, M.S. (1966). Notes on the development of basic moods: The depressive affect in psychoanalysis. In R. M. Lowenstein, L.M. Newman, M. Schur, and A.J. Solnit, (Eds.), *Psychoanalysis: A general psychology* (pp. 152-168). New York: International Universities Press.

Schur, M. (1972). *Freud: Living and dying*. New York: International Universities Press.

The Fullness of Emptiness

Edward A. Wise

SUMMARY. The experience of loss is explored as a universal and integral part of life. Therapeutic opportunities and possibilities for change are described. Benefits for therapists who allows or themselves to remain open to the intensity of their experiences are mentioned, along with ways in which grieving therapists can enhance their work with others. The healing nature of solitude is also addressed. Finally, a seven part poem entitled "The Fullness of Emptiness" is offered as a commentary on several aspects of the loss experience, including loneliness, grief, search for meaning, and creativity.

Loss, suffering and grief are inevitable human experiences, just as are attachment, pleasure, and joy. They are all parts of an organic whole of the Yin-Yang variety. No one escapes unmarked by the pain of grief, though not all allow themselves the freedom to heal. Going into the depths of one's despair, allowing the world and ourselves to shatter, is a terrifying experience. Giving in to the terror of shattering is a surrender of the self to the unknown pain that lies ahead. It requires an abandonment of the self in the face of death.

While standing on the threshold of despair, there is a universal resistance to maintain control, to prevent oneself from shattering. Such counterforce creates considerable somatic tension, anxiety, and fear as one would expect. The psychotherapist's task at this stage is to patiently join the client. A soothing presence from a

Edward A. Wise received his PhD in clinical psychology from the University of Wyoming in 1980 and his BA in 1975 from Washington University in St. Louis, MO. He is currently affiliated with the University of Tennessee at Memphis and is in full time private practice, working with adolescents and adults. Address correspondence to the author at 74 No. Cooper St., Memphis, TN 38104.

guide who trusts the client's experience and values the evolutionary adaptive capacity of the individual conveys the expectation of hope and provides the support necessary for the journey through the pain.

The actual leap into the abyss is a time of great outpouring and relief. Wailing cries of pain surface from the years and depths of attachment. Previous losses may also be recalled as the old pains join in the cries for relief. Although the intensity is overwhelming at times, in a unique way it is a sign of being alive. As the intensity subsides in its ebb and flow, it becomes clearer that the grief is a way of being, and as a living-being experience requires integration into one's daily existence. Developing the capacity to listen to and to tolerate the emptiness, to hear the old voices from the past echo in the seemingly empty present, can be greatly enhanced and facilitated in the therapeutic process. These are times of great therapeutic potential in which the client reexcavates the past and may turn to the therapist for assistance in reintegrating previously unresolved issues. The therapeutic opportunity is to assist the client in achieving an understanding and integration of those aspects of the self and the past as they are examined, while knowing that the client simultaneously integrates or introjects the soothing exploratory nature of the process as well. Grieving can be an experience that is lived creatively and as an affirmation of existence.

For the psychotherapist who experiences and accepts the pain and suffering of grief at this level, one's relationship with humanity is deepened. The sense of all of us being "in the same boat," of sharing universal realities, emerges more into the foreground of life. Recognizing that we are all more alike than we are different, and that pain is an inevitable part of all of our lives, creates a greater sense of belonging and of being a part of humankind. A deepened sense of compassion and a desire to reach out to fellow sufferers can develop, which allows for a greater acceptance and embrace of others both in and out of their pain.

As a therapist, allowing oneself to go through such intense experiences provides an opportunity to gain new understandings of the human condition and of the role of psychotherapy in the life process. It can provide the bedrock of genuine acceptance — and even embrace — of pain and suffering in working with others. Therapeutic postures that have previously been adopted and integrated into the daily work of one's therapy can be reexamined in new meaningful light and altered accordingly. By going through their own grief, therapists can develop a deepened sense of unobtrusive respect for others in their aloneness and loneliness at a level that is otherwise inaccessible.

Such an experience also forces one to reexamine issues that ultimately relate to the value of one's existence in solitude and in relationship to others. The meaningless aspects of one's life become even emptier and heavier to carry out, making them easier to give up and replace with more fulfilling and satisfying endeavors. Similarly, for the therapist experiencing such grief, unsuccessful ways of being with the client are easier to drop, while waiting for new avenues to unfold. Uncertainty and ambiguity are easier to tolerate as one joins the process to see what emerges. The adventuresome nature of the work becomes even more compelling as one looks inward more openly to see what might develop, while providing the client the same opportunity.

At times in the mourning process existence becomes aloneness and loneliness, possessing the potential for greater self-awareness through confrontation with oneself and with the empathic resonance of the therapist. Negative aspects of the self, previously disowned or minimized, can be examined as one recalls the past. These "self-condemnations" should not be summarily dismissed as transient guilt reactions, but genuinely explored as opportunities for change and forgiveness. In the solitude of aloneness one can come to depths of understanding about oneself and others that are otherwise much more difficult, if not impossible, to access and accept. Confronting these aspects of the self is one way in which the individual begins to experience a greater sense of possibility, which gives rise to hope. It also provides an opportunity to accept some aspects of the self as unfortunate, and to forgive oneself for the past. Letting go of the self in the past, of course, facilitates the emergence of a new way of being, and thus brings with it hope for regeneration and renewal. As Moustakas (1961) eloquently states, "Let there be loneliness, for where there is loneliness, there is also love, and where there is suffering, there also is joy" (p. 103).

REFERENCE

Moustakas, C.E. (1961). *Loneliness*. Englewood Cliffs, NJ: Prentice Hall.

THE FULLNESS OF EMPTINESS

i

There are times
Walking around in this immense loneliness
When your voice softly echoes through me
Or I find myself waiting for you.

I have come to respect the loneliness
For it brings even greater meaning
To the love we shared
As it intensifies the emptiness.

The empty lonely expanse
Clarifies what was and is.
Bringing greater focus and perspective
To the full love-joy that could have been.

Making even more irrelevant
The day to day dissatisfactions
So minute and petty
The awe of love drowns them.

ii

I failed
To hold your hands
While gazing into your eyes
To the pure center of your soul.

To worship, feed, and nourish,
Accept, embrace, and support
Encouraging more
Of you.

The place of reverence
From which all flows
Through which is only peace
Where we are all one.

Where I am you
We are one.
The pure essence
Of all life.

iii

Having cried for days
The sadness of loss
Wells up like the ocean
Washing through me more.

On and on infinitely,
While I stand as humbly as I can
Feeling death of love and life
And my startling insignificance.

The universe
Though weeping with me
Moves on and through me
Maintaining its splendor.

The sadness of humanity
Now I know
As never before
For she is ever gone.

iv

I cry each day
Until there are no more tears
And I go on
Empty, lonely through the day.

Yesterday was the same
Tomorrow will be filled with tears
Living with the pain each day
Of losing you.

Letting go of our past
Forgiving each of us
My sadness is pure
It is all that is.

So complete and entire
It is my last gesture-gift to you;
I say goodbye with great and pure sorrow
Wishing you peace.

v

I cry a million tears;
A universe of sadness
Washes through me
Seemingly never ending.

Sad weeping
Is all there is
Pure in feeling
Being now.

Living and breathing
Loneliness;
The creative depths
Emerge . . . transcend.

From deep in my bowels
Where I live
Accepting in sad peace
Your goodbye.

vi

Wandering around
In the immense loneliness
The sadness of your leaving
Is all there is.

Is all I am
In a strange new peace
As I allow the deep, deep cries of pain
To emerge unscathed, pure.

Therein lies creation
Through the feelings
So deep and strong within
That come bellowing out.

The center of my being
A mere vehicle
For this awesome intensity
This oneness.

vii

It is through loss,
The mourning
The grief
That life takes its meaning.

The other levels of being
The pervasiveness of life
Come to be real
Only through loss.

The tragic drama
Through which life unfolds —
We are only one small dying part
Through which now springs life.

Bursting, teeming-blood-through-the-veins
Tears-swelling-through-chest-and-eyes.
Saying goodbye
Only to say hello, to be, now.

Letting all of the past go
Saying goodbye to all that was
Deeply grieving
But cleansing.

Letting go
Emptying self
Into nothingness
Through which life flows.

Letting the burst of now
Surge
Alive
Ahhh . . . shine on.

The tears of deep, deep sadness
Turn to breaths of awe
In humbling recognition
Of life.

The tears of sadness
Turn to tears of wonder
(Keep being all there is)
Turn to joy.

(Keep going)
being all of it
Feeling it surge
Love, sadness, empty, awe, loss, full.

More tears,
Moving on
Through it
With it, with life, changing.

Moving freely
Letting it all go
Letting it happen
Truly being, now.